AFRICAN MAROONS IN
SIXTEENTH-CENTURY PANAMA

AFRICAN MAROONS IN SIXTEENTH-CENTURY PANAMA

A History in Documents

EDITED BY

Robert C. Schwaller

UNIVERSITY OF OKLAHOMA PRESS : NORMAN

Note on the cover image:
The cover features an aquatint made after François Jules Bourgoin's painting *The Maroons in Ambush on the Dromilly Estate in the Parish of Trelawney, Jamaica.* It depicts a scene from the Second Maroon War fought on Jamaica (1795–96). This image captures some sense of what European-maroon conflict may have looked like. Yet it is important to note that this image was created by a European artist and illustrates a war fought two hundred years after the events covered in this book. While it offers a valuable visual analog for events in sixteenth century Panama, the image both reflects and perpetuates European stereotypes about Africans and maroons.

Library of Congress Cataloging-in-Publication Data

Names: Schwaller, Robert C., 1981– editor.
Title: African maroons in sixteenth-century Panama : a history in documents / edited by Robert C. Schwaller.
Description: Norman : University of Oklahoma Press, [2021] | Includes bibliographical references and index. | Summary: "Historical exploration of African resistance to slavery in the sixteenth century in Spanish Panama through a selection of primary sources documenting Spanish-maroon conflict, from which the maroons succeeded in negotiating peace with Spanish authorities and established the first two free-black towns in the Americas"—Provided by publisher.
Identifiers: LCCN 2021010539 | ISBN 978-0-8061-6933-0 (paperback)
Subjects: LCSH: Maroons—Panama—History—16th century—Sources. | Blacks—Panama—History—16th century—Sources. | Slavery—Panama—History—16th century—Sources. | Slave insurrections—Panama—History—16th century—Sources. | Panama—History—To 1903—Sources.
Classification: LCC F1577.B55 A45 2021 | DDC 972.87/02—dc23
LC record available at https://lccn.loc.gov/2021010539

The paper in this book meets the guidelines for permanence and durability of the Committee on Production Guidelines for Book Longevity of the Council on Library Resources, Inc. ∞

In memory of the men, women, and children whose lives are imperfectly preserved by the pages of this volume. Their struggles against bondage compel us to secure racial equality and reject anti-Black racism and structural violence.

Contents

Preface

I first encountered the maroons of sixteenth-century Panama during a research trip to the Archivo General de Indias in 2012. I was just beginning preliminary research on a project examining encounters between Africans, their descendants, and Indigenous peoples in early Spanish America. I was blown away by the amount of material preserving Spanish-maroon conflict in Panama and was shocked that I had not encountered this history before. In hindsight, I am certain I had run across a brief mention of Panama's maroons in Richard Price's *Maroon Societies*. As I explored the available documents, I was pleasantly surprised to find evidence for maroon contact with neighboring Indigenous communities. Yet the richness of the sources spoke to so many other aspects of African experience in the Americas. Who were these maroons, how long had their communities existed, how did they maintain their freedom, and what precipitated their acceptance of a formal peace with Spanish authorities? The search for these questions has since led me to examine maroon communities on Hispaniola and in Mexico. That research is slowly percolating into a separate monograph that I hope will make it into print sooner rather than later.

This volume began as I tried to make my way through the thousand-plus pages of material for Panama. At the time, I was caring for my newborn son, Fritz, and discovered that translating sources was a task to which I could devote my sleep-deprived brain during the dribs and drabs of time I could fit in between childcare and catnaps. This project and its translations continued on and off until the birth of my second child, Mechi, when once again the work of translating and annotating paired well with caring for a newborn.

I am grateful for all those who have supported this project. Most importantly, I am deeply indebted to my wife, Rachel E. C. Schwaller, who has

---

always offered keen insights and sage advice on my translation and annotations. I am also grateful to my father, John F. Schwaller; it has been very helpful to get translation advice from someone with an MA in Spanish and Portuguese and a PhD in Latin American History. I must also thank the undergraduate students at the University of Kansas who read early versions of this manuscript. Their advice helped me craft a more cohesive and coherent narrative. Finally, I am deeply appreciative of the advice and suggestions offered by Kris Lane and David Wheat and the hard work of Kathryn Vaggalis in helping me finalize the manuscript.

A Note on Translation
and Archival Documentation

Many of the documents in this volume come from official Spanish correspondence, reports, and directives. As such, the language used can be both formal and dry. In translating these texts, I have tried to capture their bureaucratic nature while maintaining readability and intelligibility. Sixteenth-century Spanish frequently strung together many clauses that to modern English readers would appear to be one long run-on sentence. To address this, I have tried to separate complete clauses into shorter sentences using natural break points. At other times, multiple secondary clauses can confuse the subjects and verbs of sentences. Consequently, some sentences in the English translation do not follow the same order as the Spanish original.

I have chosen to retain some Spanish terms whose semantic sense could be confused by translation. These most commonly include civic terms, titles of office, and racial categories. Although one could translate the racial category of *negro* as "Black" or *mulato* as "mulatto," the semantic meanings of these terms for sixteenth-century Spanish speakers do not correspond precisely to their modern English equivalents. To be sure, many of the same negative connotations transcend the gulf of time and language. Nevertheless, I have chosen to retain such terms and italicize them to emphasize their contextual, rather than transhistorical, meanings.

The term "Bayano" can be confusing. It first appears as the name of the leader of several maroon communities during the late 1540s and 1550s. The Spanish occasionally dubbed him King Bayano. After his defeat, Spaniards and maroons applied the term "the Bayano" to the region he had ruled. The Bayano ranged from the royal road connecting Panama City and Nombre de Dios in the west to the Gulf of San Miguel and the ruins of Santa María la Antigua del Darién in the east. Since the sixteenth century, the name Bayano has lived on, often associated with features in this region. The river known as the Río Chepo during the sixteenth century became the Río Bay-ano. In the early twentieth century, a merchant ship named *Bayano* plied the Atlantic as a banana boat of the United Fruit Company. Drafted into military service as the HMS *Bayano*, the ship was sunk in 1915 by a German U-boat. In 1976, a hydroelectric dam built on the Río Bayano flooded much of the territory once inhabited by maroons to form Lake Bayano. Near the lake a series of caves also take the name Bayano.

I have included several documents written and published in English. For clarity, and for consistency, I have modernized the spelling, including that of foreign words. As with sixteenth-century Spanish writers, English authors of the time frequently used conjunctions as punctuation. Where necessary I have also broken up run-on sentences to enhance readability.

Archival Documentation

The majority of the documents that appear in this volume are housed in the Archivo General de Indias (AGI), in Seville, Spain. The citation format for the AGI lists the item by section, volume (often termed *legajo* in Spanish), *ramo* or *libro* (bundle or book), then document number. For example, the citation "AGI, Panama 13, R. 17, N. 83" indicates that the document is in volume 13 of the section Panama, Ramo 17, Number 83. In some sections the order of Ramo and Number can be reversed. Usually documents are numbered sequentially within a volume regardless of the number of ramos. Some citations may contain folio numbers, such as "fs. 125v–28." Most doc-uments are enumerated by folio (a single page front and back). A "v" follow-ing a folio number indicates "verso" or reverse side.

Many of the documents cited in this volume can be accessed online through the Portal de Archivos Espanoles (PARES; http://pares.mcu.es /ParesBusquedas20/catalogo/search). After a recent (2020) change, the advanced search page appears in English for users accessing the site from the United States. To access a document directly, first select "Filter by Archive" and choose "Archivo General de Indias." Next enter the section, volume, ramo, and number into the "Filter by reference number" field. *Do not include spaces.* The above citation would be entered as "PANAMA,13,R.17,N.83"; if searching for a specific document, select "Full reference number." The "incomplete reference number" option can be used to see all documents at a specific level of the citation hierarchy. For example, "PANAMA,13" would show all documents in that legajo; "PANAMA,13,R.17" would show all documents in that ramo. Importantly, some crucial documents in this study are not accessible in PARES. Notably, Panama legajos 39–43 contain documents vital to this period of Panama's history but are only accessible to scholars working at the AGI.

Finally, all the documents are written by hand in sixteenth-century Castilian at a time prior to orthographic and lexicological standardization. The paleography (old handwriting) of many documents is quite clear, since they were official correspondence, and these documents can be used to help instruct students in sixteenth-century paleography. Nevertheless, even without a knowledge of Spanish, seeing the original documents reveals the hard work that scholars must undertake to access the events of this period.

Abbreviations and Frequently Used Spanish Terms and Phrases

Abbreviations

AGI: Archivo General de Indias, Seville, Spain

CDI-DCC: *Colección de documentos inéditos relativos al descubrimiento, conquista y colonizacion de las posesiones espanolas en america y occeania* (Madrid: Imprenta de Manuel de Quirós, 1864)

Spanish Terms and Phrases

audiencia: High court, composed of *oidores* (judges), appointed by the king and led by the *presidente* (president or chief justice), who often also held certain administrative or military authority in addition to judicial power.

cabildo: Municipal city council, the most important institution of local government in the Spanish world, composed of *regidores* (aldermen) and *alcaldes* (local magistrates).

cedula: Royal decree that carried the force of law.

cimarron(es): Maroon(s), commonly paired with *negro/a* (e.g., "negros cimarrones").

doctor: A title granted to individuals who had earned a doctorate, usually in law or theology. Held by some high-ranking officials.

escribano: Scrivener or scribe, often associated with an institution of government, such as an audiencia or cabildo.

licenciado: An individual who had earned an advanced university degree.

monte(s): In most instances I have translated this as "the bush." In sixteenth-century Spanish it referred to terrain that was difficult to traverse because of its topography or vegetation or both. I have retained the Spanish in contexts where the English translation may confuse the original meaning or phrasing.

regimiento: The subset of a cabildo composed of its *regidores* (aldermen).

Introduction

On June 19, 1579, don Luis Maçanbique appeared before the judges of the Audiencia of Panama. Don Luis led a community of almost one hundred *cimarrones* (maroons), runaway slaves who had resisted Spanish attempts at re-enslavement for at least a decade if not longer. He bore with him two documents. One document was a royal seal impressed in red wax on white paper, a token of safe passage granted by the *audiencia* (high court) so that he might travel from his home near the bay of Portobelo to the Spanish capital of Panama City. He also bore a written petition in which he accepted a royal promise of pardon and liberty on behalf of his people. In return for the pardon, he swore fealty to the Spanish king, Philip II. The petition described Maçanbique as "king of the soldiers of Portobelo." Don Luis was not the first maroon to swear fealty to the Spanish king in return for freedom, but he was the first African maroon leader to secure the pardon and liberty of his entire community. Two years later, a much larger community of maroons located in eastern Panama would negotiate a similar peace with the Audiencia of Panama. The treaties signed by the maroon leaders would secure freedom for over four hundred formerly enslaved Africans and establish the first two free Black towns in the Americas.

Maroons resisted Spaniards not only by running away, raiding for supplies, and defending their communities but also by forging alliances with foreigners interested in undermining Spain's claim to the mainland. In 1572, Francis Drake, the famed English pirate, adventurer, and explorer, secured an alliance with maroons that allowed him to attack Nombre de Dios and Venta de Chagres. He sought the valuable silver and gold bullion regularly shipped from Spanish Peru through the Isthmus of Panama on its journey back to Spain.

Four years later, John Oxenham, a former shipmate of Drake, returned
to the isthmus and once again allied with maroons. More ambitious even
than Drake, Oxenham traversed the isthmus and built small boats on the
Pacific side. Using those boats, Oxenham, his crew, and maroons captured
a trading ship on its way from Lima to Panama City. They went on to raid
Spanish estates on the Pearl Islands before attempting a retreat back to
their ship on the Atlantic coast. They would not succeed.

Spaniards quickly mobilized forces along both Atlantic and Pacific
coasts. These efforts to capture the English quickly escalated into a scorched
earth conflict targeting the maroons who had aided the foreigners. The
voluminous documentation created by this five-year war and its aftermath
offer the most complete picture of African maroon communities in the sixteenth century. This volume collects those documents, along with others
from earlier and later, to offer a window into the half-century conflict
between Spaniards and Africans in eastern Panama.

Despite their significance, these maroon communities and their
decades-long struggles against the Spanish are not widely known. In 1932,
Irene Wright published translations of a number of documents included
here as part of a collection focusing on English voyages to early Spanish
America.[1] In 1947, W. E. B. Du Bois noted that Panama's maroons, alongside the Brazilian maroons of Palmares, prefigured the later success of
Toussaint L'Ouverture in Haiti.[2] Since then, most historical studies have
been published in Spanish. Not surprisingly, scholars in Panama and Spain
have predominated. In 1961, Carlos Guillot's *Negros rebeldes y negros cimarrones* situated Panama's maroons in a larger history of African resistance to
Spanish rule.[3] Soon afterward, Armando Fortune published a number of
articles in which he recounted the history of Panama's earliest enslaved
Africans as well as those who became maroons.[4] Other scholars of Panama,
including Alfredo Castillero Calvo and Carmen Mena García, have discussed the issue of marronage in larger works on the social and cultural
development of early Spanish Panama.[5] In 1994, Carol Jopling transcribed
several hundred documents related to the treatment and experiences of
Indigenous peoples and Africans in early colonial Panama.[6] Using this rich
source base in conjunction with Wright's earlier work, Ruth Pike authored
the most concise English treatment of the maroons in 2007.[7] Two years
later, Jean Pierre Tardieu published the first monograph to focus solely on
Panama's sixteenth-century maroons.[8] He argued that the constant struggle against Spanish forces helped forge a unique African American iden-

tity. Building on the work of these scholars, this volume makes the struggle of Panama's maroons accessible to a broader audience by curating annotated translations of the richest primary sources. The documents that follow offer an unparalleled view of the tenuousness of European empires, the transatlantic slave trade, early African resistance, and the negotiation of sovereignty and geopolitics in the early modern Atlantic.

Conquest and Indigenous Decimation

The Spanish-maroon conflict of sixteenth-century Panama reveals the significant connections between the initial conquest of Indigenous peoples and the later rise of marronage. Indeed, the conquest of Indigenous communities established the historical conditions for marronage. Decades later, Spaniards described their attempts to subjugate maroons as conquests. Although scholars often examine marronage as an aspect of resistance to slavery, in Panama, as in other regions, marronage also challenged earlier conquests and precipitated continued campaigns of conquest.

Prior to the Spaniards' arrival, the Cueva, an Indigenous group, inhabited the eastern isthmus of Panama.[9] Anthropologists have classified Cueva political structure as hereditary chiefdoms.[10] Communities could range between several hundred to several thousand people. Most chiefdoms included a larger settlement, housing the ruling elite, and smaller dispersed hamlets.[11] Like many other groups in the circum-Caribbean, the Cueva practiced a mixed form of subsistence that included maize cultivation and hunting and gathering.[12] Chiefdoms appear to have been clustered along the many rivers and tributaries of the isthmus. Although Cueva communities controlled territory along the coast, the Cueva avoided settlement near the shoreline.[13] At the time of Spanish arrival, the Cueva likely numbered around one quarter million people. By 1550, less than two thousand would survive.[14] As a result, much of their historic homeland would lie depopulated, ripe for habitation by Africans fleeing enslavement.

Between 1501 and 1508, numerous Spanish expeditions traversed the coastline of Panama. In 1508, two conquest expeditions entered the region. Diego de Nicuesa targeted the western half of the isthmus, then called Veragua, while Alonso de Hojeda set out to conquer the Gulf of Uraba in the east.[15] Neither expedition saw much success. Hojeda's forces suffered major defeats as Indigenous resistance forced them to flee from the eastern shores of the Gulf of Uraba. In response, they targeted the Indigenous

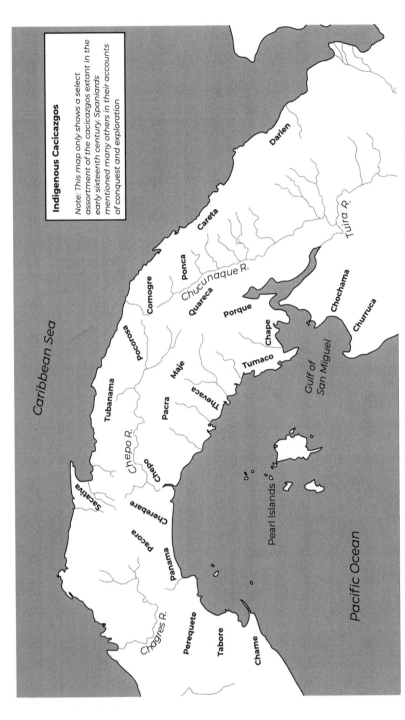

Indigenous cacicazgos of Tierra Firme, ca. 1500. *Sources:* Helms, *Ancient Panama*, 41, 52; Romoli, "El territorio Cueva, 1500–1510," in *Los de la lengua Cueva*, n.p.

community of Darién on the western side of the gulf. Subsequently they established a Spanish town named Santa María la Antigua del Darién. This community would serve as the base for Spanish conquests in the region for the next ten years. For his part, Nicuesa had even less success. His fleet became separated and scattered along the coastline. To survive, Nicuesa established a fort in a bay that he named Nombre de Dios. Eventually the survivors retreated to Santa María.

During the next three years, leadership in that settlement fell to Vasco Nuñez de Balboa, who pursued a mixed strategy of negotiation and conquest with the Cueva people of eastern Panama.[16] These efforts allowed him to gain an awareness of the geography and the complex political landscape of Cueva chiefdoms. After forging alliances, Balboa targeted Indigenous communities hostile to his allies. Eventually his growing knowledge allowed him to traverse the isthmus with Indigenous assistance.

In January 1513, Balboa informed the king that his expeditions had yielded evidence that a great sea lay to the west.[17] With Columbus's initial voyages, Spaniards had hoped to find a route to Asia. By the early sixteenth century, explorers recognized that much of the mainland of the New World lay between the Atlantic and their desired destinations in Asia. Any route, maritime or overland, that could link the two seas offered great prospects for future trade and exploration. Balboa hoped to identify just such a route.

While Balboa succeeded in his effort to reach the "south sea" (Pacific Ocean), the journey marked a turning point in Spanish-Indigenous relations. Encounters with the chiefdoms that inhabited the southern coast tended to be violent as Spaniards began to avoid diplomacy and instead demanded supplies, precious metals, and human captives that could be used for labor in Santa María or its nearby placer gold mines. Shortly after returning to Santa María, Balboa sent Andrés de Garavito down the Río Chucunaque on a campaign of "a fuego y a sangre" (fire and blood) to gather more captives.[18]

In 1514, Pedrarias Dávila arrived as a royally appointed governor of the region. The fleet carrying Dávila brought almost two thousand Spaniards to a community that had previously numbered less than five hundred. As governor, Dávila rapidly expanded expeditions to supply the much larger Spanish population and quickly secure spoils of war for the newly arrived conquistadors.

Although many Spanish conquest expeditions received royal authorization, usually the participants themselves funded their efforts, rather than the

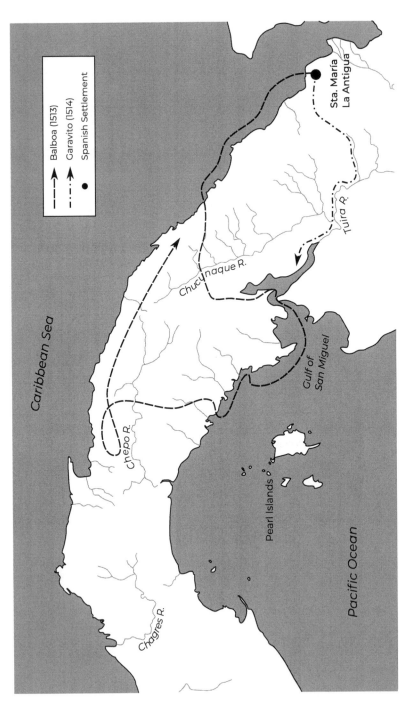

Expeditions of Balboa and Garavito, 1513–1514. *Sources:* Oviedo y Valdés, *Historia general*, 3:9–20. Sauer, *Early Spanish Main*, 221.

Legend:
- Balboa (1513)
- Garavito (1514)
- Spanish Settlement

Caribbean Sea

Pacific Ocean

Sta. María
La Antigua

Tuira R.

Chucunaque R.

Gulf of
San Miguel

Chepo R.

Pearl Islands

Chagres R.

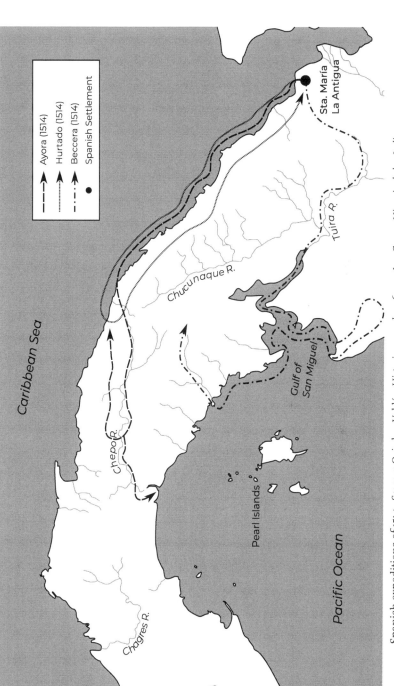

Caribbean Sea

Chagres R.

Chepo R.

Chucunaque R.

Tuira R.

Pearl Islands

Gulf of
San Miguel

Pacific Ocean

Sta. María
La Antigua

Ayora (1514)
Hurtado (1514)
Beccera (1514)
Spanish Settlement

Spanish expeditions of 1514. *Sources:* Oviedo y Valdés, *Historia general,* 3:36–40; Las Casas, *Historia de las Indias,* 4:175–79.

Spanish crown. As a result, expeditions resembled financial corporations more than military units.[19] In most cases, participants entered into a contract with the expedition organizers that stipulated how shares of the spoils would be distributed among the members. Consequently, the targeted search for valuable commodities and human captives sought to maximize individuals' profits. Under Dávila's orders, numerous expeditions "brought great trains of people imprisoned by chains, with all the gold they could find."[20]

In 1514 alone, expeditions led by Juan de Ayora, Bartolomé Hurtado, and Francisco Beçerra targeted *cacicazgos* to the west, beyond the still nominally allied Careta, and to the south through the Gulf of San Miguel and the Pearl Islands.[21] As Indigenous communities disappeared, their members scattered or captured, Spanish campaigns proceeded farther into the isthmus. In 1515, Tello de Guzmán and Gonzalo de Badajoz led campaigns against the cacicazgos of the central river valleys and western isthmus. The same year, Gaspar de Morales pillaged communities in the Gulf of San Miguel and Pearl Islands. To facilitate further western conquest, the Spanish founded a new town named Acla near the cacicazgo of Careta.

In 1517, Gaspar de Espinosa reached the populous Azuero Peninsula and secured more gold and slaves than in any previous ventures. The *entrada* (campaign) lasted over a year and traversed more territory than any prior expedition. Before heading west, Espinosa targeted the rebellious cacicazgos of Comogre and Pocorosa. In his own account of the venture, Espinosa frequently used the verb *"ranchear"* to describe the practice of burning and looting Indigenous towns. As they travelled west along the Río Chepo, squads ranged afield of the main party capturing any Cueva who fled.[22] After pillaging the Azuero Peninsula, the party began the return journey. Espinosa's own account of the expedition attests to the catastrophic collapse of the region's Indigenous communities due to warfare, flight, and starvation.[23] The party continued their retaliatory strikes against the Tubanama, Paruaca, Pocorosa, Comogre, and Pucheribuca cacicazgos. By this time, the cacicazgo of Careta had ceased to exist.[24] Bartolomé de Las Casas recounted that Espinosa returned with over two thousand slaves and eighty thousand castellanos of gold.[25]

Between 1517 and 1519, Balboa raided cacicazgos around the Gulf of San Miguel to secure laborers that could be used in building a fleet of ships in the Pacific. To replace those who died, Balboa ordered squads to round up any Indigenous persons who had fled into the bush.[26] Pascual de

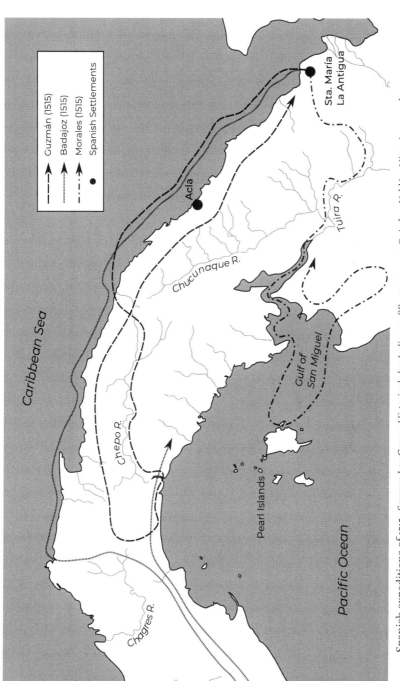

Spanish expeditions of 1515. *Sources:* Las Casas, *Historia de las Indias,* 4:188–97, 203–15; Oviedo y Valdés, *Historia general,* 3:47–50.

Map labels: Caribbean Sea; Pacific Ocean; Sta. María La Antigua; Aclá; Tuira R.; Chucunaque R.; Chepo R.; Chagres R.; Gulf of San Miguel; Pearl Islands

Legend:
- Guzmán (1515)
- Badajoz (1515)
- Morales (1515)
- Spanish Settlements

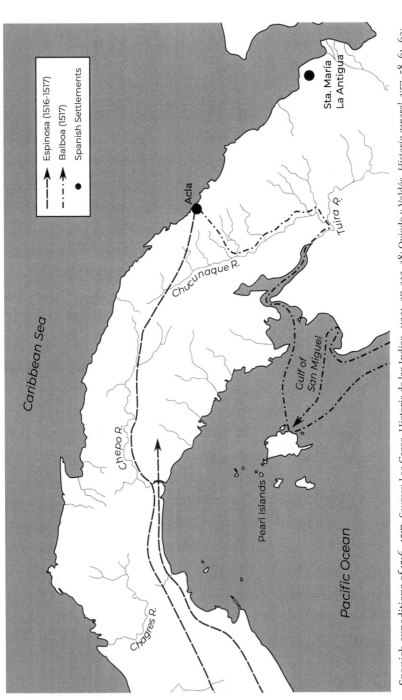

Spanish expeditions of 1516–1517. *Sources:* Las Casas, *Historia de las Indias*, 4:221–27, 232–38; Oviedo y Valdés, *Historia general*, 3:57–58, 61–62; *CDI-DCC*, 2:467–522; Fernández de Navarrete, *Colección de los viages*, 3:403–5.

Within the map:

Caribbean Sea

Acla

Chucunaque R.

Chepo R.

Chagres R.

Pearl Islands

Gulf of San Miguel

Tuira R.

Sta. María La Antigua

Pacific Ocean

Legend:
- - - Espinosa (1516–1517)
-·-·- Balboa (1517)
● Spanish Settlements

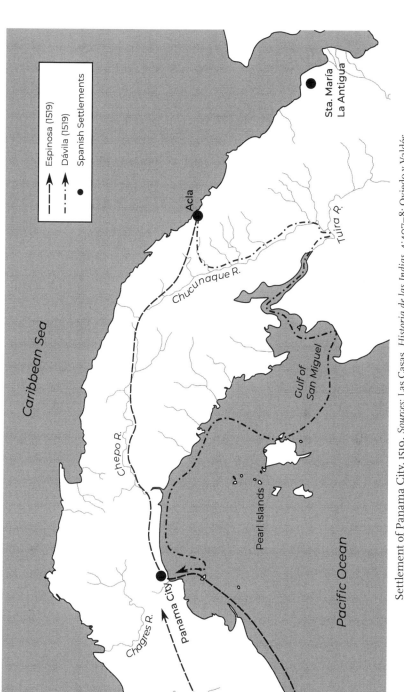

Settlement of Panama City, 1519. *Sources:* Las Casas, *Historia de las Indias,* 4:407–8; Oviedo y Valdés, *Historia general,* 3:62–64, 68–69; CDI-DCC, 20:5–119.

Andagoya observed, "The province of these *indios*, which was full of people, we decimated taking them to Acla to carry the materials for the ship, and by uprooting all of the food that they had to [feed] the carpenters and laborers."[27] The rigorous labor required of the project led to the deaths of as many as two thousand Cueva.

By 1519, eastern Panama lacked native laborers. All observers noted that for miles in any direction no Indigenous people could be found.[28] The lack of nearby labor and increasing conflicts between Dávila and the residents of Santa María led the governor to relocate the seat of government to the west. The expedition proceeded on two fronts; Espinosa led one force down the Río Chepo while Dávila ventured by sea from the Gulf of San Miguel. On August 15, 1519, Dávila founded Panama City. Soon after, more expeditions set off to raid the cacicazgos located near the new capital.[29]

Almost immediately after founding the new city, Dávila ordered the first documented *repartimiento* (division) of Indigenous captives among Spanish conquistadors. This document and a subsequent adjustment from 1522 record the near total decimation of the Indigenous inhabitants of eastern Panama.[30] Most of the over seven thousand Indigenous persons included in the division originally resided in cacicazgos that fell between Natá in the west and the Río Chepo in the east. Some communities from near Acla and the Gulf of San Miguel appeared, but none from the vicinity of Santa María. This absence likely suggests that no residents from this region survived the relocation.[31] By 1522, all of the Indigenous communities subject to the repartimiento had been relocated to Panama City. Although some Cueva may have remained in isolated hamlets, Spanish warfare, pillaging, enslavement, and overwork had systematically decimated the Indigenous population of eastern Panama within eight years of Dávila's arrival.

Without local Indigenous labor to bolster Spanish interests, even Spanish settlements in the eastern isthmus disappeared. By 1524, Spaniards had abandoned Santa María. For its part, Acla persevered into the 1530s, but the lack of Indigenous labor and the growing importance of Nombre de Dios eventually led to its dissolution. By the late 1530s, Spanish Panama was composed of the port cities of Nombre de Dios and Panama City and smaller agricultural communities, like Natá to the west. A small Indigenous village located along the lower Río Chepo represented the easternmost settlement under Spanish rule.

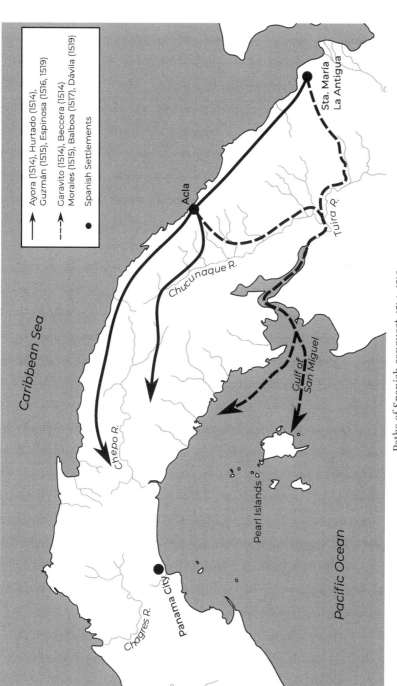

Paths of Spanish conquest, 1514–1519.

Ayora (1514), Hurtado (1514),
Guzmán (1515), Espinosa (1516, 1519)

Garavito (1514), Beccera (1514)
Morales (1515), Balboa (1517), Dávila (1519)

● Spanish Settlements

Caribbean Sea

Sta. María
La Antigua

Acla

Tuira R.

Chucunaque R.

Gulf of
San Miguel

Chepo R.

Pearl Islands

Pacific Ocean

Panama City

Chagres R.

Spanish Political Organization

The Spanish colonial system created a hierarchy of political institutions through which authorities governed subjects of the king. At the time of the foundation of Santa María, the *cabildo* (city council) served as the primary institution of governance. Spanish cabildos included both magistrates, named *alcaldes*, and aldermen, named *regidores*. During the conquest era, conquistadors frequently founded cities and elected cabildos in order to establish a more permanent institution through which they could interact with the monarchy. In many cases, the "cities" they founded were nothing more than collections of tents or huts.

In 1514, when Pedrarias Dávila assumed the governorship of the region he received the authority to name rural magistrates, commission captains to lead military expeditions, establish a royal treasury, and oversee the collection of taxes, among other powers. Existing cities such as Santa María, Acla, and Panama retained their cabildos and jurisdiction over municipal government. In 1537, as it became clear that the isthmus would serve as the primary route to newly conquered lands in South America, the king established an audiencia in Panama. The audiencia had jurisdiction over both criminal and civil cases and served as a court of appeals for cases tried by local magistrates. The king consolidated the position of governor in the audiencia, granting the chief justice, or president, many of the powers previously held by the governor.[32] This new court only resided in Panama for four years. The rapidly changing political landscape of Central and South America led the king to transfer Panama's court northward to Guatemala while simultaneously creating a new court in Lima to oversee Spanish Peru. From 1542 until 1562, royally appointed governors once again sequentially served as the chief executive in the region.

In 1563, the king reversed the earlier move, returning the audiencia to Panama. Once again, the president of the audiencia served as governor of the region in addition to his duties on the court. From this point forward, the audiencia and its president oversaw the judicial and secular governance of the region. Not surprisingly, local residents did not always see eye to eye with appointees, who frequently arrived directly from Spain. Cabildos frequently complained to the king when the audiencia did not do as they wished.

Below the audiencia existed a myriad of other royally appointed positions that could frequently come into conflict during the exercise of their duties. Moreover, after its re-creation in 1563, the Audiencia of Panama and the Audiencia of Lima did not always have a clear relationship. Although Lima had become the seat of a viceroy (the highest-ranking royal official in the Americas) and an audiencia, Panama's position as the gateway to Peru made it easier for its audiencia to communicate back to Spain. Authorities in Peru frequently complained that Panama exceeded its authority by dealing directly with Spain. Eventually, royal edicts subordinated the Audiencia of Panama to the viceroy of Peru and the Audiencia of Lima.

The multilayered structure of Spanish governance frequently created tensions, as different officials could have competing claims to particular duties. In challenging Spanish authority, African maroons and foreign interlopers often brought these tensions to the fore. Cities, frequently the targets of attacks by these groups, could use their own municipal rights to defend themselves. Yet frequently cabildos lacked the financial resources or political will to deal with the scope of such incursions. At the same time, governors and audiencias lamented having to spend royal funds to deal with maroons and foreigners, especially as they perceived that the former existed because of the failings of city-dwelling slaveowners. While officials at all levels of government had a duty to protect the kingdom, on the ground the responsibility for such duties could be quite muddled.

African Labor and Marronage

Africans first entered Panama alongside Spanish conquistadors.[33] Nuflo de Olano, a free-colored companion of Balboa, participated in the first trans-isthmus crossing.[34] As in other parts of the Americas, conquistadors owned slaves and frequently relied on enslaved persons to bolster the ranks of conquest campaigns.[35] Many Africans who arrived during the conquest era filled auxiliary positions attending to their owners or overseeing their owners' economic interests. Their duties could include managing enslaved Indigenous persons and rural estates. As early as 1515, some royally owned slaves toiled in Santa María clearing roads to connect mining camps to the city.[36] In this period, African labor was essential to Spanish interests but constituted a small fraction of labor needed in the nascent colony.

By the mid-1520s, Indigenous labor became so scarce that residents began to import Native peoples enslaved during the conquests of Nicaragua, Guatemala, Mexico, and Peru.[37] When Indigenous slaves failed to meet labor needs, Spaniards began to demand enslaved Africans to bolster the available labor supply. In 1527, the crown authorized the sale of one thousand Africans to the region to help support the construction of Panama City and to support entradas into the newly discovered region of Peru.[38]

Although quantitative data is scarce for the early sixteenth century, various pieces of evidence suggest that Africans quickly became the primary laborers in many of the region's industries. A close reading of slave ship documentation suggests that during the 1530s and 1540s Nombre de Dios received more slave ships, and likely more enslaved Africans, than any other Spanish American port.[39] Yet not all of these enslaved Africans stayed in the region. Many Africans who arrived in Panama ended up in Peru. Nevertheless, the frequency of slave ship arrivals allowed residents of Panama to readily purchase Africans. Nombre de Dios remained one of the most active ports for slave disembarkation until the 1570s, when nearby Cartagena began to take most of the trade destined to the southern Caribbean and Spanish South America.[40]

In 1575, Alonso Criado de Castilla, an *oidor* (judge) of the Audiencia, attested to the results of half a century of heavy slave importation. Writing to the crown he observed, "Those people that serve and work [here] are all *negros*, because among the *gente blanca* (White persons) none will serve or dedicate themselves to labor, for this reason the sum of *negros* who are in this kingdom is large."[41] He went on to enumerate the many occupations in which enslaved Africans toiled. Over sixteen hundred served Spaniards in Panama City; five hundred did the same in Nombre de Dios. One hundred more worked in the orchards that supplied the city. Cattle ranches relied on 150 Africans as cowboys. Almost two hundred worked as lumberjacks that supplied the cities with firewood and lumber. The mule trains that served as the primary means of transporting goods between Nombre de Dios and Panama required over four hundred enslaved Africans. Five hundred plied boats that served the maritime trans-isthmus route from Nombre de Dios down the Río Chagres. In the Pearl Islands, over three hundred enslaved Africans faced dangerous conditions diving for pearls. Even in Natá, where Indigenous labor had predominated, almost five hundred enslaved Africans labored in agricultural production or domestic service.

In his missive, Criado de Castilla did not provide a clear picture of the Spanish population. He claimed that Panama City had five hundred *vecinos*, and at times the city housed as many as eight hundred residents.[42] He made no mention of Spanish women or children, but he did report that there were around three hundred free Black residents. All told, the African and Afro-descended population of the city undoubtably surpassed the Spanish population in 1575. Within thirty years, the African population accounted for 75 percent of the region's residents.[43]

Not surprisingly, resistance through flight became common as more enslaved Africans arrived in the region. Scholars of slavery have divided running away into two types: "petit marronage" and "grand marronage."[44] Eighteenth- and nineteenth-century slaveowners in the French Caribbean used these terms to describe slave flight. "Petit marronage" applied to short-term, individual flight, often in the form of truancy. Persons engaging in such resistance sought temporary amelioration of the hardships of slavery. Enslaved persons often used truancy to negotiate greater privileges or autonomy from their owners. While Africans engaging in petit marronage could band together for support, such groups tended to be fleeting. In contrast, grand marronage involved groups running away with the intent to escape slavery and reconstitute their own societies in areas beyond the reach of their former masters. In early Spanish America, the distinction between petit and grand marronage can be hard to discern because the sources do not necessarily distinguish between short-term, individual flight and long-term, collective flight. Moreover, individuals who initially engaged in petit marronage could later become incorporated into communities engaged in grand marronage.[45]

In Panama, the first documented evidence of marronage came in 1525. During the *residencia* conducted after Dávila's tenure as governor, residents observed that Africans who escaped Panama City began to raid roadways and *estancias*.[46] Around 1530, Africans working in placer mines near Acla fled to the abandoned site of Santa María.[47] In 1535, a group of several dozen enslaved Africans working outside Panama, including slaves owned by the governor, rebelled.[48] They set fire to their owners' properties before turning to the city itself. The rebellion unraveled when another enslaved African informed the local magistrates, who succeeded in capturing many of the rebels. Subsequent investigations revealed that the group planned to flee toward Acla where they hoped to meet up with existing maroons and establish a settlement.

By the late 1540s, the scope of marronage expanded. In 1549, the first named maroon, Felipillo, led a number of enslaved pearl divers seeking escape from the harsh conditions of the Pearl Islands.[49] Felipillo and his fellow divers fled to the Gulf of San Miguel, where they joined with some remaining Indigenous persons and other runaways. They constructed a *palenque* (stockade) to defend their huts.[50] A Spanish expedition led by Francisco Carreño would capture and execute Felipillo (see document 2).

At roughly the same time, a much larger community of maroons had established itself in the upper reaches of the Río Chepo. Led by a man named Bayano, this community numbered in the hundreds and maintained at least two separate settlements. Bayano and his people situated their communities in the region that had once housed the largest Cueva cacicazgos. By this period, only a small community, known as Caricua, remained. Spanish chroniclers believed that its Indigenous residents had become slaves of the maroons. Bayano's settlements maintained their own subsistence agriculture that included local Indigenous crops. The maroons staged periodic raids on the trans-isthmus highway and the cities of Nombre de Dios and Panama to acquire manufactured products including clothes, weapons, and tools. Between 1553 and 1556, Spanish authorities commissioned at least four expeditions to defeat King Bayano (see document 5).[51] Francisco Carreño led one of those expeditions and succeeded in capturing Bayano; however, the governor chose to free the maroon king in the hopes of securing the surrender of the whole community. Such a peace did not come to fruition. In 1556, General Pedro de Ursúa led another campaign (see document 7). He succeeded but only after tricking Bayano and drugging the king and many of his men. The viceroy of Peru spared Bayano's life and allowed him to travel to Spain, where he lived out his days.

Ursúa's campaign failed to capture all of King Bayano's people. In the decades that followed, those survivors and new maroons fleeing Spanish masters once again began to coalesce into settlements dispersed in former Cueva lands from the Río Chepo to the Gulf of San Miguel. From the 1560s onward, Spaniards routinely called this region, comprising most of eastern Panama, the Bayano. Additionally, some maroons fled west to the Bay of Portobelo, near Nombre de Dios, and to the Cerro de Cabra, near Panama City. In his 1575 description of the region, Criado de Castilla estimated that there were twenty-five hundred maroons at large.[52] While the *oidor* likely exaggerated this figure, maroons certainly outnumbered Spanish residents of Nombre de Dios.

The increasing presence of foreign ships along the Caribbean coastline of Panama brought maroons into contact with French and English crews interested in gaining knowledge of the region, its resources, and its defenses.[53] In 1572, Francis Drake arrived in the region with the goal of sacking Nombre de Dios and its royal customs house (see documents 14–18).[54] After Spaniards repulsed his initial assault, Drake allied with local maroons to capture a mule train loaded with goods and bullion as it passed through the way station of Venta de Chagres. This attack also largely failed; Drake and his men fled with their maroon allies. In 1573, Drake made one last attempt to raid a mule train bolstering his English-maroon force with twenty Frenchmen led by Guillaume le Testu. This raid secured a sizable treasure, although le Testu would be captured and executed. Drake and his men returned to England with some of the treasure, having buried a large amount near the coast.

In 1576, one of Drake's men, John Oxenham, led a return voyage to the region (see document 24). Intimately familiar with the maroons who had allied with Drake, Oxenham joined with maroons and proceeded across the isthmus from the region near the site of Acla to the Gulf of San Miguel. In the gulf, Oxenham and his men built a boat that they used to plunder the Pearl Islands and to raid ships travelling from Peru to Panama City. These assaults triggered immediate responses by the Spanish, with expeditions organized in Panama City and Peru.

The campaign that began as an attempt to capture Oxenham and his men would eventually turn into a total war of *"fuego y sangre"* (fire and blood), targeting maroon communities. Knowledgeable of the land, maroons fled in advance of Spanish troops. Spanish patrols frequently burned down abandoned maroon communities and their fields. The cost of war on both sides eventually prompted a negotiated peace. Over the course of 1579–81, at least three separate maroon communities received pardons and freedom (see documents 43, 45, 56). Most of these former maroons became residents of two free-Black towns created by the audiencia, Santiago del Príncipe and Santa Cruz la Real.

Marronage did not disappear from Panama following these peace agreements, although grand marronage appears to have greatly diminished. Petit marronage remained common among the enslaved population of the region's cities and countryside.[55] In the early seventeenth century, Indigenous Guna (Kuna) peoples migrated into eastern Panama from what is now Colombia. By the eighteenth century, they had established themselves from the Gulf of San Miguel through the cacicazgo of Darién and as far as the San Blas Archipelago.[56] Spanish accounts frequently emphasized the bellicosity of the

Guna. The reoccupation of eastern Panama by the Guna likely inhibited the growth of large African maroon communities after 1600. Nevertheless, in the late colonial period at least one African maroon community, known as Palenque, formed near the abandoned site of Nombre de Dios. Although poorly attested in historical sources, at some point in the late colonial period this community transitioned into a free-Black town.[57]

Finally, maroon resistance cannot be divorced from their prior experiences in Africa. In the documents that follow, many African individuals appear with a given name, usually a Christian name, and a second name such as Congo, Biafara, or Zape. In the sixteenth century, observers tended to see these terms as indicative of African "nations" or "lands." Modern scholars frequently consider these terms ethnic categories.[58] In many cases, such designations derived from African ethnic names, ethnonyms, or place names, toponyms, but some terms were constructions applied by slave traders' beliefs of where Africans originated. Regardless of their etymology, Africans mobilized these terms in complex and elastic ways to create and/or re-create identity and community in the Americas.[59] Europeans, both in Africa and the Americas, also used such terms to create stereotypes about different groups of Africans, sometimes even influencing slave traders' and slave owners' demand for people of particular nations.

Scholars have debated the link between African societies and ethnicities and the ascription of specific categories during the slave trade and in the Americas. Some argue that these terms marked new identities that coalesced during enslavement, transportation, and chattel slavery in the Americas.[60] These scholars argue that such labels did not necessarily correlate to specific political or ethnic identities in Atlantic Africa. Instead, they grew out of shared affinities based in culture, language, cosmology, geography, and experience, among other factors. In contrast, other scholars have argued that these terms reflect enslaved Africans' own ascriptions of ethnicity rooted in their lives in Africa.[61] In part, this scholarly debate reflects the evolving nature of the slave trade and changing conditions in Africa and the Americas. Trading regions shifted, as did African states and peoples. Places of arrival in the Americas changed over time, as did the major European powers transporting enslaved Africans. All these factors make linking ascribed categories in the Americas to contemporary African societies, regions, or states a complex challenge requiring scholars to account for conditions in the Americas and Africa at any given moment. It should not be surprising that during some periods these terms show clear linkages to African ethnic groups, places, and states, while at other times the connections may have been less direct and the process of ascription more mediated by shared experiences of enslavement.

In the early Caribbean, most labels ascribed to Africans, especially those from Upper Guinea, reflected their ethnic backgrounds and societies of origin.[62] Nevertheless, even in this early period, categories applied to Africans from West Central Africa tended to be more abstracted, indicating general places of origin.[63] Thanks to their preservation of such terms, the documents that follow reveal a wealth of information about the varied geographic origins and ethnolinguistic affinities of Panama's maroons. The documents reveal that these terms played a key role in structuring maroon communities and organizing their resistance to Spanish assaults.[64]

Spanish Responses to Slave Flight

The first example of grand marronage in Spanish America occurred on the island of Hispaniola in 1519. In that year, an Indigenous leader named Enrique fled with many of his people from their Spanish encomendero.[65] In fact, the Spanish term *cimarrón* derives from a Taino word, *símara*, meaning "wild, savage, gone astray."[66] In fleeing their encomendero, Enrique and his people became the first maroons. Enrique fled to a mountainous region known as the Bahoruco, his ancestral homeland. Two years later, the first enslaved Africans rose up on a sugar estate owned by Diego Colón, a son of Christopher Columbus. While Spanish residents quickly mobilized a counteroffensive that claimed the lives of several Africans, most of the rebellious slaves joined Enrique and his people in the Bahoruco.[67]

Spanish authorities on Hispaniola quickly imposed harsh laws intended to prevent and discourage future rebellions and maroons.[68] The ordinances prohibited slaves from travelling without their masters or written permission. Slaves could not be rented out without consent of local authorities. No slave was allowed to carry any weapon other than a small knife. Owners could be fined for not reporting runaways or for being delinquent in oversight. Punishments for slaves included whippings for the first violation, amputation of a foot for the second, and execution after three offenses. The ordinances also levied a local tax to support capturing runaway slaves. Many localities copied such provisions in the years that followed.

In the 1520s, officials in Panama first sought to control marronage by compelling slave owners to track down runaways or to pay for others to do so.[69] The increasing frequency and scope of marronage prompted the king to order Governor Antonio de la Gama to promulgate slave ordinances for the region.[70] In the years that followed, the cabildos of Panama City and Nombre de Dios issued their own municipal ordinances that financed maroon policing via taxes on bread and wine. Authorities imposed particularly heinous punishments on runaway slaves. Governor de la Gama and his lieutenant governor, Pascual de Andagoya, punished runaway slaves who resisted recapture with the death penalty.[71] During this same period, punishments could also include whipping and the removal of male slaves' genitals, a practice prohibited by royal *cedula* in 1540.[72]

Beyond the threat of punishments, Spaniards employed a variety of strategies to repress, recapture, and defeat maroons. Especially in cases of violent revolt, such as the rebellion of the cacique Enrique or the 1535 plot in Panama City, civil magistrates (*alcaldes* or *corregidores*) relied on the immediate mobilization of Spanish slave owners and residents. Such efforts could foil major plots but frequently failed to recapture all participants. To counter maroon raids on Spanish settlements or transportation routes, colonial authorities could establish semipermanent patrols. During the 1540s, authorities on Hispaniola established a set of roving patrols to police the roadways between the island's Spanish settlements.[73] In Panama, no equivalent system of patrols existed, although the special tax levies did support armed guards for merchants and travelers on the road between Nombre de Dios and Panama City.

The commissioning of entradas, or sorties, represented the most frequent method of addressing marronage. When maroon raids became particularly concerning, authorities would commission a Spaniard to raise a company to proceed against the maroons in question. In practice, this system mirrored the framework of Spanish conquests and how they had unfolded and continued to unfold in the Americas. Private Spaniards received license to raise and maintain an armed company for the purposes of subjugating a hostile group. As with conquest expeditions, the commissions granted for entradas against maroons often required the leader to bear the costs of outfitting and maintaining the operation.

Although the form largely mirrored that of conquest expeditions, some differences existed. The major difference was that the targets of the entrada were *negros*, not *indios*. Another difference lay in the promised outcomes. In the case of conquest entradas, the leader frequently received authority to serve as governor and *capitán general* of the conquered region. Because the Spanish claimed dominion over regions occupied by maroons, leaders of anti-maroon entradas did not receive such promises of future office. However, most commissions granted the leader some rights over maroon captives. This privilege could take the form of direct ownership of captured slaves, the right to auction slaves, or the establishment of a reward for each returned slave. In some ways, these privileges paralleled the ability of conquest leaders to grant Indigenous communities to other Spaniards in encomienda or dispose of Indigenous persons captured in "just war" as slaves. Although legally distinct, both mechanisms allowed the commissioned leader to recuperate costs outlaid for the venture.

Importantly, Spanish efforts at policing maroons or extirpating them via armed entradas did not always succeed. In many areas of Spanish America, marronage represented an endemic problem through most of the colonial period. In cases where the threat of continued maroon depredations loomed large and the cost of continued conflict appeared unending, Spaniards considered negotiation as a means of last resort for bringing an end to maroon conflicts.

The first instance of negotiation occurred on Hispaniola in 1533. After almost fifteen years of conflict, the crown authorized Francisco Barrionuevo to negotiate with Enrique. Although there had been previous attempts at peace, none had succeeded. After several months of searching and tentative discussions, Barrionuevo and Enrique agreed to terms. In return for freedom from the encomienda, and pardon for their crimes, Enrique and his people agreed to leave the mountains and swear loyalty to the crown. They were allowed to live in their own self-governing town near the Spanish town of Azua. In the centuries that followed, Spaniards repeated this strategy of negotiation following prolonged conflicts with rebellious Indigenous or African groups. The maroons of Panama represent the first example of the application of this strategy to African maroons.

Reading Marronage with the Grain

Spaniards drafted almost all the documents that record maroon struggles in Panama. Only a precious few documents contain the voices of maroons themselves, and those voices are mediated by the Spaniard who composed the actual document. Consequently, the primary views put forward by these accounts are those of the Spanish participants. Their views were not monolithic. Spaniards in Panama came to the region with very different experiences. Some may have come from regions in Spain with few Africans. Others may have come from communities, like Seville, that had been home to numerous enslaved and free Africans for over a century. Still others may have had experience in Africa. Some may have been raised alongside Africans and their descendants. Some worked closely with Africans, while others only saw them from a distance. Yet, despite differing experience with Africans, a shared set of cultural preconceptions and prejudices shaped how they wrote about Africans and marronage.

The strategy of "reading with the grain" analyzes the sources for what they say—in other words, reading the narrative created by Spaniards. Reading in this way can be helpful because it allows us to understand the motivations that influenced Spanish choices. It reveals how Spanish perceptions of Africans, prejudiced as they were, informed decisions and actions. Nevertheless, as scholars we should be careful not to confuse what Spanish sources say about maroons with historical reality. The Spanish sources comprise a narrative rooted in Spanish prejudices and expectations. To most Spanish observers, Africans were bestial, irrational, and vengeful. Many Spaniards believed that maroons wanted to destroy Spanish cities and enslave their residents. Understanding how the Spanish thought can help us understand the context of their actions and the choices they made. The task of gaining an awareness of what Spaniards thought requires carefully reading Spanish sources and slowly building a framework for understanding their claims and motivations. Yet such windows offer a poor view into the experiences of maroons and the context of their choices.

Reading Marronage against the Grain

Unfortunately, lacking maroon-authored sources, we can only access the maroons' side through Spanish sources. To do this, scholars "read against the grain." That is, scholars interrogate and question the Spanish narrative in order to tease out historical reality from the biases and interests that shaped the documents. One must be able to recognize where biases may have altered the events or perceptions being recorded. For example, many Spanish observers described maroons as "jumping" or "leaping" in an animalistic fashion during battles. To a Spanish reader the implication was that Africans were bestial and uncivilized. Yet what were Africans actually doing? They were fighting with African martial techniques. At least one English observer of these events reveals this reality by noting that this behavior was part of the Africans' "own country wars." Similarly, despite the Spanish insistence that Africans were irrational and bestial, a close reading of the sources reveal a highly developed military strategy.[74] Africans raided for supplies as needed but when challenged directly tended to scatter and engage in guerrilla warfare. At times maroons burned their own towns to prevent Spaniards from using them as bases or pillaging them for supplies. Reading against Spanish prejudice, these actions reveal maroon strategies adapted to fighting and surviving against a superior military foe.

In all cases, reading against the grain is more difficult than reading with the grain. It requires a much greater familiarity with the sources. In many cases, it requires scholars to use additional primary and secondary sources to understand what is going on beneath the surface. In the case of African maroons, knowing the cultural practices of different African groups and cultures can help scholars see through the Spanish account. Similarly, knowledge of other maroon societies can help contextualize the events described and afford scholars with more examples to try to tease maroon experiences from Spanish accounts. Finally, what we glean from reading against the grain is often more conjectural than definitive. We may never know exactly what maroons believed or access their hopes and fears. Nevertheless, scholars can only work with the sources that have been preserved, and reading against the grain offers a method for accessing viewpoints and histories otherwise excluded from the historical narrative.

Why Are the Maroons of Panama Unique?

While the maroons of Panama were not the first example of African marronage in the Western Hemisphere, they are the most well-documented maroons of the sixteenth century. Historians have a greater volume and range of documents that afford views into the experiences of early maroons in Panama than for any other part of the hemisphere. The documents collected in this volume speak to the regional origins and diasporic identities of Africans in Panama. They offer glimpses into the social structure and ritual practice of Africans living in maroon communities. Few other sources can provide as clear a window into maroons' engagement in politics both at the scale of inter-imperial struggles and local contestations over space and resources.

In no uncertain terms, the maroons of Panama represent the first successful slave rebellion in the Americas. The maroons who lived in the communities of the Bayano, the bay of Portobelo, and the Cerro de Cabra rejected their enslavement, protected their liberty with force of arms, negotiated formal recognition as free persons, and astutely secured the right to local self-government. The towns of Santiago del Príncipe and Santa Cruz la Real represent the first two free-Black corporate communities in the Western Hemisphere.

The Spanish-maroon conflict in Panama also reveals the tenuousness of European empire in the Americas. The Spanish claimed dominion over the isthmus based on their initial conquest of the Cueva. Yet maroons' flight to depopulated regions and subsequent establishment of multiple subsistence-based communities challenged European notions of sovereignty. Did the Spanish decision to ignore and abandon the eastern isthmus effectively vacate their earlier conquests? Did maroons' occupation and defense of the region reflect an African conquest in the Americas? If so, the struggles documented in this volume can be understood as a contestation of conquests, European and African.[75] In the end, the negotiated peace acknowledged Spanish sovereignty but secured freedom and self-governance for the maroons and their descendants. Maroon exploitation of Spanish territorial weakness underpinned their success.

Telescoping beyond the scope of the documents in this volume, many of the dynamics that underpinned the Spanish-maroon conflict would repeat both in Panama and beyond. Following the peace with the maroons, Spaniards again depopulated the eastern isthmus, establishing Santiago del Príncipe near Nombre de Dios and Santa Cruz la Real near Panama City. This choice created a new vacuum, and over the next several decades Guna people (known at the time as *indios bugue bugue*) initiated a migration from modern-day Colombia into the Darién, the Gulf of San Miguel, and eventually as far as the San Blas Archipelago.[76] Their occupation again revealed the lack of effective Spanish control. Colonial authorities in the region would struggle against these new arrivals for centuries. At the beginning of the eighteenth century, two Scottish expeditions attempted to carve out a colony from a region consistently shown to be outside of Spanish control.[77]

The precedent set by the Spanish choice to negotiate with maroons, initially the Indigenous maroons of Hispaniola, then the maroons of Panama, would repeat in similar instances across the empire. In 1609, Spanish authorities in Mexico negotiated a peace with the maroon leader Yanga that established New Spain's first free-Black community.[78] Later maroons in that region would secure the establishment of San Miguel de Soyaltepeque in 1670, Mandinga in 1735, and Nuestra Senora de Guadalupe de los Morenos de Amapa in 1769.[79] In the Nuevo Reino de Granada (Colombia), maroons of the Sierra de María would secure their freedom and establish San Basilio in 1713.[80] In 1677, Spanish authorities of Santo Domingo authorized the creation of San Lorenzo de las Minas, a free-Black community composed of runaway Haitian slaves. A hundred years later, on the eve of the Haitian revolution, maroons of Santo Domingo's Bahoruco negotiated a peace that founded the free-Black community of El Naranjo.[81]

More impressive, the example of Panama's maroons spread beyond the confines of Spain's empire. In eighteenth-century Jamaica, English authorities specifically cited Spanish negotiations with maroons in Panama when they chose to sign treaties with two maroon communities located on the island.[82] For a time in the seventeenth century, authorities in Brazil sought to use treaties to manage the sizable maroon community of Palmares.[83] The French in Guiana and the Dutch in Suriname similarly negotiated treaties to end long-term conflicts with maroons during the eighteenth and nineteenth centuries.[84] While treaties often represented a strategy of last resort for European colonial powers, the maroons of Panama represented the first Africans in the Americas to succeed in forcing Europeans into negotiations.

The pages that follow reveal the struggles of sixteenth-century maroons. Although the documents record major victories for formerly enslaved Africans, readers cannot forget the difficult and dire circumstances faced by Africans when they engaged in marronage. The choice to flee enslavement weighed the continued suffering of bondage against the uncertainty of the unknown and the inhuman punishments endured by those who were recaptured. Subsistence could be tenuous. Manufactured goods, including tools, weapons, and in some cases clothing or medicine, could only be secured by raiding Spanish mule trains or settlements. Spanish forces always enjoyed better weaponry and resources. When attacked by Spanish troops, flight and guerrilla combat almost always proved most prudent. Yet, when maroons abandoned their communities, Spaniards burned their fields and homes, forcing maroons to start anew, often in less desirable locations. Even with constant vigilance, careful planning, and a tenacious desire for liberty, maroons faced uncertain futures. Their success represented nothing less than a monumental victory for enslaved peoples in the Americas.

Notes

1. Wright, *English Voyages*.
2. Du Bois, *World and Africa*, 124.
3. Guillot, *Negros rebeldes*.
4. Fortune, "Los primeros negros"; Fortune, "Bayano"; Fortune, "Los negros cimarrones"; Fortune, "El esclavo negro."
5. Castillero Calvo, *Conquista, evangelización y resistencia*; Castillero Calvo, *Historia general de Panamá*; Mena García, *La sociedad de Panamá*; Diez Castillo, *Los cimarrones y los negros*; Guardia, *Los negros*; Vila Vilar, "Cimarronaje en Panamá y Cartagena."
6. Jopling, *Indios y negros en Panamá*.
7. Pike, "Black Rebels."
8. Tardieu, *Cimarrones de Panamá*.
9. Oviedo describes the Indigenous people of eastern Panama using the phrase "de la lengua Cueva" and calls the region "la provincia de Cueva." Oviedo y Valdés, *Historia general*, 3:106, 135, 155.
10. Helms, *Ancient Panama*, 11–20; Romoli, *Los de la lengua de Cueva*, 116–21; Hoopes, "Late Chibca," 243, 248.
11. Romoli, *Los de la lengua de Cueva*, 145–48.
12. Hoopes, "Late Chibca," 242; Romoli, *Los de la lengua de Cueva*, 156–60.
13. Romoli, *Los de la lengua de Cueva*, 146.
14. Romoli, *Los de la lengua de Cueva*, 32–47; "Estructuras demográficas y mestizaje" in Castillero Calvo, *Historia general de Panamá*, 262–63. By 1550, few of the Indigenous residents were Cueva; most were peoples transported from Nicaragua to Panama to bolster the labor of the region.
15. Sauer, *Early Spanish Main*, 162–70.
16. For ethnohistorical studies of the Cueva, see Romoli, *Los de la lengua de Cueva*; Casimir de Brizuela, *El territorio cueva*; Helms, *Ancient Panama*.
17. "Carta dirigida al Rey por Vasco Nuñez de Balboa desde Santa María del Darien . . . ," in Fernández de Navarrete, *Colección de los viages*, 3:366–67.
18. Las Casas, *Historia de las Indias*, 4:133–34.
19. Restall, *Seven Myths*, 27–43.
20. "Relación de los sucesos de Pedrarias Dávila . . . ," in Fernández de Navarrete, *Colección de los viages*, 3:396.
21. Oviedo y Valdés, *Historia general*, 3:37–39; Oviedo y Valdés, *Writing from the Edge of the World*, 65–68.

22. "Relación hecha por Gaspar de Espinosa . . . ," in *Colección de documentos inéditos (CDI-DCC)*, 2:472.

23. "Relación hecha por Gaspar de Espinosa . . . ," in *CDI-DCC*, 2:519–22.

24. Oviedo y Valdés, *Historia general*, 3:58; Oviedo y Valdés, *Writing from the Edge of the World*, 92.

25. Las Casas, *Historia de las Indias*, 4:227.

26. Oviedo y Valdés, *Historia general*, 3:58; Oviedo y Valdés, *Writing from the Edge of the World*, 92–93.

27. "Relación de los sucesos de Pedrarias Dávila . . . ," in Fernández de Navarrete, *Colección de los viages*, 3:404.

28. "Relación de los sucesos de Pedrarias Dávila . . . ," in Fernández de Navarrete, *Colección de los viages*, 3:413.

29. Sauer, *Early Spanish Main*, 280–81.

30. Romoli, *Los de la lengua de Cueva*, 43–44, tabla 2. The later repartimiento recorded two thousand more *indios* largely because it included several communities not enumerated by the first division.

31. Such a process probably occurred in the Darién. The lack of cacicazgos from the region in the 1519 and 1522 documents may reflect an earlier undocumented division. Regardless, no autonomous indigenous communities remained in the Darien by 1522. Mena García, *El oro del Darién*, 575.

32. "La Audiencia de Tierra Firme" in Castillero Calvo, *Historia general de Panamá*, 207–8.

33. Mena García, *Sociedad de Panamá*, 83.

34. "Free-colored" refers to free individuals of African ancestry; this can include individuals of mixed ancestry. Fortune, "El esclavo negro," 11.

35. Restall, "Black Conquistadors"; Oviedo y Valdés, *Historia general*, 3:40.

36. Fortune, "Los primeros negros," 66.

37. Mena García, *Sociedad de Panamá*, 52.

38. Fortune, "El esclavo negro," 16.

39. Eagle, "Early Slave Trade," 143–49.

40. Eagle, "Early Slave Trade," 150–53.

41. "Sumaria descripción del reino de Tierra Firme . . . ," in Jopling, *Indios y negros en Panamá*, 13.

42. In the sixteenth century, the Spanish term *vecino* marked individuals with legally granted rights of citizenship in a community. The *cabildo* granted the status, which frequently required obligations of maintaining a home and serving in the local militia.

43. Wheat, *Atlantic Africa and the Spanish Caribbean*, 280, table 215.

44. Florentino and Amantino, "Runaways and *Quilombolas* in the Americas," 710; Thompson, *Flight to Freedom*, 53.

45. Schwaller, "Contested Conquests."

46. Guillot, *Negros rebeldes*, 136. In the Spanish political system, all royal appointees underwent a formal inquiry, termed a *residencia*, following their term of

office. This investigation sought to identify and punish officials who had abused their authority.

47. Guillot, *Negros rebeldes*, 137–38; Mena García, *Sociedad de Panamá*, 402–3.

48. Mena García, *Sociedad de Panamá*, 404–5.

49. Archivo General de Indias (Seville, Spain) (hereafter AGI), Patronato 150, N. 14, R. 2, fs. 753–54.

50. Over time the term *palenque* came to describe maroon settlements because they featured such defenses.

51. AGI, Patronato 150, N. 14, R. 2, fs. 754–56, Pike, "Black Rebels," 247.

52. "Sumaria descripción del reino de Tierra Firme . . . ," in Jopling, *Indios y negros en Panamá*, 14.

53. Lane, *Pillaging the Empire*, 40–44.

54. Pike, "Black Rebels," 255–59.

55. Castillero Calvo, "Conflictos sociales, guerra y Pax Hispana," 500.

56. García Casares, *Historia del Darién*, 162–63.

57. C. Anderson, *Old Panama and Castilla del Oro*, 14.

58. Green argues that the modern concept of ethnicity represents a foreign imposition onto categories that may have functioned more as markers of lineage and kinship, including adoptive or fictive kinship. Green, *Rise of the Trans-Atlantic Slave Trade*, 62–68.

59. Sweet, "Mistaken identities?"; P. Lovejoy, "Identifying Enslaved Africans," 8–13.

60. Chambers, "Ethnicity in the Diaspora," 28–29.

61. Hall, *Slavery and African Ethnicities in the Americas: Restoring the Links*, 23; Wheat, *Atlantic Africa and the Spanish Caribbean*, 20–23.

62. Wheat, *Atlantic Africa and the Spanish Caribbean*, 20–23.

63. Wheat, *Atlantic Africa and the Spanish Caribbean*, 103.

64. Wheat, *Atlantic Africa and the Spanish Caribbean*, 55–63; Tardieu, *Cimarrones de Panamá*, 198–235.

65. Altman, "Revolt of Enriquillo."

66. Deive, *Los guerrilleros negros*, 11–12.

67. Stone, "America's First Slave Revolt."

68. "Virrey de Indias: ordenanzas sobre los negros y sus amos," AGI, Patronato 295, N. 104.

69. Mena García, *Sociedad de Panamá*, 402.

70. Fortune, "Los negros cimarrones," 317.

71. Mena García, *Sociedad de Panamá*, 406–7.

72. AGI, Panama, 235, L. 7, fs. 122

73. Utrera, *Historia militar*, 1:265.

74. Barcia has shown that West African resistance in nineteenth-century Cuba and Brazil drew heavily from African martial practice, including methods of organization, tactics, and weaponry. Barcia, *West African Warfare*. Although the sixteenth-century sources are less detailed, the evidence indicates that the same was true in Panama.

75. Schwaller, "Contested Conquests."

76. García Casares, *Historia del Darién*, 162–63.

77. Orr, *Scotland, Darien and the Atlantic World*; García Casares, *Historia del Darién*, 250–61.

78. Archivo General de la Nación (Mexico City), Inquisición 283, exp. 26, fs. 186–87. Transcription and translation published in Landers, "*Cimarrón* and Citizen," 133–35.

79. Landers, "*Cimarrón* and Citizen," 132.

80. Cassiani Herrera, "San Basilio de Palenque."

81. Deive, *La esclavitud del negro*, 2:532–43; Deive, *Los cimarrones*.

82. Campbell, *Maroons of Jamaica*, 100–101.

83. Anderson, "Quilombo of Palmares," 562–63.

84. Bilby and Baird N'Diaye, "Creativity and Resistance," 56.

Part I
Early Maroons through the First
Bayano War (1530s–1550s)

1. Royal Cedula Authorizing Rewards for Capturing Maroons, April 29, 1536

Source: AGI, Panama 235, L. 6, fs. 24v–25.

As early as 1536, the residents of Panama complained that maroons in the region had grown numerous and dangerous. This royal cedula relates some of the earliest accounts of maroons' actions and Spaniards' attempts to prevent them. While we do not have the original petition that prompted this document, the cedula repeats much of what the city of Panama represented to the Emperor Charles V and his ministers. A key issue raised here, and consistently in the decades that followed, is the excessive cost of pursuing and capturing maroons. The residents of Panama petitioned the Crown to spend funds collected for the maintenance of the royal road to offset the costs they might incur.

• • •

Whereas Hernán Ximénez, in the name of you, the council, magistrates, and *regidores, caballeros, escuderos*,[1] officials, and gentlemen of the city of Panama, has related to me that in that land there is a great quantity of *negros* who have arrived from these kingdoms and from the islands and provinces of our Indies, and that every day they continue to rebel, wandering *cimarrones* in the bush rejecting the service of their masters, killing, robbing, and assaulting the royal roads, Christians, and other persons. In this they go about robbing estancias and committing other very grave insults and countless crimes to the disservice of God, our lord, and our own. Because the city does not have means with which to pursue and apprehend these *negros* they have not done so for lack of men.[2] [Hernán Ximénez] asked me if they might spend a moderate amount, as is necessary, from the tax levied for roadworks between Nombre de Dios and [the city of Panama] in order to apprehend and pursue the *negros cimarrones* and other criminals, because otherwise the city and land will be at risk and danger. Having been seen by those of my Council of the Indies, it was agreed that this, my cedula, should be sent. Therefore, I grant you license and authority that each year, whenever a person brings a criminal to the city to receive justice you may give them ten pesos of gold from the tax, without incurring any penalty [for doing so].[3]

1. *Caballeros* and *escuderos* were minor titles of nobility.
2. In other words, without funds the city could not recruit individuals to go out against the maroons.
3. Abuse of royal funds carried stiff penalties. This sentence clarifies that the use of the tax funds for the newly designated purpose could not be penalized.

2. Francisco Carreño's Account of Felipillo's 1549 Revolt (1562)

Source: AGI, Patronato 150, N. 14, R. 2, fs. 753–805.

In 1549, Felipillo, the first named maroon in the region's history, led a group of enslaved Africans from the pearl fisheries to escape and settle in the Gulf of San Miguel region. The most detailed account of that rebellion and the actions taken in response comes from Francisco Carreño's *probanza de méritos y servicios* (proof of merit and service). Such proofs functioned as legal records of an individual's actions and generally accompanied requests for appointment to royal office or reward for services rendered. While such proofs generally presented the individual in a positive light, they contained formal depositions of multiple witnesses and certification by local authorities.

Francisco Carreño did not represent an average Spaniard in the Americas. His father, Bartolomé Carreño, participated in some of the earliest expeditions to the islands of Dominica, Grenada, Martinique, Saint Lucia, and Trinidad. By 1525, Bartolomé Carreño had received a commission as a general of the Indies fleet. In 1538, Bartolomé conducted the first detailed exploration of Bermuda. In 1552, he took command of the annual fleet traveling to the Indies. Bartolomé would continue in royal service until his death in 1568. His son, Francisco, likely made his way to the New World alongside Bartolomé. His father's experiences demonstrated to Francisco how continued royal service could lead to reward and advancement.

In 1537, Francisco initially settled in Cabo de la Vela on the Caribbean coast of what is now Colombia, where he helped discover pearl fisheries. Eventually he made his way to Panama. He continued to search for pearl fisheries along the Pacific coastline. By the 1540s, he had settled in Panama City, overseeing a pearl fishery in the Pearl Islands. Importantly, Francisco and other Spanish pearl fishery owners did not dive for pearls themselves. Instead, they relied on enslaved Africans and enslaved or coerced Indigenous divers to do the difficult and dangerous work of scouring pearl beds. When Felipillo revolted in 1549, Carreño likely feared that such resistance might spread among his enslaved divers. Nonetheless, the slave owners did not appear to react immediately to the revolt. As Carreño's probanza reveals, his discovery and defeat of Felipillo and his community appears to have been accidental.

Sadly, we know almost nothing of Felipillo other than that he likely toiled as a pearl diver. His alliance with native laborers suggests that Africans and native divers had begun to forge social and possibly cultural ties on the Pearl Islands. These connections likely afforded Felipillo and his people local knowledge of the region and landscape that facilitated their flight.

•   •   •

In the city of Panama of this kingdom of Tierra Firme on the fifth day of September the year of our lord 1562 before the very magnificent lord, Pedro de Azevedo, *alcalde hordinario* by His Majesty, of this city . . . appeared Captain Francisco Carreño, vecino of this city, who presented a written petition and interrogatory signed with his name that follows:[1]

Very Magnificent Lord

Captain Francsico Carreño, vecino of this city, states that it is convenient to me that I should make a *probanza ad perpetum rei e memorium* . . . of the time that I have resided in this part of the Indies and how I have served His Majesty.

I request that your mercy order that the witnesses that I name be asked the questions that I present . . .

The witnesses presented on behalf of Captain Francisco Carreño shall be asked the following questions . . .

I. Firstly, they shall be asked if they know Captain Francisco Carreño and if they know that he is a vecino of this city, and for how long [have they known him], etc.

II. Item, if they know or have heard that in the past year of 49, that is thirteen years ago more or less, a negro named Felipillo rose up and fled along with other *negros* and *indios* from the island and estate of Hernando de Carmona, vecino of this city.[2] With the people that he took and other *indios* and *negros cimarrones* they arrived in the Gulf of San Miguel where they constructed a wooden palisade surrounding their huts.[3] They collected runaway *negros* who fled from the [Pearl] Islands and from this city doing great damage to the estates of the vecinos of this city. If [they] continued to grow it would be necessary to form a large force and spend a great quantity of gold pesos from the royal treasury and from private citizens to attempt to disperse and kill them.

III. Item, if they know etc. that in February of the year 1551, under the governorship of Sancho Clavijo, Captain Francisco Carreño, going in search of pearl fisheries in the Gulf of San Miguel, thirty leagues[4] from this city, ran across a canoe of *indios* and *negros cimarrones* near an island called Isle of Iguanas.[5] Taking the canoe and an *indio* who served as guide, along with two men of his house and his *negros* and *indios*, [Carreño] went to the palisade and settlement that the *negro* Felipe had built, taking the palisade, and burning the huts and food they had there. He captured all the *negros, negras,* and *indios* and *indias*, in total thirty persons, taking them to this city. Governor Sancho Clavijo punished them without awarding [Carreño] any recompense. He conducted the [expedition] at his expense. While bringing the group of *cimarrones* that he had captured he lost a new boat in which he carried the people near the island of San Telmo.[6] The boat was valued at over six hundred *pesos de oro*.[7] Captain Francisco Carreño had no other interest than to serve His Majesty and to do good work for this *republica* and its people. His dispersal of the palenque and *negros* was very well known.

The probanza goes on to describe Carreño's 1554 expedition against King Bayano (see document 5).

In many probanzas, witness testimony closely mirrors the questions posed by the solicitant. Often witnesses repeated word for word the phrasing of the question. Below are some witness statements that offer unique details not found in the original questions.

Bernaldo Gallo, vecino of Panama City

III. To the third question [this witness] said that he knows that during the aforementioned period, during the governorship of Sancho de Clavijo, this witness remembers seeing Captain Francisco Carreño going to the Gulf of San Miguel in search of pearl fisheries with some of his people. One time, this witness saw that when Francisco Carreño returned he carried with him two or three *negros cimarrones* and some *indios* who had been with them.[8] Francisco Carreño took them from the Pearl Islands to this city to be turned in to the magistrates. This witness heard that [after] Francisco Carreño turned the *negros* and *indios* in to the magistrates, one of the *negros* was quartered for having killed a Christian.[9]

Juan Bautista de Señor, vecino of Panama City

II. To the second question, [this witness] knows that at the time mentioned in the question, Felipe *negro ladino,* [slave] of Hernando Carmona, rose up and went *cimarrón* from the estate and island of his master.[10] He took with him some *negros* and *indios* and *indias* to the Gulf of San Miguel. This witness knows this because he was in the Pearl Islands at the time, and it was public and notorious that Felipe *negro* constructed in the Gulf of San Miguel a camp, surrounded with wood, with huts and fields inside.[11] He collected the *negros* and *negras* that ran away from this city and the islands. . . .

III. To the third question, [this witness] knows that at the time mentioned in the question, Francisco Carreño went in his boat to the Gulf of San Miguel along with his people in search of a canoe of *negros* and *indios,* pearl divers who had fled his island.[12] On this trip, it was public and notorious that Captain Francisco Carreño ran across a canoe of *negros* and *indios cimarrones* on the Isle of Iguanas. He captured them with the people he had brought. Having used a translator [to interrogate them], Captain Francisco Carreño went with his people to the pueblo of Felipe *negro.*[13] With the people he brought, he took [the settlement], burned the pueblo, fields, and palisade. He brought the *negros* and *negras, indios* and *indias,* to this city where this witness saw the *cimarrones.* . . .

---

1. The interrogatory formed the core of a probanza. Petitioners drafted a list of questions that officials then used to collect sworn depositions from select individuals. The Spanish called what is now eastern Panama and western Colombia Tierra Firme.

2. Interrogatories tended to pose very specific questions that include valuable details about the events they describe. That said, individuals frequently composed probanzas years or decades after the fact.

3. The Spanish term *palenque* means palisade. In the Americas, palisades became ubiquitous fortifications for maroon communities. Eventually, *palenque* would become synonymous with maroon settlements. In 1562, however, Carreño used the term *palenque* to specifically describe the fortifications built by Felipillo and his people.

4. One league is roughly three miles.

5. Isla Iguanas sits just inside the Gulf of San Miguel.

6. Isla San Telmo lies just to the southeast of Isla del Rey, the largest island in the Pearl Islands.
7. Gold pesos. In the first half of the sixteenth century, gold pesos served as the most common unit of currency in the Americas. By mid-century, the discovery of silver in both Peru and Mexico prompted a shift to *pesos de plata*.
8. Gallo's recollection of two or three captives contrasts with Carreño's claim of thirty.
9. The *negro* executed by quartering was likely Felipillo.
10. Bautista calls Felipe a ladino, indicating that he had been among Spaniards long enough to acquire fluency in Spanish.
11. The phrase "public and notorious" represented a legal standard of proof equating to "common knowledge." In context, "notorious" did not imply the negative aspect it carries in English.
12. If true, Carreño omitted that he was in pursuit of his own runaway slaves perhaps because it may have reflected poorly on him as a slave owner.
13. Bautista used the phrase *"tomado lengua de ellos."* Although the statement did not specify who served as interpreter, Bautista understood that the location of Felipe's community was conveyed to Carreño in a language other than Spanish.

3. Information Presented by Nombre de Dios, August 24, 1551
Source: AGI, Panama 29, R. 5, N. 11.

Just as individuals could solicit information for a *probanza de mérito*, cities and institutions could request that officials collect sworn testimony on their behalf, often to substantiate petitions addressed to the king. In 1551, the city of Nombre de Dios requested that the lieutenant governor collect information to substantiate a series of concerns raised by the community. The first two issues listed by the community concerned the threats caused by the growing numbers of maroons and the costs incurred by the community in attempting to suppress and punish maroon attacks.

•   •   •

In the city of Nombre de Dios in the kingdom of Tierra Firme, August 24, 1551...before Antonio Jaymes, lieutenant governor in this city..., appeared Rodrigo de la Fuente who presented a petition that follows:

Very Magnificent Lord

Rodrigo de la Fuente, vecino of this city of Nombre de Dios . . . states that for the service of His Majesty, the good of the *republica* of this city, and the administration of justice in this city, it is convenient that His Majesty be informed of several things that by his order can be remedied. . . . I ask, your mercy, to collect information using the following chapters:

I. If they know that in this kingdom and the district of this city and the road from it to Panama there are over six hundred *negros* who have risen up [and fled] to the bush and forests.[1] They wander about as highwaymen killing and robbing many persons and muleteers, those that travel by that road. Many times, they have come together to the city of Nombre de Dios where they commit murders and thefts and take a large quantity of *negros*. The *negros* that are in this city leave to join up with them and because of this every day [the *negros cimarrones*] greatly grow in number. They have caused many damages in the past and have burned this city and that of Panama many times.[2]

II. If they know that the magistrates of this kingdom have with great care and diligence sent captains with men against the rebellious *negros* to secure the roads and have killed and destroyed many of [the *negros*].[3] The Christians of this city and its funds are not enough to fight the *negros cimarrones*. The costs of doing so are great; if there were a greater quantity of funds available [for] these expenditures, more quickly could the *cimarrones* be destroyed and ended.

The remainder of the petition deals with other matters of civic governance, the administration of justice, and the oversight of officials. Most witnesses that responded to these questions mirrored the language of the petition. However, one offered a much more extensive account of the maroons who threatened Nombre de Dios.

Pero García Marqués

To the first chapter, he said that he knows that which is contained in this question. Ever since this witness has lived in Nombre de Dios he has always seen a great quantity of *negros* who have risen up in the forests. Many times, they have assailed travelers on the road between this city and Panama. In particular, they attacked a [man named] Zarate and other persons, they wounded him in the face with arrows.[4] Later [this witness] heard that the *negros* attacked the road and killed an *español* and other persons that travelled with a muleteer named Frías. They stole his animals, unloaded the [goods] he carried, and took them. This is all public and notorious. Later the people sent out by this city recovered part of that which was stolen and the head of an *español* that they carried.[5] Similarly, he has heard that about one and a half months ago the *negros* went to the Venta de las Juntas that is near this town. They entered there and robbed what they found, taking with them a little *negrillo*. Many other times, he has heard it said that the *negros cimarrones* have taken *negros* sent out for forage, and if they did not want to go with [the *cimarrones*], they killed them.[6] They have killed some and, in this way, have gathered many *negros* and caused much damage to this city. Many other times they have come to the river of this city and taken many *negras* who go there to wash [clothes]. They take [the *negras*] and the clothes by force, and in the place where they go for water, that is El Chorillo, they have taken many *negras* of the vecinos of this city. In all this they do great damage. They have taken a *negra* from this witness and have taken them from many others. . . .

To the second chapter, he said that he knows that with all possible diligence the magistrates of this city have sent people in pursuit of the *negros* and in search of them many times. They have killed and captured many *negros*, meting justice on them. In this conquest, they have spent many funds and . . . these expeditions have cost more than has been raised by the tax set aside for them.[7]

---

1. This is the earliest estimate for the number of maroons in the region. While the number is likely exaggerated for effect, the number of maroons likely exceeded the Spanish population of Nombre de Dios.
2. No other known reports suggest that maroons burned down either city, although they may have set fire to outlying buildings during raids or skirmishes with authorities.
3. Unfortunately, no known documents shed light on the expeditions alluded to here. We do not know who led them, how many soldiers they took, how often they set out, or whether they succeeded in capturing or killing maroons.
4. The specificity of this detail lends credence to the witness's account, as others may have likely remembered these victims.
5. In contrast to the previous two victims, the lack of information about the decapitated Spaniard may indicate that the witness has chosen to engage in some hyperbole intended to further justify the requests of the petition. No other witness offered such a vivid and gruesome account. It is unclear why the maroons would want to take the head of a Spaniard, since the goal of the attack was to capture clothing, weapons, and other manufactured goods.

6. Such strategies for recruitment appear in later resistance movements. Barcia, *West African Warfare*, 125.

7. The witness is referring to the tax authorized in 1536.

4. Alvaro de Sosa to the Crown, May 15, 1553

Source: AGI, Panama 39, N. 29, fs. 162. Also AGI, Patronato 192, N. 1, R. 56.

Soon after arriving in Panama to take up the governorship of the region, Alvaro de Sosa reported his initial impressions to the king. In this long letter, he mentioned the plight of the dwindling city of Acla, its association with maroons, and initial attempts to combat the problem.

This account and the previous documents suggest that maroons had effectively carved out a territory that extended from Nombre de Dios southeast toward Acla and then across the interior to the Gulf of San Miguel. This territory comprised what had once been the Cueva heartland. By the 1550s, maroons had multiple settlements nestled along the region's foothills and rivers. From these locations, they could raid the major transisthmian trade routes, the two port cities, and what was left of Acla.

•   •   •

The city of Acla, which was the first one to be gained in this land,[1] has continued diminishing every year because the vecinos who have chosen to stay are few. I believe they do not number ten, counting *españoles* and *mestizos*. There have been times when there were one hundred vecinos, which was when it served as the port for this land. When that moved to Nombre de Dios, the decline began.[2] Several of the vecinos have told me that unless Your Majesty provides for their maintenance so they do not suffer, they will have to relocate. I have written to them telling them that Your Majesty ordered me to take particular care in the support of the city, and that Your Majesty ordered me to send an account of what Your Majesty can do [in this]. In the meantime, I sent them some people and food. Those that went informed me that those that live there have enough food from their fields and mines. They have *negros* that work [to sustain them]. The principal trouble they have comes from the *negros cimarrones*, for the land itself is good. The [*negros cimarrones*] are the ones that bring unrest to the city. The *negros* that wander in the bush surpass eight hundred and have very good

settlements. We have begun to issue orders to stop them. We have ordered
that every year they undertake an expedition. In the past this was done with
many men and cost a great deal but bore little fruit, costing four thousand
pesos.[3] Now it appears to us that it is better to send fewer men many times
during the year, to two or three areas searching for them. [Recently] from
one of these groups we have news that they arrived at a pueblo of the
negros. Before they arrived, they captured two *negros*, and through inter-
preters learned that the settlement was very large. The captain that led our
[men], not being very valiant, informed us of what had happened and
asked for more men, and having done so I told him to venture where he
wished.[4] We do not know what will come of this. [5] Turning back to what
must be done with this city of Acla, what I believe now is that whenever
such a force leaves here, they should leave men hidden. . . . I am thinking
of sending fifteen or twenty men, giving them some maize to eat. [With
these men] in place, [the *negros cimarrones*] will not be able to leave [their
settlements]. Having these men there the land will be safe from the *cimarrones*. It is possible that they could lead better expeditions from there than
we can from here [Nombre de Dios], even if it would cost more. In the
meantime, Your Majesty should order that which is most appropriate to
your service. . . .

1. Santa María la Antigua was the first formal city founded in the region. In the 1530s,
   after Santa María had been abandoned, some of its residents moved to Acla where
   they merged the two communities' governments, becoming Santa María del Antigua de Acla. Governor Sosa may have counted Acla as the first settlement because
   Acla had inherited Santa María's earlier claim. Ceballos, "New World Civitas,"
   34–35.
2. Furthermore, the lure of new conquests in Peru and westward into Central America
   drew many residents away from the city during the 1530s and 1540s. Although an
   important city during the conquest of the Cueva, Acla quickly became a backwater
   only connected to other areas via coastal trade and lacking local labor or industry
   other than gold placer mining.
3. For a single expedition, especially one that saw little success, this was an exorbi-
   tant cost.
4. Sosa clearly expresses frustration that the captain did not press the attack.
5. The not-valiant leader of the expedition may have been Captain Morcillo. The next
   documents reveal that Morcillo would attempt an assault, only to be killed along
   with most of his men.

5. Francisco Carreño's 1554 Expedition against Bayano (1562)

Source: AGI, Patronato 150, N. 14, R. 2, fs. 753–805.

Over the next three years, Governor Alvaro de Sosa would implement his plan to send smaller, more frequent expeditions against the maroons. These expeditions would reveal that the maroons not only had multiple settlements but were also led by a king, named Bayano. Sosa's plan to use small expeditions to defeat or constrain the maroons did not account for their numerical superiority and social and political organization. These were not small groups of runaway slaves but rather a socially complex, hierarchical society capable of subsistence and self-defense.

Unaware of the nature of their opposition, or overconfident in their superiority, four Spanish expeditions set out between 1553 and 1555. The first, likely alluded to in the previous document, ended with all but three or four Spaniards being killed. The second, led by Francisco Carreño, avoided combat and instead sought to peacefully negotiate with Bayano. Yet the fleeting peace secured by Carreño would not last.

Likely mistrusting Spanish intentions, Bayano appears to have chosen to ignore the terms of the agreement. In response, Governor Sosa sent out another expedition led by Captain Lozano. The maroons defeated Lozano, sending his men fleeing. In the hopes of reestablishing the peace, Sosa once again sent Carreño to Bayano. Although this overture occurred peacefully, Bayano did not leave his territory. Instead, he sought to appease the Spanish by turning over one of his maroon captains and several *negras* that his captain had stolen from the Spanish.

After three years and four expeditions, the Spanish would make no progress against Bayano and his people. This document, Carreño's probanza from 1562, offers the most candid and detailed account of these expeditions. Although no formal record of the tentative peace between Sosa and Bayano exists, this probanza, and the testimony it contains, offers clues as to the nature of the terms.

• • •

IIII. Item, if they know, etc. that in the year 1554, Alvaro de Sosa sent [Francisco Carreño] as captain with certain men in search of *negros cimarrones* that, according to Captain Morcillo, had a settlement up the Río Chepo in the foothills of the mountains.[1] The settlement was ruled over and commanded by a *negro* named King Bayano who had a great quantity of *negros* and *negras cimarrones* and many fields and huts. When Morcillo and his soldiers arrived, the negros fought them, killing the captain and his men such that only three or four men escaped.[2]

V. Item, if they know that when word arrived in this city [Panama City] of the defeat and of the great multitude of *negros cimarrones*, there was much unrest and scandal in this kingdom because the location of the settlement was so notorious and all the *negros* wished to rise up and leave the service of their masters; they fled every day, going to join up with Bayano. If no remedy could be found for the terror felt [by the vecinos] and the many *negros* who had risen up, this kingdom would experience terrible misfortune and perdition; no one would be able to have estates in the countryside or walk the roads without great risk and the deaths of many.

VI. Item, if they know, etc. that same year, in order to remedy that which Bayano had done and to prevent the harm that could come, Governor Alvaro de Sosa and the cabildo of this city, named Francisco Carreño a captain. He went with his men of war to the pueblo of Bayano. He brought Bayano, who was called king, and other captains of his, to the city of Nombre de Dios and Governor Alvaro de Sosa.[3] In doing so he did a great service for His Majesty and to this kingdom. Captain Francisco Carreño did this without payment from the royal treasury, nor did any vecino of this city or any other person pay him a salary or reward for this, instead Captain Francisco Carreño spent over eight hundred pesos of his own wealth and estate.[4]

VII. Item, if they know etc. that Governor Alvaro de Sosa, having made peace with Bayano and sending him back to his pueblo, sent Captain Francisco Lozano against [Bayano] with many men, at the expense of the cities of this kingdom. When Lozano arrived, he could not defeat Bayano as he and his *cimarrones* had burned their pueblo and all the food, after which Francisco Lozano returned to this city having lost over forty men on the expedition.[5] To fix this, Governor Alvaro de Sosa ordered Captain Francisco Carreño to take no more than three men and return to the bush to seek out Bayano. He found Bayano and entreated peacefully. Bayano gave him *negras* that have been stolen from the city of Nombre de Dios along with one of his captains who had taken [the women].[6] Captain Francisco Carreño brought the *negras* and the *negro* to Nombre de Dios and turned them in to the lieutenant [governor] Gonzalo de Avila who brought some of them to justice. In all this Francisco Carreño spent much of his estate and never received any salary or reward other than serving His Majesty and this *republica*.

The probanza goes on to describe Francisco Carreño's services defending Nombre de Dios from French attacks in 1559, preparing for a possible attack by Lope de Aguirre in 1561, and serving the king by discovering pearl fisheries and enriching the treasury, among other services. Below are excerpts from witness testimony that expand on Carreño's questions.

Bernaldo Gallo, vecino of Panama City

VI. To the sixth question, [the witness] said that he knows that in order to remedy the damages done by Captain Bayano, the other rebellious *negros*, and to disband them, the magistrates and *regimiento* of this city sent Captain Francisco Carreño with soldiers to capture and disband them. This witness saw Captain Francisco Carreño with the men given to him leave on the expedition in two ships.[7] It seems to this witness that within one or two months, that Captain Francisco Carreño returned to the city of Nombre de Dios and brought with him Captain Bayano and other captains of his who he brought with peaceful entreaties. [Captain Carreño] turned them over to the magistrates of the city of Nombre de Dios. . . .

VII. To the seventh question, [the witness] said that he knows that when Captain Francisco Carreño brought the *negro*, Captain Bayano, and the other *negros*, his captains, he agreed to a peace with them. This witness does not know the details. This witness has heard that having received license from the magistrates to return to their pueblo to bring other *negros* and people who lived there, it was public and notorious that Captain Bayano went to his pueblo and did not return. This witness went in his own boat to the Gulf of San Miguel where Bayano resides to see if he would return by boat with his people, having brought supplies for the voyage. When this witness arrived at the landing, he found a Christian who had gone [there] as a messenger for the magistrates to call upon Captain Bayano. When this witness arrived [the messenger] was dying of hunger and told him that they should leave because Captain Bayano had told him that he would not come.[8] This witness left. Later this witness saw that the magistrates and *regimiento* of this city sent Francisco Lozano as a captain with soldiers to bring Captain Bayano [as a captive] and defeat [the *negros*]. This witness saw Francisco Lozano and his men depart on the expedition. Within a few days this witness knows and saw that Captain Lozano returned to this city without any captives and that it was public and notorious that several soldiers died of hunger and thirst. . . .

Juan Bautista de Señor, vecino of Panama City

VII. To the seventh question, this witness knows that after Captain Francisco Carreño brought the *negro*, King Bayano, Alvaro de Sosa, governor, made peace with them under certain terms. King Bayano and his captains returned to their pueblo with the understanding that they would come back after several days. After that time had elapsed, and having seen that the *negro*, King Bayano, had not returned, Alvaro de Sosa, governor, raised another force to go against them, under Captain Francisco Lozano. This witness saw Francisco Lozano and his men depart on their journey. It was public and notorious in this city that King Bayano *negro* did not want to return [because] before he arrived, they had burned the pueblo. Therefore, Captain Lozano returned to this city. This witness knows that the expedition cost [public funds] and that some soldiers died. Governor Alvaro de Sosa having seen what had happened once again called Captain Francisco Carreño to go to the pueblo of King Bayano. This witness knows that [Carreño] went on the expedition and that entreated peacefully with King Bayano. [Carreño] turned over some *negros* and *negras* that King Bayano had given him to the magistrates of the city of Nombre de Dios. . . .

1. This location offered security and access to much of the isthmus. The Río Chepo allowed easy transit toward Panama City. From any point along the river, overland travel west would lead to the overland transisthmian trade route between Nombre de Dios and Panama. Crossing the ridgeline to the north, maroons could reach the Caribbean. Crossing foothills to the east, maroons could travel down various river systems to the Gulf of San Miguel.
2. Later accounts note that the maroons used lookouts. Morcillo and his men may have been ambushed by maroons alerted to their presence.
3. Carreño's description is painfully vague. Did Carreño initially fight Bayano's men? Did Carreño take initiative to negotiate with Bayano? It appears that Carreño or Bayano made the choice to attempt a peaceful solution.
4. Carreño's commission stipulated a reward for captured maroons. Negotiation removed the possibility of recouping his investment. AGI, Panama 150, N. 14, R. 2, fs. 806.
5. Bayano and his people likely feared that the knowledge of their location would increase the likelihood of further Spanish attacks. Burning the community and relocating represented an attempt to ensure their own safety.
6. This may reflect terms of the agreement between Bayano and Sosa. Frequently, treaties between colonial authorities and maroons stipulated that maroons had to return any runaway slaves who arrived after the signing of the peace.
7. At this time, the Spanish believed that the best way to reach Bayano's settlement was to travel by ship to the Gulf of San Miguel and then up one of the many rivers that empty into the gulf.

8. Bayano may have been fearful of Spanish treachery or unconvinced by the terms. Did the peace offer freedom and pardons to all his subjects? Did the Spanish expect him to return subjects who had more recently fled the Spanish or who had been liberated by other maroons? Where did the Spanish intend for the community to settle? With so many possible points of conflict, and Spanish accounts so universally vague as to the terms, Bayano's reticence was well-founded.

6. Alvaro de Sosa to the Crown, April 4, 1555
Source: AGI, Panama 29, R. 6, N. 25, fs. 4–4v.

After several years of commissioning expeditions, Governor Sosa wrote to the king, updating him on those efforts. Although this letter was less detailed than Francisco Carreño's probanza, the governor wrote it soon after the events that it describes. The letter does not discuss Carreño's second expedition to Bayano, suggesting that it may have been written prior to or during that undertaking.

After seeing how the maroons responded to his plans, Sosa recognized that in the face of Spanish military force maroons tended to disperse instead of confronting the expedition. Maroons would continue to use this tactic, dispersion and evasion, to minimize Spaniards' ability to recapture or kill their number. In response, Sosa suggested that the Spanish establish a settlement in the region. While he did not explain his rationale thoroughly, such a strategy endeavored to occupy lands otherwise under the control of maroons, denying them resources and limiting their mobility. Additionally, a settlement could serve as a permanent base of operations to drive the maroons farther from the vital transisthmian trade routes and the two major port cities.

. . .

I have also written to Your Majesty about the great trouble that this land has of the *negros cimarrones*, in this I have worked mightily and spent many funds. I have ordered three expeditions against them, which to all has appeared to be the best attempt so far. In these, there have been some misfortunes both with the captains that have gone and because the land is so sterile and lacking in food. The first captain that we sent [Morcillo], the *cimarrones* killed, he was the most well prepared and a man most suitable for the task. The other captains have tried to negotiate with the *negros* or at least one of their leaders.[1] It appears that there has been division among them, because they have not come to conclude the peace.[2] Now, I continue to search for another way to rout these people. It is to settle fifty or sixty men near them. Half of these should be *negros* of whom we have total confidence, purchased with our funds, and who will receive their freedom after a time of service.[3] The *cimarrones* are a people that unless one constantly sends expeditions against them it will not be enough because during the expedition they scatter, but once it has returned they regroup. This has cost much and there are few funds; the vecinos are very bothered by financing the expeditions and by renting out [their] *negros* to them because when they have [the *negros*] die on the expedition.[4] Your Majesty would be served to order how best to finance these efforts.

The proposed settlement would not come to fruition during Sosa's tenure as governor, although the suggestion would resurface during later periods of Spanish-maroon conflict.

1. This statement seems to imply that Captain Lozano's ill-fated expedition had orders to reestablish negotiation with Bayano.
2. Sosa likely based this assessment on reports by Carreño and others. Although Spaniards frequently considered Bayano to be king of his people, his authority may not have been absolute. In the 1570s, the maroon communities of the region appeared to form a confederation of subgroups defined by shared diasporic experiences. The leaders of these subgroups had their own hierarchical relationships. Wheat, *Atlantic Africa and the Spanish Caribbean*, 55–63; Tardieu, *Cimarrones de Panamá*, 198–235. If a similar structure existed in Bayano's time, he may have been the highest-ranking maroon leader but not an absolute monarch. The division described by Sosa may indicate that internal politics among maroons impeded the establishment of a peace.
3. This plan's reliance on enslaved African labor reinforces the centrality of African labor to Spaniards in Panama. Even when attempting to combat African maroons, Spaniards could not envision establishing a community that did not rely on coerced African labor for its basic subsistence and survival.
4. With little to no available Indigenous labor, these expeditions relied on enslaved Africans as porters and to provide other manual labor. Since private citizens owned most slaves in the region, captains had to rent out slaves to serve the needs of the expedition.

7. Excerpts from Pedro de Aguado's *Historia de Venezuela* Describing the War against King Bayano, ca. 1556 (1581)

Source: Aguado, *Historia de Venezuela*, vol. 2, 183–229.

In 1556, the newly appointed viceroy of Peru, the Marques de Cañete, passed through the isthmus on his way to Lima. When apprised of the region's maroons, the viceroy attempted to address the problems that had so plagued Governor Sosa. He immediately authorized the expenditure of thirty thousand pesos. Half would be spent fortifying the port of Nombre de Dios. The other half would fund an expedition against the maroons. The viceroy prevailed on Pedro de Ursúa, a veteran conquistador to lead this expedition. Ursúa had participated in conquests in the New Kingdom of Granada (modern Colombia) where he founded several towns and had experience fighting insurgent Indigenous groups. The viceroy bolstered Ursúa's troops by offering pardons to Spanish prisoners awaiting trial for treason and rebellion if they chose to go on the expedition. As a result, Ursúa's forces greatly outnumbered any prior efforts to militarily defeat the maroons.

Pedro de Aguado, a Franciscan friar who chronicled the early exploration and settlement of Venezuela and Colombia, preserved this account of Ursúa's efforts. In the larger history, Aguado recounts Ursúa's exploits in in the conquests of the New Kingdom of Granada through his death at the hands of the traitor Lope de Aguirre. Although written from a Spanish perspective, the account contains valuable descriptions of how Panama's maroons lived. At the same time, the author's biases against Africans color the narrative. Readers must be careful to disentangle Aguado's prejudice from the events that he recorded.

•   •   •

Chapter Nine

In those same days, the vecinos of Panama and Nombre de Dios, especially the merchants who lived off trade and commerce, were filled with a terrible fear because for many days many *negro* slaves, fed up with the servitude and captivity their masters held them in, had taken to hiding in the depths of the most remote forests and mountains, with the desire to preserve their liberty or die for it. There they had built a pueblo and fortress, keeping in that safe place their wives, children, and other weak persons. The most valiant and courageous *negros* go out to the royal road between Nombre de Dios and Panama, where mule trains carry goods to Panama. They rob and pillage the muleteers and passengers, stealing all they carry, so much that they have ruined many great estates. With such evil deeds they have shown that they would like to completely destroy and ruin these two fertile cities. Although some persons were charged with disciplining and destroying this gathering of *negros*, lured with great promises of reward and recompense, none has left to undertake it, as the *negros* are entrenched and fortified in a stronghold, so knowledgeable and skilled in the land, which by its nature is harsh and obscure, that they go about almost daring someone to find them. They have arrived many times with shameful temerity, confident in their nimbleness, at the gates and watering holes of Nombre de Dios to take and steal *negras* and other persons that go out for the things they need, without fear of punishment. . . . [1]

Aguado then praises the appointment of Pedro de Ursúa as captain of an expedition to go out against the *negros*. After receiving support from merchants and leaders in Panama City, Ursúa travelled to Nombre de Dios to assemble his forces.

Pedro de Ursúa went to Nombre de Dios, where he raised a flag and with the sound of a drum began to gather men. He made Francisco Gutiérrez his *maestre de campo*, a native of Seville but not practiced in the art of war, having no experience. Yet he was very motivated, valiant, and of quick intellect so that despite his inexperience in short time he learned what many others never do, as later he would show. Ursúa named his *capitanes de infantería*: Francisco Díaz, a relative of his who would later lose his head in the Motilones, and Pedro de la Fuente, a man practiced in this land for having served with other *españoles* pursuing and hunting the *negros [cimarrones]*.[2] He named García de Arze *alférez* of the expedition, a good soldier, excellent harquebusier who later died at the hand of Lope de Aguirre on the journey down the Marañón.[3] Francisco de Cisneros and Pedro de Peralta he made squad leaders.

It took several days for Pedro de Ursúa to assemble and organize the men for this war. During that time, Pedro de Mazuelos, the elder, sent four thousand pesos worth of goods in two mule trains to Panama—with less protection than calamitous times like these require. When the muleteers arrived at a river beside the Sierra de Capira, a gang of over twenty *negros cimarrones* came out onto the road, armed with bows and arrows, machetes for swords, and some thin spears.[4] In order to spread fear in all those passengers who might travel through in the future, the *negros* desired to slaughter the pack animals and passengers and spread their bodies along the road so that this abominable example of cruelty might terrorize all the residents of Panama and Nombre de Dios.[5] But the *negros* were prevented from doing this cruel deed by one of their leaders. Hoping to show his humanity and clemency, he not only freed the muleteers and the *españoles* who travelled with them but also gave them the majority of pack animals so that they could continue to travel. They only kept some of the sturdier and better-looking mules along with all of the goods. Later, they separated from the goods the most useful and helpful items: Rouen fabric, canvas, machetes, scissors, knives and other items of quality. The rest they threw in the banks of the river, and [they] returned to their hideout with what they carried, leaving some items hidden so they might return for them.

The news of the assault reached Nombre de Dios, where it moved all the residents to complain of the negligence and carelessness of those that governed. Despite their duty to remedy such unrest and safeguard those who travelled, with drowsy sloppiness and deaf dissimulation they allowed the evils of the *negros* to occur, not considering the damage and irreparable dangers that could transpire from these underestimated actions. The magistrates, believing the issue of the *negros* to have been entrusted to Pedro de Ursúa, excused themselves saying that the remedy and relief that everyone requested lay in his hand. Pedro de Mazuelos, who had been particularly put out by the robbery perpetrated by the slaves, proposed to Pedro de Ursúa that should he quickly dispatch his men to where the attack had occurred and, following the *negros*, recapture the stolen merchandise, he would give them part of the goods, or otherwise pay them a certain salary for their work in searching.

Ursúa immediately sent out Captain Pedro de la Fuente with fifteen men. He not only entrusted him with the recovery of Mazuelos's merchandise but ordered that they acquire a *negro* alive who might serve as a guide to find the settlements and camps of the *negros* so that they might not go out blind or haphazardly to search for them in the impenetrable mountains of Nombre de Dios. Pedro de la Fuente, guided by muleteers, arrived at the place where the robberies had occurred, finding all manner of clothing, including silks, velvet, taffeta, and other things of value, spread out on the ground. [Fuente] ordered that they collect all the goods. As they did so, they heard the din of a large gang approaching them from the mountain. Captain Fuente, wanting to know what it was, ordered his men to assemble without a sound and hid with them. There they waited next to the bank of the river and the mountain until out of the forest emerged ten agile *negros* well-armed according to their manner. They waited until the [*negros*] left the woods and came into the open. Once they were in a suitable position [the *españoles*] charged them, crying "SANTIAGO."[6]

The *negros*, not disturbed to see the *españoles* overrunning them, readied their weapons and waited in good form, similarly crying out the name "SANTIAGO" like the *españoles* who charged them.[7] [The *negros*] wishing to encourage one another, so that they might have a victory that would be honorable and beneficial to themselves and their companions, could only cry out "For today, for today," as they were incapable of properly pronouncing Castilian, and were not able to say anything else. They meant to say, "Today is the day to win a complete victory over our enemies, who we can vanquish if fortune does not leave us!"[8] And it appeared so, even though at the moment they were fewer in number than the *españoles*, in other ways [the *españoles*] were not their equals but inferior, the agility of those barbarians was so great that in their hand was the choice to wait, attack, or flee. Beyond this, the weather and land were to their advantage, it being a dark and overcast day and light rain having begun to fall, wetting all the land. Where they were was rugged and full of large slippery rocks, which allowed the *negros* to easily and agilely jump from rock to rock and place to place while making it very difficult for our men.[9] Consequently they could not engage their enemies in combat. Seeing this, the *negros*, from the high ground that they favored, let fly arrows and rocks from greater safety and with greater strength than our men. Moreover, the harquebuses that the *españoles* carried were completely useless because the light rain had dampened the powder in the flash pans so they would not fire.[10]

Small river similar to the scene described by Aguado. *Photograph by the author.*

The fight went a long time without fortune favoring one side. Early, the *negros* had wounded one or two *españoles*, leading some of the *negros* to assume they were more courageous and that they had a much greater advantage in one-on-one combat. From different sides three of them came upon three *españoles* who had been separated from the rest. The success of two [of these] *españoles* killing two of the *negros* who came at them, while leaving the third to fight with their companion, was of immense encouragement to our side and put great fear into the other [*negros*] as their leader and captain had been slain. Not wanting to wait for another group of *negros* that was coming behind, they turned to flee, escaping with nimbleness into the mountain and forest that favored them, leaping with great speed and ease from rock to rock, almost mocking the *españoles* that tried to follow them. Yet, [Captain Fuente], wise in such combat, did not allow a single soldier to follow the *negros*, instead gathering their weapons and beginning to interrogate the *negro* that remained in their hands. They asked if the *negros'* hideout or settlement was nearby. He responded no but [that], after him and his companions, fifteen other *negros* would shortly arrive and that those who had fled would not return to the location of their main settlement out of fear.[11] The safest thing that the *españoles* could do was return with haste unless they wanted to be killed or captured by the *negros* who would be coming, including a valiant captain, a bishop,[12] and other notable valiant men of his company. Not only would they have the numerical advantage over the *españoles*, but also their strength, valor, and skill at arms was greater. Nevertheless, it would take them time to arrive.

Captain Fuente believed what the *negro* had told them, but, not showing fickleness or cowardice, instead placing his trust in immortal God to give him a complete victory over these thieves that would harm and injure Christians by assaulting them and robbing them on the roads, he stayed put with his men, arms at the ready, awaiting the arrival of the *negros*.

Chapter Ten

The seven *negros* that had fled the first skirmish encountered the fifteen that were on their way. Having given them news of what happened, how few *españoles* were, and how tired they were from the fight, they all returned [to the site of the first battle] together. They distributed the arrows and other weapons that remained among their number. Accelerating their pace with great nimbleness and desiring to set themselves against the *españoles*, they closed on them with large leaps and shouts of joy, throwing themselves in the air and over great rocks, by their appearance very agile leaps, in the hopes of instilling fear into the *españoles* and causing them to flee. They were so focused on this, that even though they spied our men from far off, they did not desist until they had fallen upon them, firing an infinity of arrows and saying in their garbled way, that imitated Castilian speech, "Today, Christians, Santiago, at them!"

The soldiers received and rebuffed this fury by the slaves with singular valor. Not only did they not receive any arrow wound, but Captain Fuente y Vega, *español*, firing two harquebuses that he had on hand, aimed them expertly so that the two balls killed two valiant *negros* that led the advance. One of them being the captain or figure that the *negros* held as their leader. With this they lost some of the verve that they had initially shown when they saw the *españoles*, perceiving this first exchange to be a bad omen. Nonetheless, they did not stop fighting or shooting arrows or barbs at the *españoles*. For their part [the *espanoles*] did not relent, although they had reason to fear the vigor of the *negros*. Once again firing his two harquebuses, Fuente y Vega employed them so well firing various times he wounded and killed other *negros*, such that they lost their zeal.[13] Seeing how timidly and loosely the slaves fought, Captain Fuente y Vega dropped his harquebuses and took up sword and buckler, lashing out at them so furiously that they turned and fled. The *españoles* gave chase and captured five *negros* alive.

So great was the fear of the slaves that they could not look our men in the face.[14] With this victory the countryside being safe, the *españoles* took the *negros* captive and along with the recovered merchandise returned to Nombre de Dios, where their arrival spurred great happiness and contentment in the pueblo that only a little while earlier had been fearful and terrified.

Later a small scandal began between residents and slaveowners and the royal treasury officials and soldiers who captured the slaves. The vecinos who had previously owned the [maroons] desired to return them to their prior servitude so they might benefit from them once again, believing their claims to be most valid. The royal treasury officials, by an unclear and twisted claim, asked that they be sold, and the funds placed in the royal treasury. The soldiers, who did the work of capturing these bandits and the risk of defeating them, also wished that they be sold as a reward for their efforts and believed having been captured in war and combat their claim was the most just in law. But all these litigants put aside their claims to the fulfilment of justice and the laws. [The *negros*] having been placed in the jail, the lieutenant governor or royal magistrate condemned them for their crimes, sentencing them to be set upon by dogs before being hanged, a severe punishment, yet a deserved one because of the cruelty of the delinquents. . . . The punishment was done in this way: placing a thick rope in the public plaza between a post and the nearest window on the plaza and strung with six iron collars, they put the *negros* into the collars naked from neck to waist with small bars in their hands.

Readers should be aware that the following two paragraphs contain explicit descriptions of the maroons' public execution.

Among these slaves was one who they held to be their spiritual leader and who held the honor of being called "bishop." This one, in a superstitious and heretical manner baptized, instructed, and preached doing other manner of ceremonies that they call celebrating or saying mass.[15] In these things, and other abominable superstitions they take for religion, all the *negros* were so fanatical and devoted that despite being exhorted to renounce and return to the Catholic faith, and welcome the baptism that they had received, they did not wish to do so even at the point of death.[16] Instead, in imitation of other Lutherans, they believed that their rustic and vain ceremonies were the true religion.[17] This was particularly true for the *negro* bishop. When he and others were extorted to receive death as Christians, confessing and receiving absolution, so with contrition they might be saved through the mediating grace of the death and passion of the Son of God, the barbarian responded, with signs of a bedeviled spirit, that he already desired death, because with his death and that of his companions he hoped to receive complete vengeance against the people of this pueblo for when his spirit arrives in his land it will bring a horde of people who will destroy and devastate the city. He never thought to give up the religion that he and his held, instead choosing to live and die in it.

The other *negros* gave the same response as their bishop. With that the executioner released some mastiffs, dogs of enormous size kept for this reason.[18] These, as they had already been taught to bite human flesh, at the moment they were released began to bite and rend. As the *negros* had small bars in their hands to defend themselves from the dogs without being able to do damage to the animals, they began to fight and take vengeance upon the mastiffs. These animals, more irascible than any other, with great fury set upon the miserable *negros* with teeth and strength of limbs, rending large chunks of flesh in all directions. Even though through these agonies the *negros* were called to return to the faith, they did not wish to do so.[19] After they had been ripped up and bitten by the dogs, they were removed from the collars and carried to gallows set apart from the pueblo. There they were hung, ending the well-deserved punishment for their rebellion and treason.

The way that they celebrate matters of their religion is this: in order to imitate the mass, the bishop dresses in a black shirt with a crimson tunic. He then approaches a type of altar that they had made in their sanctuary, and in the presence of all the bystanders who have come to hear and see, he puts a jug of wine and a roll of bread on the altar. He sings a type of song in his maternal tongue to which all those present respond, and in their presence he eats the bread and drinks the wine. Having eaten the bread and drunk the wine his service concludes, and everyone is satisfied, having watched and listened with great attention and devotion.[20]

In his sermons and preaching he tries to persuade the listeners to maintain their obstinate liberty, defending their pueblo and the land they possess with arms, supporting their king, who they call Bayano, revered and obeyed by all as their natural lord in the same manner as other people, and that he might maintain them and govern them with justice, defending them from the *españoles* that desire their destruction. They baptize their infants in this way: many *negros* and *negras* come together as godfathers and godmothers, taking the child to the sanctuary. There they have all the wine they can, they drink, dance, and sing. At the same time the bishop takes a jar of water and dumps it over the infant, after which everyone dances, sings, and drinks. Once this is done, they return to the home of the recently baptized. They have many other vain and crazy ceremonies like these, all of which are rustic and unworthy to be recorded.[21]

A few days after the execution, a squad of very nimble *negros* left the mountains to attack the outskirts of Nombre de Dios, believing that the *españoles* would be caught unawares by their arrival—they were not mistaken. They arrived at the vegetable garden owned by Alonso Peréz and encountered some *negras* and other people who were washing. Taking with them most of the clothes, they practically winked at the gates of Nombre de Dios. They incited a great scandal in the pueblo, because they did this at midday when the sun shone most strongly and the people left the streets, for walking in the sun at that hour can cause illness and is bad for one's health. All the residents were resting or sleeping in the cool and shade of their entryways and hall-ways.[22] Suddenly hearing the sound of bells, the signal for men to gather with arms in the case of sudden attack, everyone was shocked, fearing that enemies were already in the city. Quickly mobilizing, a group of soldiers gave chase to the *negros*, but with their agility and knowledge of the land the *negros* had a great advantage over the *españoles* in pursuit. The [*negros*] did not come to any harm, nor should they have had much fear, for later, still close [to the town], they hid, disappearing so they could not be found.

The residents of Nombre de Dios, fearing that the *negros* come so near and regularly commit robberies and assaults at the very doors of their homes, ordered that guards and patrols, on foot and horse, keep watch day and night over those areas where the *negros* might approach. But even with these guards, such is the shamelessness and daring of the *negros* that they came from the mountains to areas unwatched, not even considered. With nimbleness and incredible speed, they committed the damage they could to the unprepared people they encountered, quickly returning to hide in the mountains.

Chapter Eleven

Of those captured by Pedro de la Fuente, one slave appeared docile and well-disposed to be a translator and guide, knowledgeable of the land where the *negros* had established themselves and of other information that would be needed in the future. This one gave a long account of where the hideout of the runaway slaves was located. He acknowledged that there were over three hundred of them, and that there had been such discontent that they elected and raised up from among their number as headman or leader, a *negro* of good temper and strength, very fluent in Castilian, who they called King Bayano.[23] They serve and respect him with the veneration due a prince, mix-ing rites and ceremonies from Guinea, as were used with their kings and rulers, with those that later they saw *españoles* use with their judges and superiors.[24] And like this, King Bayano governs them in a manner similar to a magistrate, although barbaric, dealing with all those subject to his power making them obey, fear, and fulfill all that he commands.

Near to where [the *negros*] were fortified, there was a pueblo of *indios* named Caricua.[25] Their residents had been subjugated and placed in servi-tude with rigorous violence [by the *negros*], taking from them their daughters and wives and mixing with them.[26] Mixing themselves, men with women, from which they engendered another type of people, who in color are dissimilar to the father and the mother, even though they are called *mulatos*—and by appearances they are—they bear such a slight resemblance to the children of *negras* and *blancos*. And as a result, those who are properly called *mulatos* call those of this mixture—that of *negros* and *indias*—*zambaigos*, such that they are a people that do not deserve the honorable name of *mulatos*.[27]

The shamelessness and haughtiness of this King Bayano grew so great that several times he constrained and forced the governor of the pueblos of Panama and Nombre de Dios to parley, to consent that he come and talk and engage in negotiations over his survival and his liberty, as if this land was actually that of his ancestors and that the *españoles* had usurped and taken that [which] was theirs by natural and common right.[28] But, the Governor carefully considering the strength of these fugitive slaves, the great damages they had caused to many places, the unrest [they caused] in the pueblos, the impediment to travel, concealing the affront caused by their rustic and vile acts, granted them an audience. He respected the truce that brought them to the towns, so long as [neither Bayano] nor any of the slaves that accompanied him committed any afront or excess, faithfully keeping [the truce], despite the unworthiness of these *negros* and slaves, who did not honor the servitude of their masters and owners to which they had been obligated.

For the many times that they had taken up arms and come against [the cities] to destroy and devastate them, not contenting themselves with the theft and robbery committed with the tyrannical liberty that they possesses, [the Governor] not only did not need to keep the peace, but by whatever means and through whatever deception they could be tricked and lured, as through false promises, would be just. One could do so without breaking the faith that otherwise accompanies those bound to promises of truce, meting upon them whatever punishment the occasion deserved.[29] In this respect, in breaking [the truce, the Governor] would not expect greater damage to be caused to the *republicas*. Later, Pedro de Ursúa would order such [treachery] to defeat the gathering and uprising of these *negros*. This was beneficial as will be thoroughly explained.

[Ursúa] understood, from the slave [guide], that the settlement in which the King Bayano perpetually resided was down the coast, a little way inland from the sea. The land being very closed and rugged, the General Pedro de

Ursúa sent munitions, victuals, and other heavy war materiel difficult to carry by sea. He would travel with the men by land with what they could carry. Even though the number of soldiers that he had gathered was very small and fewer than the sum of *negros*—he had wanted to assemble one hundred men—the clamor of the pueblos was such that he was almost forced out of Nombre de Dios, in the month of October, still lacking many things and with only forty men. Earlier he had sent Francisco Gutiérrez, his *maestre de campo*, with another thirty men, munitions, and victuals to a landing, or predetermined bay, to await those coming by land.[30] He arrived there after four days of sailing and awaited Pedro de Ursúa. For his part, Ursúa was delayed eighteen days as he explored the land, sending scouts this way and that to see if on those ventures they could find a settlement or cave occupied by an isolated group of these thieves. Despite searching with all due diligence, he did not find anything. While it was useless to dispatch squads, it greatly benefited his soldiers, because walking and trekking with their weapons from one part to the next without any rest except for a short break, they came to be as accustomed to the work as if they had previous experience.[31] When later they began to pursue and destroy the assembly of *negros*, they did their work without laxity or carelessness, [which] was a great reason that they would achieve victory in their efforts.

After arriving at the beach where those sent by ship awaited, Pedro de Ursúa consulted and debated what to do. With all speed, General Pedro de Ursúa sent Captain Fuente with twenty-five well equipped soldiers to spend three days travelling through the mountains and sierras learning the land and its disposition, returning to report on what they learned so that he might better order what should be done.

On the second morning after leaving the maritime base, Fuente found some signs of *negros* that led him to a relatively deep swamp difficult to traverse. Fuente set out to cross it. After some of his men had started out, a squad of *negros* that had spent the night nearby sensed them. They set themselves upon those *españoles* who had passed through the water, forcing them back across to their companions. In this first encounter, the attack of the *negros*, even though outnumbering the *españoles*, was not as effective as they believed, not causing any damage to the soldiers. Instead, it gave them space to group together, [and] fortifying themselves one to another they defended themselves with singular valor for many days. The *negros* of this first encounter saw that the *españoles* did not show weakness or cowardice.

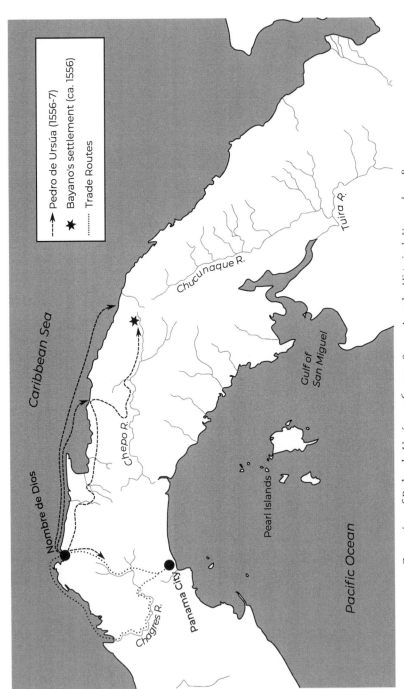

Campaign of Pedro de Ursúa, 1556–1557. *Source:* Aguado, *Historia de Venezuela,* 2:183–229.

Caribbean Sea

Nombre de Dios

Chepo R.

Chucunaque R.

Tuira R.

Gulf of
San Miguel

Pearl Islands

Panama City

Chagres R.

Pacific Ocean

→ Pedro de Ursúa (1556-7)
★ Bayano's settlement (ca. 1556)
⋯⋯ Trade Routes

They did not show any sign of retreat, fighting with their harquebuses and other arms. Breaking off from the *negros*, who the [*españoles*] hoped to defeat and take captive, a scout set off with great speed to ask for aid and assistance from the other *negros* and their king. He sent new reinforcements and a great abundance of arrows and other projectiles that they use.

Together they now numbered ninety forbidding *negros*. Some, having been assailed and wounded by our weapons and harquebuses, did not dare come close enough to be caught. Instead, they attempted to surround our [soldiers] and close off any route of retreat, constricting them day and night so that they could not put down their weapons. By this way, they hoped to deny the *españoles* food, causing them to lose physical strength, rendering them unable to wield their weapons and easier to defeat and vanquish.

Captain Fuente and his men spent eight days this way.[32] After which, Pedro de Ursúa, suspecting that some ill fate had delayed them, sent Captain Francisco Díaz with another twenty-five men to follow the route taken by the first group. Soon after leaving their camp, Francisco Díaz changed his route, leaving the path taken by Fuente to one side, and taking another that was more open. He crossed the swamp at a more accommodating location but far from where the *españoles* had attempted to cross. Leaving the place behind and continuing ahead he found a field full of banana trees that the *negros* had made.[33] Wandering from one place to the next, in search of signs of the *negros* or their camp, they heard the clamor of the harquebuses that Fuente and his men fired to defend themselves from the enemy. Francisco Díaz, fearing the worst, gave orders to his men informing them of what he heard and inspiring them to do what as *españoles* they were obligated to do. They entered the terrain ahead following the path with such luck that after a slight detour, approaching in complete silence—hands muffling anything that might make a noise—they arrived without the squad of *negros* sensing them. Coming from behind they killed some, frightening the rest and scattering them so they could not reunite.

The encircled *españoles*, seeing the relief that had come unannounced, struck back at their enemies to turn the tide of battle, even though they were very weakened since in those days they had only eaten *bijao* buds and green plantains.[34] But the *negros*, who being unharmed and having lacked nothing during those days, awaited the counterattack of those weak soldiers without fear. Without much work they repulsed the attack and regrouped. The *españoles* united and began to fight as one with their harquebuses and the *negros* with their crossbows. Even though the harquebuses dissuaded some *negros*, the rest showed such good spirit that they did not notice those that left. They stood fighting the one side against the other until night brought a ceasefire. With that, the *negros*, unnoticed by anyone, retreated, travelling through the night by unknown paths. At sunrise, they reached the camp of Pedro de Ursúa, who had stayed with his remaining companions. The [*negros*] arrived so suddenly and unperceived that they caught the soldiers unaware, but not as much as might have been.[35] Thanks to the swiftness and good order of Pedro de Ursúa the surprise and shock did not have as great an effect. Gathering men he found close by, the general ordered them to take up arms, turn toward the enemy, and rush into the mob of *negros*, bringing an end to their shameful state. They succeeded in stopping [the *negros*] and forcing them to regroup, for they had already begun to pillage the camp to take what they could.[36]

After the *negros* assembled themselves and turned to face the General, they believed being so few they could easily defeat them. But, as they advanced, Pedro de Ursúa, with a harquebus in hand, and the *alférez*, García de Arze, with another, and Juan de Arles, a good soldier, with his, they began to fire with such luck that the first shots took down three *negros*, and they quickly reloaded with shot. The *negros* who were coming to attack also had eyes toward their flanks, they feared that the remaining *españoles* whom they had left at the swamp had not remained but followed them and would shortly arrive to surround and assail them. They began to lose the will to fight and began an orderly withdrawal, entering the thick foliage.[37] Ursúa harried the enemy on their flight for as long as he thought wise. When [*negros*] had secluded themselves in the bush, he gave up the chase, satisfied that the *negros* had paid for the daring and the shame they had caused with the blood they had spilled, the corpses they left behind, and those wounded whose blood fell on the path, a clear sign of their injuries.

At the start of the battle, and for a time afterward, the General did not cease to worry about the fate of the other *españoles* sent with Francisco Díaz and Fuente. The men had tarried several days at the *negros'* banana field to heal wounds and regroup, gathering much food.

Chapter Twelve

The principal settlement of the *negros* was located somewhat inland fifteen leagues down the coast from where they were.[38] General Ursúa determined to press forward as near as the disposition of the land and its ease of travel would allow, so that from that point he might do what the circumstances and fortune would allow. Before leaving he sent Francisco Gutiérrez, his *maestre de campo*, by sea to Nombre de Dios, to acquire some jugs of wine that had been mixed with drug or poison and some merchandise from Spain that he might lure and trick [the *negros*] with gifts and praise, cautiously double-dealing to achieve what he wished without bloodshed. Putting this all into the hands of Mars it would be difficult to achieve, as all things appeared to go against the *españoles*.[39] Their enemies had great advantage, in number and in nimbleness; one must admire the speed with which they quickly scale the sierras and hills and climb and bound large rocks. To the [soldiers], it seemed that the slaves could attack or flee whenever they wished, always traveling within sight but at a distance, mocking the men who hoped to bring their weapons to bear by never allowing them to do so.

Francisco Gutiérrez left for Nombre de Dios to undertake this task. Ursúa ordered him not to return to their current port but to go farther down the coast to a bay or shoreline closer to the slaves' settlement where he would find Ursúa and his men. Ursúa and his men needed several days to regroup and heal the men wounded by the *negros* following the fights mentioned above. [Afterward,] he left with a guide who took them over a rough and difficult path. It was difficult work for the soldiers, who not only had to carry their swords and bucklers but also other weapons and war materiel and all of the food and victuals they would need on their journey. However, they did not prepare as well as they should have, believing that they would find some fields or plantings of the *negros* from which they could supply themselves. This did not occur. Instead, they encountered swamps, thickets, mud patches, and mangroves that afflicted them and harried them greatly. This caused their travel to take far longer than they had imagined, it took over twenty-five days to cover only fifteen leagues. Once Ursúa arrived near the settlement or camp of the *negros* he set up camp in a convenient place near the coast and then ventured to spy on the settlement of the slaves. It was situated on a tall, tree-covered ridge, naturally fortified and surrounded on all sides by cliffs, natural or man-made, such that one could not climb them, and if by chance someone would fall from that height, he would be broken into innumerable pieces before reaching the ground.

On the two approaches to the hill the *negros* had built narrow paths such that a few stones could be released to block the advance of any number of men regardless of their zeal. In addition to this, at the top of the two paths, they had fortified the entrances with palisades and so constructed it would not be easy for our men to dislodge them even if they could climb the path.[40] Above, on the top of the hill, the houses and huts of the *negros* were built, crisscrossing the width of the ridge, with little room to spare. Between the houses in some low points they had made pits or silos full of all manner of food that they had collected or cultivated for their subsistence.

This stronghold only held King Bayano and his men of war, who from there went out on their forays and assaults on the roads frequented by *españoles*, even though they were far away. Away from here, in the interior, there was another settlement or fort, where they had their women, children, and other people unsuited to war, situated in a very hidden place, such that it was never seen by *españoles* until after King Bayano was captured and the *negros* thwarted.

Considering how futile it would be to attempt to subjugate the *negros* through war, given the great advantages described above, General Ursúa chose to intercede with them and their *negro* king through negotiation and commerce. Since beginning his uprising and tyranny, [Bayano], with his rustic brazenness, many times entered into treaties and agreements with the Governor of Panama and Nombre de Dios, and with barbarous arrogance entered into agreements with these cities. He would certainly do the same with Pedro de Ursúa, entering into negotiation and trade with him, coming to a shared accord to send some of his captains to stay and wait at the camp of Pedro de Ursúa and agreeing to allow some *españoles* to enter his settlement. Nevertheless, in these negotiations and conversations, Bayano always stayed alert, leaving his most of men just within sight, arms in their hands, as he and some of his allies came to deal with Ursúa, who with no less sagacity and awareness dealt and conversed with [Bayano] to bring about the agreement with gentle words designed to captivate and incline the hearts and spirits of the barbarians to continue their stay. Pedro de Ursúa, never losing sight of his plan, shrewdly told them that his only reason for coming was to establish terms so that the two *republicas*, of *españoles* and *negros*, could come to a perpetual accord and from this point forward no longer do harm to one another, nor pursue each other, nor rob from each other.[41] In order to more favorably incline them, he suggested to the *negros* that their efforts had been favored by fortune, they had never been overrun nor injured nor defeated by the *españoles*. Without a doubt this was a sign that immortal God had permitted this and wished that they retain their past liberty, in which God had created them, like all other peoples of the world.[42] Moreover, royal ministers had granted him full and sufficient authority to enter this agreement because it was so necessary. Bayano and his seconds dawdled so much in these negotiations that few days would pass without them coming to eat and entreat with General Ursúa, whom they treated with all their ability and courtesy, even respecting the soldiers.

During this time, Francisco Gutiérrez arrived from Nombre de Dios, with all that he had been entrusted to bring, including more soldiers, food-stuffs, and munitions, all of which were greatly lacking. General Ursúa took the opportunity to give more gifts to Bayano, the king, and other presents that signified his friendship, begging him that he had achieved all his ends and desires, that he and his *negros* should celebrate an upcoming feast day with a banquet in their settlement befitting their friendship and alliance because it would greatly please [Ursúa] to do so. Bayano was already so trust-ing that he granted Pedro de Ursúa what he asked, with the caveat that his *negro* soldiers would be pleased to receive some Rouen cloth shirts, machetes or axes, red caps, and other items, because they had become such lords of the land that whatever people entered, be they *españoles* or *indios*, they were obligated to grant them homage, recognizing their lordship over the land.[43] Ursúa promised to do all of it fully. Appearing that this and the rest that he intended to do would be successful, he thought it prudent to inform his sol-diers and companions. He gathered them together, saying to them:

> Gentlemen and companions, our efforts, taking up arms against these fugitive and traitorous slaves, will be to no effect if we are unable to bring about their destruction and ruin by any means. This is impossible to achieve fully through force of arms, you have all seen that they are trained and have clearly made it known that they have placed all their strength in the summits and roughness of these mountains and in the cover afforded by the dense bush and thickets. With the agility and skill of brutes born in these lands they aim to hide and retreat, showing themselves to us only when they wish. They

are like men who through much awareness and knowledge of this land inhabit and live as natives. If we trust our hope of victory to our weapons, intending to turn them to this purpose and cause, we will not realize our goal nor achieve victory in this war, and will return to Nombre de Dios [unsuccessful]. We cannot sustain ourselves much time in this place, the land lacks what we need for sustenance, and resupply from the cities of Nombre de Dios and Panama would tarry greatly being so far from this region. [Should this come to pass,] a double misfortune would befall these two cities. This horde of *negros* believing themselves to be victorious through only their efforts and the strength of their spirit would with greater shamelessness and redoubled daring leave their hidden settlements and caves, not only attacking the roads and their passengers, robbing and killing travelers, but they would [also] enact that which they have attempted many times, that is to burn the cities of Nombre de Dios and Panama, achieving the ultimate end and ruin that they possibly can.

To remedy this and prevent these misfortunes, I have considered how these *negros* and their chief or headman, whom they call king, so confidently entreat and converse with us under the terms I have given. Taking advantage of the fortune presented to us by these circumstances, according to orders I have already given, we will offer them splendid food and drink, with luck they shall be drowsy from a drug that we will put in their drink. With this, their king will be captured and the most valiant and important leaders of their company killed. If some escape, the [drug] will allow us to collect them and bring them to subjugation with the least work and risk possible. I have wanted to share this with all the company, because you are the best, most experienced soldiers there are.

Do not be dissuaded by any scruples that may arise after this business, that capturing and killing these *negros* is a thing that goes against the honor of soldiery and military virtue. I believe and understand that there is no one so lacking in understanding that they cannot see the rationale. With fugitives and traitorous slaves, purchased with our own money, we have the right and justification to use any falsities and double-dealings necessary and convenient to subjugate them and restore them to the servitude to which they previously held and are obligated. Especially since this horde of *negros*—against all laws and rights human or divine—intend not only to become lords of this land, where they are not native, nor raised, nor did any of their forebears possess it, but to raise up from among them a king and lord who will govern them and maintain justice according to their manner of life.[44] What is most excessive and puzzling is that the majority of these *negros* having been baptized and through their baptism subjected to the law and faith of almighty God, and the Roman Church, have turned heretics and in matters of religion have made laws and statues based on their prior gentility. They live according to these, naming among themselves bishops and other ministers of their false religion, to extort and catechize them and to encourage them to live according to these beliefs.[45] Only this final reason serves to free us from keeping any faith [with them] and doing as we wish without doubt that our honor be imperiled. With men who break the faith of the Church to which they have sworn and promised with such ease, all the more we can and should break our word in order to capture them so that they may be punished.

What Ursúa had proposed appeared good and well-reasoned, and they approved it, agreeing that each man would do their part as ordered. With this the speech ended, Bayano and some of his *negros* entered the camp to visit with Pedro de Urúsa. He went to greet them and received them with great happiness. That night, [Bayano] and his *negros* stayed to sleep. [Ursúa] gave them excellent food and drink, leaving them full and drunk. The next day they returned to their stronghold confident that the *españoles* would always do likewise and very happy because General Ursúa, speaking with great familiarity to Bayano, had gifted him a cape made of fine green cloth, two Rouen cloth shirts, a cap, and a machete, and to his *negro* captains he gave each Rouen shirts, trousers from Anjou, and red caps. After this they went around among themselves praising the largess and good nature of Pedro de Ursúa.

Chapter Thirteen

Near the hillock or mountain where the *negros* had their settlement, or almost at its foot, there was a piece of land or beach, very sandy with dunes. Here Bayano met and negotiated with General Ursúa and his men. Bayano ordered his *negros* to construct some houses and huts where the *españoles* could reside. The conversation, one side to the other, was both frequent and polite. Almost every day many *negros* could be found with the *españoles*, exercising together, jumping, running, relaxing, and competing in other peaceful pastimes to see who would win. There was never a lack of someone with whom to drink, and many returned home drunk. During this time, it was necessary for Francisco Gutiérrez to return to Nombre de Dios for more gifts for the *negros*, and to get more wine and drug, because that which had been brought before had weakened and lost some of its potency. With the return of Gutiérrez, the *negros* and the *españoles* celebrated greatly, because they looked forward to enjoying the gifts and refreshments that he had brought. Always, until the feast day, food and drink never lacked since the soldiers with the consent of their captain always shared with the *negros* who came to the camp of the *españoles*. Similarly, some *españoles* climbed to the fort and camp of the *negros* under the pretext of friendship to see and reconnoiter that which it held. Other times soldiers and *negros* went out together to hunt boar or other game in the jungle, more so to explore the land than for recreation of the hunt.[46] With these diversions, the day of the feast approached. On that day, Bayano came down with at least forty of his greatest and most important *negros*. The rest of the rotten *negros* stayed in their homes, suspicious that the friendship with the *españoles* would do them harm. All things necessary for the food had been prepared and the tables set. Some harquebusiers and footmen had been hidden in Ursúa's quarters where they would hopefully not be seen but would not be forgotten. The remaining soldiers wandered about the camp seemingly without concern, at least to the eyes of the *negros*, but inside they were torn up and anxious for the meal to be over and the *negros* defeated so they might take any riches they could find.

General Ursúa, with some of his officers, sat at the table, with them Bayano and all the *negros* that accompanied him. He was given the best food that could be prepared in such a place. Some waiters went about giving wine to the party, one carried a flagon of clean wine for the *españoles*, another a pitcher of poisoned wine for the *negros*. In this way, the deception would not be perceived, nor would the *españoles* be endangered, nor was there a risk that a disturbance at the table could reveal the deceit of our side.

The conclusion and unmasking of this deceit came after the meal. Ursúa feigned a desire to give some gifts to all the *negros* who had dined. Francisco Gutiérrez and Francisco Díaz got up from the table and entered Ursúa's quarters, where there was a quantity of shirts, caps, machetes, and other items for this purpose. One by one, the *negros* entered and received a shirt and machete, or something else they wished, from the hands of the captains. With this they further demonstrated great friendship by offering a glass of wine mixed with the drug. They almost all left the table drunk, the drunkenness brought about greater thirst, and these unfortunates drank all that was offered without looking at it. In this way, one left [Ursúa's] quarters with their gifts as another entered. They continued thanking each until only Bayano, three captains, and three or four other *negros* remained. One of these entered for his share, as the others had done, but it went badly for him because as Francisco Gutiérrez approached to give him a shirt, under which he had hidden a dagger, he stabbed [the *negro*] in his left side. Reaching the heart, [the *negro*] did not have time to protest or cry out, mutely falling to the floor and dying at once. Concealing this, they called another *negro* of those that had stayed at the table with Bayano. As he entered, they attempted to do the same as before, but sensing or seeing the hoax he became agitated, yelling, "Treachery, treachery." Bayano and the rest who remained, hearing this, began to rise, joining his cries, but they found themselves put upon by the men that Ursúa had hidden and were taken prisoner. Binding [Bayano] and the others to keep them quiet, [the *españoles*] went about capturing the rest.

The other soldiers who were there awaiting the first sounds of struggle readied the weapons they had on hand, joined their captains, and with all the swiftness in the world turned to take the fort and settlement of the *negros*. They climbed up and entered without resistance. Those that had remained in it seeing from above what had transpired below and recognizing the danger that could come to them became worried and lost any spirit or will to take up arms and resist our men, which they could have done easily [our men] being so few, their position so favorable, and the climb so exposed. But as the turmoil of such stunning events can quickly remove all prudence and reason and suspend the effects of one's will, no matter how strong, such occurred to all these *negros* who fled in opposite directions from where the *españoles* ascended.[47] They left the entire settlement and fort empty, none of those who chose to flee remained. Yet some *negros* that had been at the feast had already ascended, as they climbed up the effects of the drug reached their heart, they were found scattered on the ground nauseated and shaking with anger and pain, almost at the point of death. The soldiers ended their lives with many slashes and thrusts [of their swords]. The soldiers found other *negros* on the path, beginning to feel the effects [of the poison] but not yet incapacitated, but thankfully suffering so they could not flee or leave the path. These soldiers, like the others, proceeded to stab them with swords without restraint. These blows were made so forcefully that many thrust their swords into the bodies of the drugged *negros* up to the hilt. Like this they left bodies behind them from one place to the next, with wounds that were certainly mortal, even without the poison they had taken, sufficient to bring a quick end to them all.

After taking the heights, the *españoles* controlling the pueblo and fort, Captain Pedro de la Fuente took twenty soldiers to follow the *negros* who had fled. They found [the *negros*] occupied in crossing a raging river that impeded their passage.[48] The *negros*, turning to look behind them, and blocked in front unable to advance, began to defend themselves and fight like ones already sentenced to death. They wished to make their deaths as costly as possible or to preserve them through force, and so they fought to defend themselves mightily. But the *españoles*, with harquebuses that they carried, struck down eight *negros*, greatly terrifying and afflicting those who remained, who by way of escape and defense only had the rising river at their backs. Into it they went retreating, entering bit by bit with great speed so that all together and in droves they entered the current and channel of the river and quickly passed to the other side. From there they could more securely defend and hinder the passage of our men, who after doing what they could returned to the fort and settlement of the *negros* where General Pedro de Ursúa had already ascended with Bayano and the other prisoners. They had collected and returned to the fort many old *negros* and *negras*, who through the weakness of their condition could not follow the path of the rest, along with a horde of children.

The soldiers, accompanied by some [captive *negros*], went out to patrol the fields and plantings that the *negros* had nearby. They found and captured the workers who kept them and other *negros* and *negras* present there, all of whom were caught unaware. These slaves had made huge banana stands for their sustenance, not counting the maize, yuca, sweet potato, and . . . legumes that they planted and cultivated for their food.[49] The loot found by the soldiers did not come to much, and so the soldiers made little profit from this war.

Ursúa, seeing that it would be fruitless and vain to march with his men through these mountains and sierras hunting *negros* as it would only tire and trouble his soldiers for no great profit, he honestly but cautiously entreated with Bayano, asking that he order all his people, the *negros* that wandered at large, to reunite and gather with him there. Together they would go to Nombre de Dios and, with the consent of that city and of the city of Panama, they would settle a pueblo in a convenient place along the river named Francisca, well suited for travel and for the comfort of the *negros*, with this condition: henceforth, King Bayano and his *negros*, the [pueblo's] residents, would need to return all the *negros* that fled from Nombre de Dios or Panama to their masters within three days. They would also have the responsibility for supplying passengers, muleteers, and beasts of burden with necessary supplies at a fixed, moderate price.[50] [Ursúa] intermixed other cautious words that helped calm and entice Bayano very much as well as those who were captive, it appeared to them that [Ursúa] would bring it about and fulfill it to the letter. Soon after, [Bayano] began to send word to all parts [so] that the rest of the *negros* who remained alive began to gather little by little at the call of their king. At the end of fifty days, they were together in the fort. [Ursúa] informed them of the plans, and to them it appeared good and very certain, and with the promises they were much reassured. After two months of rest in the fort, Pedro de Ursúa left with them. Along the way, he removed Bayano's restraints in order to inspire fealty in the bandit. Yet, later, having arrived in Nombre de Dios, the *negro* king, Bayano, and his captains were arrested.

From there, they were sent with all caution and guard to Peru, the city of Lima, where the viceroy resided. The viceroy happily received Bayano and honored him, giving him gifts and treating him well. From there [Bayano] was sent to Spain.[51] The rest of the *negros* were arrested and taken as slaves of the king. They were ordered to be separated and sold outside of Panama, so that they would not once again join together and there would be no sign of their evil seed.[52]

The vecinos and merchants of these cities celebrated with great fiestas and public gatherings the defeat and capture of these slaves, giving many signs of thanks to Pedro de Ursúa and offering him large sums of money for his great diligence in this war and for the impressive work he did in cleaning the land of such a teeming gang of thieves and criminals. Afterward, never again did another gathering of *negros* in this land engender as much suspicion or fear in these pueblos as the one which I have just related.

When he wrote those lines, in the years before 1581, Aguado was likely unaware of the second War of the Bayano that was being fought on an even larger scale than the events he related. Moreover, almost as soon as Ursúa concluded his campaign, the cabildo of Nombre de Dios lamented the return of earlier problems. Writing in March 1557, the cabildo of Nombre de Dios related, "[The maroons] dare to disquiet us and do us as much damage as possible knowing as they do that the Captain General Pedro de Ursúa has just retired, having completed what Your Majesty commanded."[53]

1. This synopsis, although omitting specific expeditions, largely conforms to the official reports from the early 1550s, suggesting that Aguado's chronicle derived from relatively accurate firsthand accounts.

2. The Motilones, or Barís, were an unconquered Indigenous group native to the region between Colombia and Venezuela. They resisted Spanish military conquest well into the eighteenth century.

3. In 1560, Pedro de Ursúa received permission to conduct a conquest campaign from Peru down the Río Marañon into what is now Brazil. On that expedition, Lope de Aguirre revolted along with a number of the men, killing Ursúa and proclaiming himself "Prince of Peru, Tierra Firme and Chile." Werner Herzog loosely adapted the story of Lope de Aguirre's murder of Ursúa in his 1972 film *Aguirre, Wrath of God*.

4. The Sierra de Capira is the mountain range that divides Nombre de Dios from Panama City.

5. Aguado emphasizes European stereotypes against Africans. While the maroons certainly wanted to dissuade military attacks by Europeans, they depended on raiding to acquire finished goods and other items that they could not produce themselves.

6. Santiago (Saint James the Greater) was the patron saint of Spanish soldiers, and "Santiago!" was their common battlefield cry.

7. Most Africans who entered the slave trade did so as captives taken in war. As a result, enslaved Africans in the Americas may have had some martial experience before their enslavement. Thornton, *Africa and Africans*, 98–100. Importantly, not all Africans suffered enslavement through warfare. Individuals could also face judicial enslavement for debt or criminal accusations, including witchcraft. Candido, *An African Slaving Port*, 227–33; Spicksley, "Contested Enslavement"; Ferreira, *Cross-Cultural Exchange*, 52–87.

8. Aguado almost certainly embellishes for the reader.

9. This description of the maroons' physical prowess further reinforced stereotypes that Africans had almost bestial attributes. Coupled with his statements about their speech, Aguado's narrative emphasized their brutishness.

10. Wet powder plagued many Spanish conquests and military expeditions. In many cases crossbows represented a more consistent ranged weapon in conditions such as these.

11. The text is not clear whether the *negros* would fear retribution for having failed to defeat the Spaniards or were fearful that the Spanish might be pursuing them.

12. Aguado uses the Christian title "bishop" to refer to the religious leader of the *negros*.

13. Given the earlier problem of dampness coupled with the difficulty of reloading sixteenth century firearms, this account pushes the realm of plausibility.

14. The maroons had good reason to be afraid. They would be certainly be re-enslaved, possibly tortured, and maybe brutally executed.

15. It is not surprising that Aguado, a minister of the Catholic Church, used the language of Christian religion to describe the maroons' religious practices.

16. Catholic clergy baptized enslaved Africans either when embarking or disembarking from their transatlantic crossing.

17. The comparison to Lutherans suggests that Aguado, and possibly those present, perceived maroon religion to be a heretical form of Christianity rather than a form of paganism.

18. Mastiffs also served as war dogs during campaigns of conquest.

19. If the maroons had repented and called for absolution, they would have received the appropriate sacraments before being executed by garrote, a punishment deemed quicker and less painful than hanging.

20. The practice being described appears almost identical to Catholic masses of the time. Only rarely did Catholic laity consume the elements of the Eucharist. While Aguado includes the description as a way of demonstrating the twisted nature of the maroons' beliefs, the possibility exists that the maroons did practice a form of African Christianity that incorporated African religious beliefs, knowledge, and philosophies in a Christian framework. Thornton, *Africa and Africans*, 235–71. This melding of belief and practice occurred most visibly in Central West Africa in the Kingdom of Kongo and the Portuguese Kingdom of Angola. Unfortunately, we do not know the African origins of Bayano or those of his community. Given the timing of their arrival on the isthmus (1540s–1550s), their African origins likely fell in Upper Guinea (modern Senegal, Gambia, Guinea, and parts of Sierra Leone), Cape Verde (an island off the coast of Upper Guinea), or São Tomé (an island off modern Equatorial Guinea). Eagle, "Early Slave Trade," 142–49. These provenances suggest that if the practices being described here represent a form of African Christianity, the process of melding African and European beliefs primarily occurred in the Americas, beginning when Africans experienced Christianity while enslaved and continuing independently in their maroon communities.

21. The baptism described here does not differ greatly from the Catholic sacrament. Aguado appears to see vanity and frivolity in the social celebration that accompanied the service.

22. Hallways offered greater chance for a breeze in the heat and humidity.

23. The reference to discontent and election may suggest that the community had several distinct subgroups. Bayano's rule was not absolute but grounded in his perceived ability to govern and adjudicate between different factions.
24. Aguado recognizes how groups of diverse Africans integrated various African and European traditions to form new African American ones.
25. This Indigenous name did not appear in any Spanish documents during the conquest period. Nevertheless, given the location along the upper Río Chepo, the Indigenous people of this community may have been Cueva people who successfully evaded Spanish conquistadors.
26. One might question the origins of this claim. In the 1580s, Spaniards would once again find a maroon community physically and socially linked to an Indigenous one. In the later example, no evidence of violent subjugation exists. Spanish perceptions of African violence, and their association with wars of enslavement, may have colored the interpretation of the presence of an Indigenous community near that of a maroon community. In contrast to Aguado's claim, the close association of the two communities may have begun as the first maroons found shelter among the Indigenous community. Eventually, as the number of maroons grew, they established their own settlement.
27. In other parts of Spanish America, the term *mulato* could be applied to both those of African-European descent and those of African-Indigenous descent. Schwaller, "*Mulata, Hija de Negro y India.*" Aguado's description suggests that in Panama and neighboring areas, *mulatos* of African-European descent may have emphasized difference with individuals of African-Indigenous ancestry by ascribing them the term *zambaigo*.
28. This appears to be a recounting of Carreño's expedition and the earlier negotiations between Bayano and Governor Sosa.
29. Aguado foreshadows events to come, offering his opinion of the morality of breaking truces with maroons.
30. Unfortunately, Aguado does not mention any geographic features, such as rivers or bays, that might help locate the rendezvous point.
31. Aguado alludes to the reality that, raising companies as they did, captains had no guarantee that the men who joined had prior military experience or training. Many likely did not but, like their captains, saw the opportunity as a means to serve the king and gain reward or social advancement.
32. This claim seems far-fetched, designed to accentuate the tenacity of the Spaniards.
33. An Old World food, bananas were a common food staple in coastal Africa, and their cultivation would have been known to many enslaved Africans in the Americas. The first recorded introduction of bananas to the Americas came in 1516 when Fray Tomás de Berlanga planted cuttings from the Canary Islands in Santo Domingo. Little is known about their broader diffusion, although the transatlantic slave trade helped to facilitate their transplantation to the Americas from Africa, a process in which enslaved Africans likely played a central role. In some parts of Latin America, bananas are called *guineos* because of their link to Africa and Africans in the Americas. The groves described by Aguado were undoubtably planted by the maroons,

possibly from plantings taken from Panama City or Nombre de Dios. Carney and Rosomoff, *In the Shadow of Slavery*, 40–44, 114.

34. *Bijao* probably refers to *Canna indica*, although this term could describe various other tropical plants.

35. The maroons' choice to attack the Spaniards' main camp suggests that they had already reconnoitered the region and knew where the Spaniards had arrived.

36. The tools, weapons, and supplies of the camp would have been invaluable to maroons as they could not fabricate such items in their settlements.

37. Aguado's description of the maroons' hit-and-run tactics further reinforces the reality that the maroons desired supplies more than the complete destruction of the Spanish. They did not lose the will to fight but instead chose to retreat after having achieved their goal.

38. This would place the settlement along the upper Río Chepo or upper Río Chucunaque.

39. Mars, the Roman god of war. Aguado implies that a purely military victory may be impossible even with divine help.

40. These defensive fortifications bear a striking similarity to those of the maroon settlement of Yanga in Central Mexico. Alegre, *Historia de la provincia*, vol. 2, 175–82.

41. Rarely did Spaniards consider Africans in the Americas to have constituted their own *republica*. Aguado's use of the term here highlights the Spaniards' awareness that the maroons had established their own sociopolitical order.

42. Aguado references the theological and juridical belief that the state of enslavement was not a natural condition but rather a state brought about by human circumstance.

43. Aguado uses the phrase *señores de la tierra*. This concept could apply to the rights held by nobility in Iberia just as it could apply to Indigenous rulers and elites in the Americas. Spanish political theory recognized the sovereignty of "natural lords." Even after their incorporation into the Spanish empire, Indigenous leaders retained privileges and rights befitting their status as "*señores de la tierra*." In this context, however, Aguado mocks the Africans' pretension to sovereignty by emphasizing their desire for presents over other aspects of lordship.

44. Notably, this monologue omits the justification of sovereignty used by the Spanish to claim their American possessions, that of conquest. If Spaniards could claim sovereignty over a foreign land in which they were not natives, nor had forebears, could not Africans do the same?

45. This description echoes Catholic critiques of Protestantism common to this period.

46. They probably hunted peccary, a small pig-like animal native to the Americas, although domesticated pigs may have escaped to the region from Spanish settlements and become feral.

47. Again Aguado considers the maroons' choice to flee to be a sign of fear or weakness. Maroons were acutely aware of the punishments they might face if captured. Flight represented the most logical strategy for survival in the face of the Spaniards' deception.

48. These events transpired in the final months of 1556. In Panama, the rainy season runs from May through December. The account's description of rainfall and swollen rivers conforms to the typical weather pattern of the region.

49. Maize, yuca (cassava/manioc), and sweet potatoes (*Ipomoea batatas*) are all indigenous to the Americas. The maroons may have learned how to cultivate them from the Caricua or acquired such knowledge from the few Indigenous people that survived in Panama City or Nombre de Dios.

50. This plan loosely mirrored the Spanish policy of *congregación*, which consolidated and relocated Indigenous communities in order to more effectively integrate them into the fiscal and economic regime of the colonial order. Nemser, *Infrastructures of Race*.

51. The Peruvian chronicler Inca Garcilaso de la Vega attests to this outcome, as did *oidor* Alonso Criado de Castilla. AGI, Panama 13, R. 21, N. 137, fs. 2; Vega, *Historia General del Peru*, 277.

52. The policy of separating rebellious slaves and mandating their sale to other regions was typical across Spanish America.

53. AGI, Panama 32, N. 10.

Part II
Maroon Resurgence (1560s–1570s)

8. Governor Luis de Guzmán to the Crown, August 28, 1562

Source: AGI, Panama 29, R. 9, N. 37, fs. 2–2v.

Despite Ursúa's campaign, *cimarrones* continued to occupy the eastern isthmus, and their numbers grew as more enslaved Africans fled from Nombre de Dios and Panama City. This letter by the governor of Panama written only five years after Ursúa's campaign attests to the persistence of maroons in the region. Some maroons certainly escaped Ursúa's efforts. Aguado's account notes that multiple communities had existed. Ursúa's duplicitous victory meant the defeat of only one of those. In the years after Ursúa's departure from Panama, additional runaways helped reestablish sizable communities.

• • •

In that which touches on the castigation of the *cimarrones*, things are such that it is more necessary to attempt to destroy them than to punish them because we have heard news that over five or six hundred of them have established settlements that grow larger every day. The danger they pose is great if at any time some bad men would organize them and they agreed.[1] I have conveyed the remedy for this to the city government and persons long-resident in these parts. In order to destroy them, it is necessary to make constant war on them for over a year without allowing them rest or recuperation until they are completely finished. For this, one hundred men, or thereabout, are necessary. The cost to these parts is very great because there are not leaders who will go for less than double hazard pay, and at a minimum each solider needs his monthly salary and maize and footwear. These the men have need of fifteen or twenty *negro* porters to carry the food. Considering everything, it appears to us there is no recourse more certain or more expansive than to nip the problem in the bud. After all, these *negros* have passed through here because of the merchants, who are quite wealthy from their businesses and profits. Your Majesty would be served to grant these cities and kingdom the right to impose a small tax of one percent, for two or three years, on all the merchandise that is loaded in Nombre de Dios and all that is loaded in Panama destined for Peru. From this, one can remedy the damage without costing the treasury of Your Majesty or the merchants because the cost will pass on to their sales, and they always sell at a profit. This seems the least burdensome option that conscience will allow.

In extirpating and dislodging these *negros*, there is always a need for eight to ten men to traverse the bush near Nombre de Dios and others in Panama to prevent [the *negros*] from approaching and to deal with those that have been scattered.[2] The [maroons] knowing that *españoles* patrol the bush is a great deterrent; Your Majesty being served to grant to these cities a part of that which Your Majesty receives from the penalties levied by the officers of your treasury on unregistered clothing.[3] The other portion will [come from] the vecinos contributing of their free will. This will be enough funding for the future.

---

1. The "bad men" described by the governor were disaffected Spaniards frustrated with increasingly restrictive royal governance and desirous of greater economic success. Guzmán's fear was well-founded; such frustrations had led to civil war and rebellion in Peru during the 1540s and 1550s. Panama had seen a series of smaller rebellions and revolts in 1544, 1545, 1550, and 1556. Only months after writing this letter, Rodrigo Méndez would attempt to overthrow the government because of enmities that had arisen with the previous governor, Rafael de Figuerola. Many residents knew of Méndez's anger, and Guzmán may have had Méndez in mind when writing this letter. Mena García, *Sociedad de Panamá*, 301–6.

2. Earlier in this letter, Guzmán identified the need to clear the bush and foliage within a half league of Nombre de Dios to allow greater vigilance and defense of the city. He proposed that the king purchase fifty slaves from Cabo Verde, one quarter of which would be female. While the enslaved men toiled at cutting down jungle, the women would grow crops and prepare food.

3. Given the high profits of selling European merchandise in the Americas, and the multilayered tax regime of the Spanish empire, many merchants and ship captains attempted to import more merchandise than had been declared, and taxed, on ships' manifests. When treasury officials discovered such subterfuge, they confiscated the goods and imposed fines on the offenders.

9. Attack on Pedro González de Meceta, September 1569

Source: AGI, Patronato 151, N. 5, R. 1. Transcription in Jopling,
Indios y negros en Panamá, 338–39.

In November 1569, Pedro González de Meceta submitted a *probanza de méritos y servicios* for having served the crown for almost two decades. After arriving in Panama sometime around 1555, González de Meceta quickly joined a campaign under Francisco Vásquez intended to conquer the region known as Veragua. In that conquest, he served as captain of a squad of fifty men and helped found the cities of

Santa Fé and Concepción. Later he helped put down the revolt of Rodrigo Méndez. In 1565, the city of Nombre de Dios granted González de Meceta a plot of land near the Cerro de Nicuesa, a hill under which ships anchored. Living here, two harquebus shots' distance from the city, González de Meceta became a target of maroon raids.

• • •

XXI. Item, if they know that one day this past September, already being night, Pedro González de Meceta was in his house with his wife and family eating dinner when a great quantity of *negros cimarrones* arrived and attacked him, his wife, and the people of his house, firing many arrows.[1] This caused a great danger to his wife and people who were in his house, and unless it had been God's will that they be protected and their quick response they would have been killed or captured. [The *negros*] stripped naked his wife and another woman who had a small child, but through their own efforts [Meceta and the women] were able to escape to the pueblo and bring word to the magistrates. . . .

XXII. Item, if they know that in addition to the previous, the *negros* wounded many *criadas* and killed a young man who lived with Pedro González de Meceta.[2] They carried off a *negra* in his service that had cost him three hundred pesos of assayed silver.[3] They took all the clothing, house furniture, weapons that he had, and burned the home in which he lived. With this all the rest of his property was burned and a large quantity of silver lost, all told over three thousand pesos worth. . . .

XXIII. Item, if they know that in maintaining a populated house, Pedro González de Meceta brought great assistance and benefit to the city of Nombre de Dios and its vecinos because it was located on the route used by the *negros* and prevented many damages by hindering the approach they used to commit robberies and carry off *negros*. This has prevented them from taking as many *negros* as they would like into the bush. Certainly, the principal intent of the *negros* in burning the house was to reopen the route so they could be unseen as they entered and exited the town to commit their robberies and other crimes, such as stealing *negros*. . . .

XXIIII. Item, if they know that Pedro González de Meceta built his home and cultivated his land at great cost and effort. The harm he received from the *negros* left him without even the shirt on his back.[4] He and his wife have

Bay of Nombre de Dios. View from site of sixteenth-century port toward the Cerro de Nicuesa (*on left*). *Photograph by the author.*

been left poor, indebted, and in need, such as no one else has ever been or is currently. . . .

XXV. Item, if they know that living in their house in the countryside, an old *negro cimarrón* named Duarte came to Pedro González de Meceta and he took [the *negro*] and brought him to the magistrate.[5] The *negro* has been of profound utility and benefit to the city because by his efforts they have made sorties against *cimarrones* and have dissipated and killed many. Every day, [the city] receives great assistance from the *negro* against the *negros cimarrones* because he is very old and a great guide. He knows the locations of the hunting grounds and fields of the *negros cimarrones* and all else that can be used to bring them harm. . . .[6]

Meceta also noted his service capturing seven French corsairs and patrolling the coast and sea for more.

Alonso de Solis, procurador *and* mayordomo *of Nombre de Dios*

XXII. The witness said he knows what is contained in the question because he was present at the mustering and saw the wounded youth and the burning house. None of Meceta's property could be saved from the house, which was roofed with palm and cane; the fire that burned and consumed it went quickly because it was located on the shore of the sea and the breeze fanned the flames.[7] The *cimarrones* took a *negra* he had in his service, for she has not reappeared. . . .

Diego Núñez Pinto, vecino of Nombre de Dios

XXI. The witness said that one night, in the aforementioned month, there was a muster against *cimarrones* in the pueblo. This witness saw from his house that the house and hut where Pedro González lived was burning. He heard may persons say that *negros cimarrones* had put fire to it and placed Meceta and his wife in great danger. They had taken the *negros* and the clothing from a woman who was living there. They escaped through the good work of the women and Meceta. This witness saw him arrive wet and almost naked, bringing word of what happened to the *justicia*. . . .

In November 1569, attacks like those against González de Meceta led the Audiencia of Panama to name a *capitán general* to lead an expedition against the maroons.[8] While a typical captain only had authority over the company he raised, a *capitán general* could commission multiple captains to raise multiple companies of men. The audiencia granted Captain Esteban de Trejo broad powers to name his own officers, structure his forces, and pursue his campaign as he saw fit. The commission even addressed the possibility of his settling new towns and negotiating a peace with the maroons.

After receiving his commission, Trejo negotiated with the cabildos of Panama and Nombre de Dios, asking that they pay eight thousand pesos to support the expedition, with half the amount being paid up front. Yet the cities did not disburse the pledged funds. In February 1570, Trejo initiated a suit against the city of Nombre de Dios for not providing its two-thousand-peso payment. He claimed that the lack of funds would delay the expedition and prevent him from recruiting men. By March, Trejo and his men had set out on their campaign.

---

1. Wealthy Spaniards frequently maintained large households composed of immediate and extended family, servants, and slaves.
2. *Criada* could describe paid female servants or female dependents such as extended kin.
3. González de Meceta avoids saying "slave," although the woman was enslaved.
4. Spaniards used claims of abject poverty to solicit royal aid, although Meceta's claims were likely more truthful than most.
5. Although offering assistance to Spaniards was a rare occurrence, some maroons saw doing so as a means to gain freedom and rejoin Spanish society.
6. Duarte may have aided the expedition of Esteban de Trejo, organized only weeks after this probanza.
7. This description suggests that the home of Meceta was a thatched cabin.
8. AGI, Panama 32, N. 14a.

10. Licenciado Carasa, *Fiscal* of the Audiencia of Panama, to the Crown, March 31, 1570

Source: AGI, Panama 13, R. 10, N. 30.

This letter briefly describes the size of Esteban de Trejo's forces as he undertook his campaign. Importantly, it also reveals tensions among the region's officials. Trejo did not enjoy universal support, nor did all officials believe that a single campaign could eradicate the maroons. Some feared that the cost of such wars would be excessive. This letter paints a vivid picture of how well-informed maroons could be of Spanish plans.

• • •

That which is most in need of remedy in this kingdom is the dispersal of the *negros cimarrones* that have rebelled in the forests and uninhabited areas. They are great in number and of such temerity and audacity that they come to the roads that travel between this city [Panama City] and Nombre de Dios [and] kill travelers and rob them of what they carry, be it clothing or wine. Until now they have not taken money. They threaten to burn the two pueblos and have even come within an eighth of a league of them. Many times, they have taken *negras* who were washing clothes in the rivers that supply the pueblos with water. Similarly, they take *negros* who are collecting firewood and encourage others to flee from their masters, as they do every day. For this reason, no master will dare punish a slave nor order them to do more than [the slave] would wish.[1]

To remedy this great evil, when don Francisco de Toledo, viceroy of Peru, was in this city he consulted with this audiencia and the city, and [he] ordered that a captain be named to lead two hundred men against the principal settlement of the [*negros cimarrones*], which is the Bayano, thirty leagues from the city of Nombre de Dios, and once uprooted from there to settle [the region] with *españoles*. This was put into effect, naming Esteban de Trejo as the captain of the expedition. He set out with one hundred forty men, one hundred of whom were harquebusiers. At the moment it is believed this plan will bear fruit, even though there is no way to sustain this enterprise with the support that comes from this city or that of Nombre de Dios, which amounts to 8,000 pesos, considering that Pedro de Ursúa spent 27,000 pesos and was unable to dislodge them, even if his expedition was of much success.[2]

At the time that the leadership of the expedition was being discussed, I opposed the naming of Trejo because he was young, of little experience or capacity, and lacking authority. To this they responded that no one else would do it for so little money, and so they concluded the matter. After fifteen years in these parts and having experience with these *negros*, I believe that if Your Majesty does not support this enterprise with a tax on the merchandise that passes through Nombre de Dios [then] the money that is raised here will not be enough. If the remedy is delayed, I am certain that the damage will be irreparable as the multitude of *negros* only grows, and from all parts they gain allies. Every day they become bolder and more unified. So great is their boldness that, having spies in this city, when the captain left with his men they set up a gallows eight leagues down the road and hung it with knives, saying that on it they would hang the captain and cut off the heads of all who went with him. Your Majesty would be served by resolving this matter as would be best for you and your subjects. . . . Panama, the last day of March 1570.

1. This statement illustrates how marronage, petite or grand, represented a tool for negotiating the master-slave relationship. Even if most enslaved Africans did not flee or become maroons, all masters had to weigh the possibility of flight when they considered punishing slaves. In this sense, the very existence of maroons helped moderate the severity of punishments received by all slaves in the region.
2. The ranking Spanish prosecutor revealed that many of King Bayano's people remained at large despite Ursúa's capture of Bayano.

11. Licenciado Diego de Vera to the Crown, August 1, 1570
Source: AGI, Panama 13, R. 10, N. 35 fs. 2v–3.

This brief note by the president of the audiencia offers a glimpse at how Trejo pursued his campaign. It appears that during the first five months, Trejo had some success penetrating the region inhabited by the maroons. Although future letters mention Trejo's campaign, none offer a clearer picture of the campaign. Despite the hopeful claims that Trejo appeared close to victory, events of the next few years suggest that once again the Spanish confused the maroons' mobility and tactical flight as a sign of defeat.

•   •   •

Captain Trejo has made two good assaults in his campaign [against the *cimarrones*] and has hemmed them in toward the south sea.[1] A captain has been ordered to flank them. This venture has been very productive because the *negros* wander about divided and have even killed one another.[2] We also understand that *indios de guerra* have pursued them.[3] God willing this venture will achieve its objectives.

In November, Vera reported that some of the maroons captured by Trejo had been publicly executed.[4]

---

1. The Pacific. The campaign likely progressed through the Río Chepo and Río Chucunaque valleys, advancing toward the Serranía de Majé, a mountain range along the coast just to the west of the Gulf of San Miguel.
2. Divisions among maroons likely resulted from differing opinions over how to deal with Spanish assaults. Additionally, the Spanish may have perceived the maroon strategy of scattering in the face of entradas as disorder rather than a calculated measure by which to evade capture and defeat.
3. These may be some of the earliest encounters with Guna peoples.
4. AGI, Panama 12, R. 10, N. 36, fs. 1.

12. The Cabildo of Panama City to the Crown, May 25, 1571
Source: AGI, Panama 30, N. 12.

By the 1570s, problems with the maroons became compounded as foreign interlopers in the region sought to profit from the lucrative trade that passed through Panama. For many residents the problem of corsairs and maroons revolved around money. Military expeditions and costal defense cost money. According to this letter, the depravations of the enemy made it impossible for the residents to supply the needed resources.

•   •   •

There is a great necessity for Your Majesty to order a solution to the great calamities and misfortunes of the past five years or more. At the moment, the fatigue and affliction of this kingdom moved this cabildo of Panama to send Your Majesty notice of these things so that Your Majesty can order that which will be most convenient to his royal service.

Much of the cause of these troubles has been widespread knowledge of the great wealth of this land, and this city, from which all of the gold and silver and pearls from Potosí, Chile, and other parts of Peru is carried to Spain. From this city, all of it is sent to the city of Nombre de Dios, by way of the Río Chagres and the Casa de Cruces, five leagues from this city by land. There are many corsairs, French and English, most Lutherans, enemies of the Holy Catholic Faith, who have come to rob the city of Nombre de Dios and the boats that from this city carry gold and silver along the Río Chagres to Nombre de Dios as well as those that go from Nombre de Dios to the Casa de Cruces, in which is carried the majority of goods brought from Spain. . . .

The cabildo continued by recounting corsair raids up the Río Chagres, targeting ships traveling between Nombre de Dios and the Casa de Cruces, a river port that served Panama City. They also described a recent attempt in which corsairs captured ships carrying over seventy thousand pesos' worth of goods.

On top of all this, the people of this land cannot do anything to prevent the raids or great damages, robberies, and deaths caused by the *negros cimarrones* that every day take place on the road from this city to that of Nombre de Dios, and to the Casa de Cruces. They are so bold that they sneak into this city and Nombre de Dios by night to steal and carry away *negros* and *negras* into the wilderness. Six nights ago, in the city of Nombre de Dios, *cimarrones* killed two *españoles* near the House of Trade and were able to leave the city unpunished. From the Chorillo, where *negras* go to wash clothing, about a harquebus shot from the city, the *cimarrones* carried off thirteen *negras*, and they do the same from the river of this city every day.[1]

The contributions made by the inhabitants of this city and that of Nombre de Dios do not suffice for the expenses required to secure the roads and break up the *cimarrones*. From this day forward it will be impossible to contribute more because for over a year and a half these cities have been supporting the expenses of the General Esteban de Trejo and his hundred and fifty men of war who have been occupied in dispersing *cimarrones*. From this have resulted many captures and deaths of *cimarrones*, but considering their great multitude more assistance is needed.

We have petitioned the audiencia for aid, but none has been forthcoming because it would be paid from the Royal Treasury and they do not have authority to do so, even though they understand the great evil and damage caused. They have ordered us to inform Your Majesty so that you would be served to remedy the problem, for which at the moment there is none for the above reasons. . . .

In this, these cities have spent all they had and have gone into great debt besides. The vecinos of them are, for the most part, very poor and in need, because in addition to the great robberies that corsairs have committed—which have left many poor and destitute—in the past year many ships have been wrecked in the south sea [Pacific Ocean] in which many fortunes were lost. As a result of this and the increase in royal taxes, the land and people are so lacking that it is impossible to contribute as they have until now against the *cimarrones* and corsairs. . . .

---

1. Despite all the Spaniards' efforts, maroons continued to engage in many of the same strategies for raiding Spanish settlements and freeing enslaved people there. Twenty years before, in 1551, Pero García Marqués complained that the maroons had done exact same thing (see document 3).

13. Panama City Slave Ordinances (1570–1572)

Source: AGI, Panama 30, N. 15. Abridged transcription in Jopling, *Indios y negros en Panamá*, 353–55.

To address the rising problem of marronage, the cabildo of Panama City drafted new ordinances for the city. A number of these were designed to better prevent marronage and punish maroons and those who assisted them. This document records the back-and-forth process by which the ordinances received approval from the king and his ministers. The cabildo of Panama likely drafted the original ordinances sometime in 1570, and the Audiencia of Panama initially authorized their implementation. In 1571, Juan de la Peña presented the ordinances to the king and requested royal approval. The king and his ministers identified several ordinances about which they needed more information. On January 10, 1572, Alonso Cano, mayordomo and *procurador* of the city, presented the royal cedula requesting further information to the audiencia and requested that the judges evaluate the ordinances. After the audiencia adjusted several of the ordinances, the cabildo of Panama drafted a more comprehensive set of ordinances designed to specifically address marronage.

•   •   •

Royal Cedula

The King. President and *oidores* of our Royal Audiencia that resides in the city of Panama in the province of Tierra Firme, named Castilla de Oro, be aware that Juan de la Peña, in the name of the cabildo, magistrates, and *regimiento* of that city of Panama has presented in our Council of the Indies certain ordinances that the cabildo [of the city] appears to have drafted for the good governance of it and that have been approved by you. He has requested that we confirm them. Among the ordinances are some that follow:

- Also, [they] ordered and mandated that insomuch as in this kingdom it has been seen and is notorious the dangers that have resulted from the *negros cimarrones* who wander in rebellion in the hinterlands and forests and other parts and on the roadways and paths that upon which one travels and trades, [and] in this city and kingdom there have occurred deaths of Christian *españoles* and robberies various times of many estates including entering in this city to abduct *negros* and *negras* who serve as well as many other diverse affronts and damages that [the maroons] have committed and make them worthy of contempt and castigation to that end in order to remedy [this, they] ordered and mandated that any *negro* or *negra* that wanders absent from the service of their master four days be given fifty lashes tied to the pillory and that they stay tied there from the time that [the lashes] are meted out until sunset. If they are absent eight days or more, outside of this city a league, they shall wear a *calza al pie de hierro con un ramal* that weighs twelve pounds.[1] This must be worn openly for six months. The penalty for removal shall be two hundred lashes, maiming of a foot, and exile from the kingdom. If their owner removes it, the [owner] incurs a fine of fifty pesos to be divided in thirds, one third to the denouncer, one [third] to the judge, and one [third] for the public works of this city, and the *negro* shall wear the *calza* for the remainder of the sentence.[2]
- Item, any *negro* or *negra* that has fled and absented themselves from their master's service for a period of thirty days shall be given one hundred lashes and have their right foot maimed.
- Item, any *negro* or *negra* that wanders absent from the service of their master six months or more shall be hanged until they die naturally.
- Item, any person, vecino or resident, of this kingdom or anyone employed in the administration of an estate shall be obligated to report any *negro* or *negra* who has absented from the service of their master to the *escribano de cabildo* within three days. If the master of the slave does not report within the said time, they incur a fine of twenty gold pesos to be divided in thirds, public works, judge, denouncer . . . [the *escribano*] shall keep a separate book for such declarations.

The cedula lists other ordinances pertaining to the regulation of butchers and public processions.

- Item, insomuch as in this city there are a great number of freed *negros* and *negras*, and each day more receive their freedom and live in this city where they have their homes, this great quantity of freed *negros* and *negras* in this city and *republica* results in many damages and robberies that they commit or cover up, they have hidden in their homes enslaved *negros* and *negras* who have absconded from their masters, and they cover up the thefts [the slaves] commit.[3] All this requires remedy as well as the many other inconveniences and damages that such a quantity of freed *negros* and *negras* cause this city. Attentive to this, [they] ordered and mandated that within thirty days [the freed *negros* and *negras*] leave this city and gather to settle on an island or other designated place because in this city they only go about loitering without working or serving a master.[4] Settling together in a fixed place, the aforementioned damages can be avoided, and they will have their fields and cultivate the land, sowing and reaping *maize*, raising fowl and pigs and bananas, and [engaging in] other livelihoods with which to sustain themselves. They can come to this city to sell [their produce], which will result in great benefit and profit for them and the city.

The cedula lists other ordinances pertaining to civic magistrates and public roads.

- That no freed *negra* or enslaved [woman] or *mulata* may wear gold, silk, or pearls, but if she is married to an *español* she may wear gold earrings with pearls and a [gold] necklace.[5] Her skirts may have velvet fringe, but she may not wear a buratto cloak nor anything other than a shawl that reaches just past the waist under penalty of having the gold jewelry, silks, and cloak confiscated.[6]

The cedula lists a final ordinance regulating the contracting of household labor.

Having reviewed the above-mentioned ordinances, those in our council not having knowledge of what should be approved have ordered that they be remitted to you [the audiencia], and we order you to review what they contain and to authorize that which serves the good government and ennoble-

ment of the city, paying attention that no one be aggrieved through this. . . .
In Madrid, February 11, 1571.

On September 15, 1572, the Audiencia of Panama acknowledged receipt of the royal
cedula. After reviewing the ordinances, the judges made several minor amend-
ments. Most changes sought to slightly moderate the punishments by reducing
their duration or severity. They also suspended the ordinance that would have relocated the city's free African residents to an island pending the outcome of a legal
challenge brought by those residents. The audiencia enacted the revised ordinances
and sent a copy to the king for royal approval. On September 15, 1572, the cabildo of
Panama submitted a separate, more comprehensive set of ordinances designed to
address the problem of marronage.

Cabildo's Petition and Ordinances

Very Powerful Sir

The cabildo, magistrates, and *regimiento* of this city of Panama state that
having seen the great harm that in this city and in all this kingdom of
Tierra Firme has transpired and continues to occur on account of the many
negros that have fled from the service of their masters and risen up in the
bush, forests, and plains of this kingdom, and that even though they have
attempted to capture, castigate, and remedy the damages that [the *negros*]
commit, they have not been effective even though great expenses have been
incurred on entradas against the *negros cimarrones* led at various times by
Francisco Loçano, Francisco Carreño, Pedro de Ursúa, Diego de Fuentes,
[and] Esteban Trejo, who with commissions as generals have gone out
against the *negros* and more regularly this city and that of Nombre de Dios
have sent out many soldiers with a commander, and even though in these
entradas they have captured and killed some *negros cimarrones* there are so
many of them that the damage incurred by the *negros* was small, but very
great have been the damages and losses to this kingdom and its vecinos and
residents.[7] The *negros cimarrones* have with great temerity and shamelessness entered this city and that of Nombre de Dios whenever they wish
under dark of night, entering the houses of vecinos and stealing *negras* who
they take to the bush, and by day they [steal *negras*] from the rivers where
they wash [clothes]. On the roadways of this city and Nombre de Dios, and
at the Casa de Cruces, they have committed great robberies and killed many
travelers, and had many fights with soldiers sent against them by this city

and that of Nombre de Dios, killing many soldiers. Ultimately on the day of Our Lady, September 8, they killed Alonso Fernández Pacheco at his cattle ranch, one league from this city.[8] They stole four *piezas de negros* and all else they could carry.[9] They have committed other such damages and murders that are so numerous that all cannot be declared here. All the vecinos of this city and Nombre de Dios are terrified; no one dare travel the roads without many men [or] dare visit their rural estates or [go] to work the gold mines of this kingdom.[10] It is abundant[ly clear] that the owners of the *negros cimarrones* are dispossessed of their slaves' service. The service of these slaves is the most important and necessary thing to this kingdom because without them one [can neither] plant fields of *maize*, [nor] cut wood in the forest for building, nor conduct mule trains, nor navigate ships along the Chagres River or ships in the south sea, [and neither] can cattle ranches be sustained without *negros*, [likewise] the orchards, pearl beds, fisheries, and other livelihoods of the land. Also, the *negros cimarrones* have been greatly aided by enslaved *negros*, [especially] those that gather firewood and forage for this city.[11] When they go out for firewood or forage, they warn [the *negros cimarrones*] when this city plans to go against them, and they procure weapons and supplies for the [*negros cimarrones*]. When the [*negros cimarrones*] come into the city, the [enslaved *negros*] hide them in their huts. Similarly, it is known that the freed *negros* that live in this city hide them, such that the [*negros cimarrones*] are well prepared to commit the damages, robberies, and murders that they have committed and continue to commit each day. In order to remedy this, we have conversed and conferred many times, and by order of Licenciado Diego de Vera, your president of this Royal Audiencia, governor and *capitán general* in this district, we held a *cabildo abierto* [public discussion] so that all vecinos and residents of this city could share their opinion concerning the things contained in the chapters listed below.[12] [They] gave their opinion on the matter and signed their names, which we present with this petition, all of which has been seen, discussed, and conferred [on] and appeared to us that the following should be ordained:

Ordinances concerning the *negros cimarrones* drafted by the *cabildo abierto*:

- Firstly, we order that any person of any state or condition, be they free or enslaved, *blanco* or *negro*, that captures a *negro* or *negra cimarrón* that has been absent from the service of their master for four months, regardless of whether they were taken by force,[13] shall gain ownership of the *negro* or *negra cimarrón* [and] from that point forward can do what they wish [with the *negro cimarrón*] for they will be their slave. The person who so captures a *negro* or *negra* shall be obligated to take them to the prison of this city and present them to the magistrate so [the *negro cimarrón*] can be seen, the time of their absence verified, and they may be punished according to the applicable ordinances of this city. If such a person instead would prefer fifty pesos of assayed silver for the return of the *negro* or *negra* they have captured, then they shall be given fifty pesos of assayed silver from the income of the city for each piece [person], and the *negro* or *negra* will become a slave of this city. If the *negro* or *negra cimarrón* absent for four months and captured would appear to this city to be a useful and convenient guide or pathfinder [for expeditions] against the other *negros cimarrones*, the city may claim them paying the soldier or person who captured them that which is deemed appropriate by the magistrates of this city or such persons charged with this task according to the value and disposition of the *negro*.

- Item, if the *negro* or *negra cimarrón* captured and brought to the prison had previously committed a crime that according to the ordinances of the city merits the death penalty and the penalty is meted out, the city is obligated to pay fifty pesos of assayed silver from its income to the person for every *negro* or *negra* they captured that was executed. The same shall be done if a punishment, although less than the death penalty, results in the death of the *negro* so that the [captor] is not left without a reward for capturing a *negro cimarrón*.[14]
- Item, if such *negro* or *negra cimarrón* has not been absent four months, the person who captured them shall be given that which is mandated by the ordinances of the city according to the time of their absence. The master of the *negro* shall pay; however, if the *negro* or *negra* did not flee of their own volition but had been taken through force by *cimarrones*, and this is proven, the master of the *negro* shall give the person who captured [the *negro*] fifty pesos of assayed silver as a reward for the capture so long as the captive had

been absent for more than four months. If the captive had been absent for less than four months from the day they were taken away by force until the day they were captured, [the master] shall pay that which is mandated by the ordinances of the city according to the length of the absence except that the master shall pay the person who captured [the *negro*]. In whatever above-mentioned case, the person who has captured such a *negro* or *negra* shall be obligated to take them to the prison of this city and present them to the magistrate, if they do not do so they many not receive or claim any reward for the capture. . . .

- Item, that whenever a *negro* or *negra cimarrón* who at any time leaves the bush for this city and brings with them another *negro* or *negra*, the *negro* that left of their own volition shall be freed and half of those [slaves] brought shall be slaves of this city and the other half slaves of the master of the slave who brought [them]. Those brought shall have executed upon them the penalty they deserve [according to their absences]. For every *negro* brought, the *negro* [who brought them] shall receive twenty pesos in addition to their liberty, if the *negros* had been absent four months; if they had been absent less time [the *negro* that brought them] shall be rewarded according to the ordinances of this city. It is understood that this should be the case when the *negro* who brought another has been absent for over four months. If the *negro* [who brought another] has been absent less than four months, he shall be free, but the [one brought] shall not become a slave of this city but a slave of the master of the *negro* that came of their own volition, the city shall not pay the twenty pesos reward unless the slave that was brought dies, in which case the master of the slave that brought them shall receive the reward.[15]

- Item, whomever gives information about a *negro* or *negra cimarrón*, but who cannot capture them, if the information results in the capture of the *negro* or *negra*, the person who gave information should receive the third part of the reward and . . . the other two-thirds go to the person that captured [the *negro*].[16]

- Item, if any *negro* or *negra* or *mulato* or *mulata* from this day forward persuades or advises any slave to hide themselves or hides the slave themselves for four months with the intent to present them later and to have them as their own, they shall receive the death penalty. If an *español* does so they shall be exiled from the Indies in addition to any other punishments afforded by law, if the slave is hidden less than four months they shall receive punishment according to the circumstances of their crime.

- Item, if any person trades with, converses, gives food, hides, or gives warning to a *negro cimarrón*, if they are a *negro* or *negra* or *mulato* or *mulata*, free or enslaved, they shall incur the same punishment as the *negro* or *negra cimarrón* in addition to the loss of half their property, to be applied to the cost of war against the *cimarrones*. If they are an *español*, they shall be exiled perpetually from the Indies in addition to any other punishments afforded by law.

- Item, by ordinance of this city, it has been ordered that any person whose slave has fled must report [the flight] within three days to the *escribano del cabildo* [clerk of the municipal council] who shall maintain a book for such declarations. . . . We order that the same be done for any *negros* that before now have fled, that they should be reported to the *escribano del cabildo* within ten days, declaring how long [the slaves] have been absent from their service under penalty that those who do not report shall lose all rights to their absent *negros* or *negras*.[17]

- Item, in order that captive *negros* do not have reason to absent themselves from the service of their masters with the intent of searching for *negros cimarrones* to capture, we order that no captive slave may go without license of their master and the magistrates in search of *negros cimarrones*. If they should go without license they shall receive no reward for capturing [a *negro cimarrón*], and the [captured] slave shall be taken by their master, excepting if the capture happened while the [captured] slave was going to fetch water, forage, [gather] firewood, or [act on] some other purpose by order of their master.[18]

- Item, we order that if any *negro* or *negra* from this day forward willingly flees from the service of their master and returns of their own volition with captured *negros cimarrones*, they shall not receive liberty or any other reward; instead they shall be punished according to the ordinances of this city. The *negros* or *negras* that they bring shall be for this city if they were *cimarrones* for over four months.[19]

A final ordinance prohibited other *escribanos* from initiating any legal cases or paperwork concerning *negros cimarrones*, mandating that all such cases had to be taken to the *escribano del cabildo*.

Therefore, we request that Your Highness be served to review these ordinances and appearing convenient to your royal service and to the good of this kingdom and its residents that Your Highness order them confirmed so that they may be published and placed in force because if we must make personal representation of them to your royal person, much time will pass, and in the interim the many damages, murders, and robberies would continue so long as the [ordinances] are not applied. . . .

Audiencia's Response

In this city of Panama, September 18, 1572, the *señores*, *presidente* and *oidores* of the audienca and royal chancellery of His Majesty that in [this city] resides concurring with the magistrates having seen these ordinances and what has been requested by the city of Panama concerning their confirmation, stated that they order that the ordinances drafted by the cabildo, magistrates, and *regimiento* be put in force and applied as they are written while they await confirmation by His Majesty by order of this Royal Audiencia. . . .

When the documents arrived at court, the Council of the Indies recommended that the king confirm the ordinances as approved by the audiencia.

1. This describes an iron fetter clasped around the leg or ankle connected to a heavy chain.
2. The tripartite division of financial penalties was common for many crimes.
3. The Spanish term *republica* referred to the social order, not a type of political system. In this case, the sense is that freed Africans are damaging to the fabric of society.
4. The plan mirrors Ursúa's proposed settlement for the Bayano maroons.
5. This represents the first sumptuary restriction placed on women of color. Although drafted by the cabildo of Panama City, after having received royal approval, this ordinance would take the force of law throughout the empire because it would later be included in the two most significant compilations of Spanish colonial law, the *Cedulario de Encinas* (1582) and the *Recopilacion de leyes de los reinos de las Indias* (1680). Encinas, *Cedulario indiano*, 4:387; *Recopilación de Leyes de las Indias*, 2:369.
6. Buratto cloth was a popular fabric usually made from silk or linen that could be embroidered.
7. No known documents attest to the expedition led by Diego de Fuentes.
8. The Feast of the Nativity of the Virgin Mary.

9. The phrase *piezas de negros* ("pieces of *negros*") was commonly used in the transatlantic slave trade to dehumanize enslaved Africans by emphasizing their commodification.

10. While there were some placer mines in Panama, most of these were located to the west, not to the east where the maroons were most numerous.

11. Networks of communication between maroons and enslaved or free Africans living in Europeans cities were common throughout the Americas. Such networks provided vital information to maroons and could allow for trade in stolen goods or for the acquisition of necessary items. Schwaller, "Contested Conquests," 622, 628; Diouf, *Slavery's Exiles,* 97–128.

12. A session of the cabildo conducted with the public present.

13. That is to say that slaves abducted by maroons would still be held accountable for absences greater than four months.

14. Many of the penalties listed—such as hundreds of lashes, hamstringing, and mangling limbs—could easily have resulted in excessive blood loss or infection leading to death.

15. Because of the severity of the punishments, captured maroons could die. In this final example, the master of the slave who brought others receives some compensation for the freedom granted to their slave.

16. This ordinance is unclear about how a third of the reward could be granted in cases where the capturer chooses to keep the slave as their own.

17. This ordinance suggests that many slave owners had been complacent in reporting the absence of their slaves. Additionally, these newly mandated reports could help the authorities better estimate the size of the maroon population on the isthmus.

18. This clause prevented slaves from attempting to capture other slaves who might be outside of the city carrying out legitimate duties assigned to them by their owners.

19. Presumably, slaves absent for less time would receive the punishment according to the ordinances and returned to their owners.

Part III
The Second Bayano War:
Maroons and the English (1572–1578)

14. Excerpts from "Sir Francis Drake Revived," Drake's Alliance with Maroons, January 1573

Source: Nichols, "Sir Francis Drake Revived," 173–87.

The first few years of the 1570s saw increased attacks on Spaniards in Panama by foreign corsairs. One of the most famous participants was Francis Drake, an English captain who would make a name for himself raiding Spain's colonies. He had likely been part of the raids described by the cabildo of Panama in 1571. Following those successes, he returned to the region in 1572 with grander plans.

Drake and his crew reached the Caribbean side of the isthmus in the summer of 1572. Soon after arriving, Drake captured some enslaved *negros* gathering wood from the Isle of Pines (Isla de Pinos), southeast of Nombre de Dios. These slaves told them of the disposition of Nombre de Dios, which they raided in July 1572. After Drake was gravely wounded, he and his men cultivated alliances with maroons through the fall and winter of 1572. Maroons assisted in the construction of a palisaded camp named Fort Diego. In January 1573, the maroons informed Drake that the Spanish fleet had arrived in Nombre de Dios. Instead of sacking Nombre de Dios, Drake and the maroons decided to raid the mule trains that would be bringing gold, silver, and merchandise from Panama City. This excerpt begins as the maroons guided the English into the interior of the isthmus.

Philip Nichols compiled this account from firsthand accounts of Drake and his men. Nichols published it in 1628. The excerpts below trace a raid made by Drake and his maroon allies in which they attempted to capture a caravan transporting goods and silver from Panama City to Nombre de Dios.

• • •

We were in all forty-eight, of which eighteen only were English; the rest were Cimarrons, which beside their arms, bore every one of them, a great quantity of victuals and provision, supplying our want of carriage in so long a march, so that we were not troubled with anything but our furniture. And because they could not carry enough to suffice us altogether; therefore (as they promised before) so by the way with their arrows, they provided for us competent store from time to time.

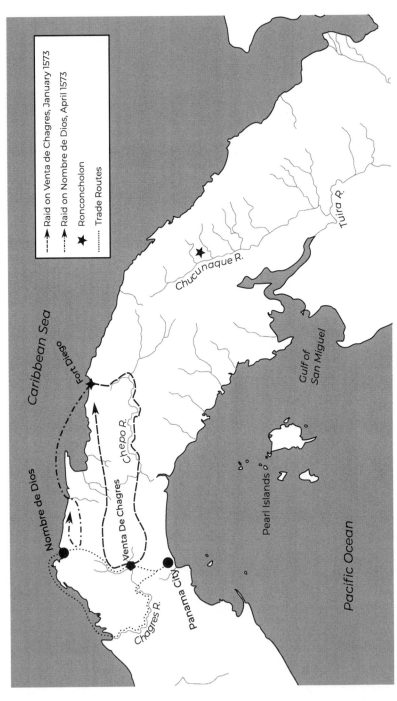

Approximate routes of English-Maroon raids, 1573. *Source:* Nichols, "Sir Francis Drake Revived," 173–202.

They have every one of them two sorts of arrows: the one to defend himself and offend the enemy, the other to kill his victuals. These for fight are somewhat like the Scottish arrow; only somewhat longer, and headed with iron, wood, or fish bones. But the arrows for provision are of three sorts, the first serveth to kill any great beast near at hand, as ox, stag, or wild boar: this hath a head of iron of a pound and a half weight, shaped in form like the head of a javelin or boar-spear, as sharp as any knife, making so large and deep a wound as can hardly be believed of him that hath not seen it. The second serveth for lesser beasts, and hath a head of three-quarters of a pound: this he most usually shooteth. The third serveth for all manner of birds: it hath a head of an ounce weight. And these heads though they be of iron only, yet are they so cunningly tempered, that they will continue a very good edge a long time: and though they be turned sometimes, yet they will never or seldom break. The necessity in which they stand hereof continually causeth them to have iron in far greater account than gold: and no man among them is of greater estimation, than he that can most perfectly give this temper unto it. [1]

The expedition marched in the morning from sunrise till ten, rested from ten till after noon, then travelled from noon until four. After the day's march, the maroons prepared shelters.

As soon as we came to the place where we intended to lodge, the Cimarrons, presently laying down their burdens, fell to cutting of forks or posts, and poles or rafters, and palmito boughs, or plantain leaves; and with great speed set up the number of six houses. For every of which, they first fastened deep into the ground, three or four great posts with forks: upon them, they laid one transom, which was commonly about twenty feet, and made the sides, in the manner of the roofs of our country houses, thatching it close with those aforesaid leaves, which keep out water a long time: observing always that in the lower ground, where greater heat was, they left some three or four feet open unthatched below, and made the houses, or rather roofs, so many feet the higher. But in the hills, where the air was more piercing and the nights cold, they made our rooms always lower, and thatched them close to the ground, leaving only one door to enter in, and a louvre hole for a vent, in the midst of the roof.[2] In every of these, they made for [the] several lodgings three fires, one in the midst, and one at each end of every house: so that the room was most temperately warm, and nothing annoyed with smoke, partly by reason of the nature of the wood which they use to burn, yielding very little smoke, partly by reason of their artificial making of it: as firing the wood cut in length like our billets at the ends, and joining them together so close, that though no flame or fire did appear, yet the heat continued without intermission.

Near many of the rivers where we stayed or lodged, we found sundry sorts of fruits, which we might use with great pleasure and safety temperately: Mammeas, Guayvas, Palmitos, Pinos, Oranges, Lemons, and divers other; from eating of which they dissuaded us in any case, unless we eat very few of them, and those first dry roasted, as Plantains, Potatoes, and such like. . . .

The third day of our journey, they brought us to a town of their own, seated near a fair river, on the side of a hill, environed with a dyke of eight feet broad, and a thick mud wall of ten feet high, sufficient to stop a sudden surpriser.[3] It had one long and broad street, lying east and west, and two other cross streets of less breadth and length: there were in it some five or six and fifty households; which were kept so clean and sweet, that not only the houses, but the very streets were very pleasant to behold. In this town we saw they lived very civilly and cleanly. For as soon as we came thither, they washed themselves in the river; and changed their apparel, as also their women do wear, which was very fine and fitly made somewhat after the Spanish fashion, though nothing so costly. This town is distant thirty-five leagues from Nombre de Dios and forty-five from Panama. It is plentifully stored with many sorts of beasts and fowl, with plenty of maize and sundry fruits.[4]

Touching their affection in religion, they have no kind of priests, only they held the Cross in great reputation. But at our Captain's persuasion, they were contented to leave their crosses, and to learn the Lord's Prayer, and to be instructed in some measure concerning GOD's true worship.[5] They kept a continual watch in four parts, three miles off their town, to prevent the mischiefs, which the Spaniards intend against them, by the conducting of some of their own coats [i.e., Cimarrones], which having been taken by the Spaniards have been enforced thereunto: wherein, as we learned, sometimes the Spaniards have prevailed over them, especially when they lived less careful; but since, they [watch] against the Spaniards, whom they killed like beasts, as often as they take them in the woods; having aforehand understood of their coming.[6]

We stayed with them that night, and the next day till noon; during which time, they related unto us diverse very strange accidents, that had fallen out between them and the Spaniards, namely one. A gallant gentleman entertained by the Governor of the country, undertook, the year last past (1572), with 150 soldiers, to put this town to the sword, men, women, and children.[7] Being conducted to it by one of them, that had been taken prisoner, and won by great gifts; he surprised it half an hour before day, by which occasion most of the men escaped, but many of their women and children were slaughtered, or taken: but the same morning by sun rising (after that their guide was slain, in following another man's wife, and that the Cimarrons had assembled themselves in their strength) they behaved themselves in such sort, and drove the Spaniards to such extremity, that what with the disadvantage of the woods (having lost their guide and thereby their way), what with famine and want, there escaped not past thirty of them, to return answer to those which sent them.[8]

Their king [chief] dwelt in a city within sixteen leagues southeast of Panama; which is able to make 1,700 fighting men.[9]

From the maroon town the company proceeded toward Panama, where, using spies, they hoped to learn when the mule trains would leave for Nombre de Dios. After learning that the treasurer of Peru would be travelling along with many pack trains, the English and maroons travelled to the rest stop of Venta de Chagres to set up an ambush. Nichols confuses Venta de Chagres for Casa de Cruces. The attack took place at Venta de Chagres, and Spanish accounts are unequivocal on this fact. Additionally, from the maroon's territory, Venta de Chagres represented the closer and more accessible target.

Being at the place appointed, our Captain with half his men [8 English and 15 Cimaroons], lay on one side of the way, about fifty paces off in the long grass; John Oxham[10] with the Captain of the Cimarrons, and the other half, lay on the other side of the way, at the like distance: but so far behind, that as occasion served, the former company might take the foremost mules by the heads, and the hindmost because the mules tied together, are always driven one after another; and especially that if we should have need to use our weapons that night, we might be sure not to endamage our fellows. We

Río Mamoní, a tributary of the Río Chepo. One of the many rivers Drake may have traversed on his way to Venta de Chagres. *Photograph by the author.*

had not lain thus in ambush much above an hour, but we heard the Recuas [mule trains] coming both from the city to Venta Cruz, and from Venta Cruz to the city, which hath a very common and great trade, when the fleets are there. We heard them by reason they delight much to have deep-sounding bells, which, in a still night, are heard very far off.[11]

Unfortunately for the raiding party, a drunk Englishmen revealed their location to a scout from Venta de Chagres who then warned the mule trains carrying gold to return to Panama. The party still captured some animals carrying basic supplies and a small amount of silver. Frustrated, Drake resolved to leave by way of Venta de Chagres, rather than travel the longer distance through the forests.

Our Captain understanding by our Cimarrons, which with great heedfulness and silence, marched now, but about half a flight-shot before us, that it was time for us to arm and take us to our weapons, for they knew the enemy was at hand, by smelling of their match and hearing of a noise:[12] had given us charge, that no one of us should make any shot, until the Spaniards had first spent their volley: which he thought they would not do before they had spoken, as indeed fell out.

For as soon as we were within hearing, a Spanish Captain cried out, "Hoo!" Our Captain answered him likewise, and being demanded "*Que gente?*" replied "Englishmen!" But when the said Commander charged him, "In the name of the King of Spain, his Master, that we should yield ourselves; promising in the word and faith of a Gentleman Soldier, that if we would so do, he would use us with all courtesy." Our Captain drawing somewhat near him said: "That for the honour of the Queen of England, his Mistress, he must have passage that way," and therewithal discharged his pistol towards him.

Upon this, they presently shot off their whole volley; which, though it lightly wounded our Captain, and divers of our men, yet it caused death to one only of our company called JOHN HARRIS, who was so powdered with hail-shot, (which they all used for the most part as it seemed, or else "quartered," for that our men were hurt with that kind) that we could not recover his life, though he continued all that day afterwards with us.

Presently as our Captain perceived their shot to come slacking, as the latter drops of a great shower of rain, with his whistle he gave us his usual signal, to answer them with our shot and arrows, and so march onwards upon the enemy, with intent to come to handy-strokes, and to have joined with them; whom when we found retired as to a place of some better strength, he increased his pace to prevent them if he might. Which the Cimarrons perceiving, although by terror of the shot continuing, they were for the time stept aside; yet as soon as they discerned by hearing that we marched onward, they all rushed forward one after another, traversing the way, with their arrows ready in their bows, and their manner of country dance or leap, very singing *Yo peho! Yo peho!* and so got before us, where they continued their leap and song, after the manner of their own country wars, till they and we overtook some of the enemy, who near the town's end, had conveyed themselves within the woods, to have taken their stand at us, as before.[13]

But our Cimarrons now thoroughly encouraged, when they saw our resolution, brake in through the thickets, on both sides of them, forcing them to fly, Friars and all! Although divers of our men were wounded, and one Cimarron especially was run through with one of their pikes, whose courage and mind served him so well notwithstanding, that he revenged his own death ere he died, by killing him that had given him that deadly wound.

We, with all speed, following this chase, entered the town of Venta Cruz, being of about forty or fifty houses, which had both a Governor and other officers and some fair houses, with many storehouses large and strong for the wares, which brought thither from Nombre de Dios, by the river of Chagres, so to be transported by mules to Panama: beside the Monastery, where we found above a thousand bulls and pardons, newly sent from Rome. . . . [14]

While the guards which we had, not without great need, set, as well on the bridge which we had to pass over, as at the town's end where we entered (they have no other entrance into the town by land: but from the water's side there is one other to carry up and down their merchandise from their frigates) gained us liberty and quiet to stay in this town some hour and half: we had not only refreshed ourselves, but our company and Cimaroons had gotten some good pillage, which our Captain allowed and gave them (being not the thing he looked for) so that it were not too cumbersome or heavy in respect of our travel, or defense of ourselves. . . .

But our Captain considering that he had a long way to pass, and that he had been now well near a fortnight from his ship, where he had left his company but weak by reason of their sickness, hastened his journeys as much as he might, refusing to visit the other Cimaroon towns (which they earnestly desired him) and encouraging his own company with such example and speech, that the way seemed much shorter. For he marched most cheerfully, and assured us that he doubted not but ere he left the coast, we should all be bountifully paid and recompensed for all those pains taken: but by reason of this our Captain's haste, and leaving of their towns, we marched many days with hungry stomachs, much against the will of our Cimaroons: who if we would have stayed any day from this continual journeying, would have killed for us victuals sufficient.

In our absence, the rest of the Cimaroons had built a little town within three leagues off the port where our ship lay. There our Captain was contented, upon their great and earnest entreaties to make some stay; for that they alleged, it was only built for his sake. And indeed he consented the rather, that the want of shoes might be supplied by means of the Cimaroons, who were a great help unto us: all our men complaining of the tenderness of their feet, whom our Captain would himself accompany in their complaint some times without cause, but some times with cause indeed; which made the rest to bear the burden the more easily.

These Cimaroons, during all the time that we were with burden, did us continually very good service, and in particular in this journey, being unto us instead of intelligencers, to advertise us; of guide in our way to direct us; of purveyors, to provide victuals for us; of house-wrights to build our lodgings; and had indeed able and strong bodies carrying all our necessaries:

yea, many times when some of our company fainted with sickness of weariness, two Cimaroons would carry him with ease between them, two miles together, and at other times, when need was, they would show themselves no less valiant than industrious, and of good judgement.

After several days travel the English arrived back at their coastal camp and the newly built maroon town. They would spend the next two months recovering while gathering supplies and information along the coast.

1. Maroons could only access iron by raiding Spanish mule trains or cities. To forge the arrowheads they melted other iron items down.
2. Comments such as these reveal the extent to which maroons adapted their shelters to the conditions of the landscape and climate.
3. This description very closely matches Aguado's account of Bayano's settlement, suggesting that the maroons either reinhabited Bayano's site, possibly adding fortifications, or the maroons chose a new site with similar geographic features. The latter case may be more probable, since maroons would have had reason to fear that Spaniards might return to Bayano's settlement.
4. These distances do not offer much help in identifying the location, as they are based on overland travel along rivers and ridgelines which cannot be easily reconstructed.
5. While Aguado perceived maroon religion to be a twisted form of Roman Catholic rites, the Protestant English saw the maroons as practicing a form of devotion similar to their own. The simplicity of maroon practice mirrored the "low church" practices that had become common in Protestant England.
6. Brackets in original. These comments likely refer to maroons recounting of Ursúa's campaign.
7. This certainly refers to Esteban de Trejo's campaign.
8. If true, this embarrassing outcome could explain why Spanish sources do not mention the conclusion of Trejo's campaign.
9. Brackets in original. The political organization of the maroons of this period is unclear. The English suggest that there may have been a new king. Subsequent Spanish sources similarly identified a singular leader but only occasionally referred to him as king.
10. This is the same John Oxenham that would return several years later.
11. First set of brackets in original.
12. Harquebuses used match cord, or slow match, a slow-burning cord, to ignite the gunpowder in the flash pan.
13. Probably, "Yo peleo," meaning "I fight." Nichols, unlike Aguado, recognized that the maroons' fighting style derived from African martial practice.
14. Venta de Chagres, as its name implies, also sat at the intersection of the Camino Real and the Río Chagres. Although most riverine trade passed through Casa de Cruces, boats did navigate farther up the river to Venta de Chagres. This may explain some of the confusion in the English sources.

15. The Cabildo of Panama to the Crown, February 24, 1573

Source: AGI, Panama 30, N. 14. Abridged transcription in Jopling,
Indios y negros en Panamá, 350.

This excerpt of a letter from the cabildo of Panama City recounts the Spanish view
of Drake's raid on Venta de Chagres and illustrates the fear that the alliance between
the English and the *cimarrones* caused in the region.

•   •   •

At present this kingdom is so terrified and the souls of everyone are so disturbed that we do not know what words will express to Your Majesty what
we wish to say. Nevertheless, we believe that it is certain that there is great
risk in any delay in remedying the situation, which we will explain as briefly
as possible.

On the ninth of July of last year, with the residents of the port of Nombre
de Dios being unprepared for what would befall them, four launches of the
English Lutherans landed at night, carrying almost eighty men. Arranged
into two units, they captured the city and held it, doing as much damage as
they could. The assault resulted in the deaths of four or five men and many
more wounded residents, who were powerless to resist or attack them
because the attack was a surprise. . . .

On the last day of January of this year, at least twenty of the English,
along with forty *negros cimarrones* with whom they are allied, assaulted the
road that passes between this city and that of Nombre de Dios in addition to
the Venta de Chagres, which is six leagues from this city by land. The result
of which was the deaths of three *españoles* and a friar of the Order of St. Dominic. Five men, *blancos* and *negros*, who were travelling the road died of their
wounds. They burned Venta [de Chagres] and stole and burned a great
quantity of clothing and merchandise owned by private persons. They
would have stolen over 80,000 pesos of gold and silver being carried by a
pack train to the city of Nombre de Dios had God not miraculously saved it
from them. About a half-league before arriving into the hands of the enemy,
the pack train noticed the [raiding party] and fled, returning to this city,
saving all the gold and silver that it carried.

Because of this daring by the English, to have come by land so close
to this city and to have allied with the *negros cimarrones*, this kingdom is as
disturbed as we mentioned above, since the damage that might arise is

apparent. The English have so shamelessly opened a door and a path by which they can attack, whenever it suits them, the pack trains that frequent this overland route, which, by necessity, carries the gold and silver of Your Majesty and of private persons to Spain and the merchandise that from there is taken to this kingdom and Peru.

The worst of all is that there is dependable news that these English and the *negros cimarrones* with whom they are allied and confederated are established in a port on this coast, located thirty leagues from here, from which they leave to commit their assaults.[1] We are certain the principal design of the English is to see and study the land, and the defenses that it has, so that returning with more people from England they might plunder and occupy it. . . .

The alliance of the English and the *negros* has been a very detrimental thing to this kingdom, because the *negros* are very skilled in the things of this land and so deft in the wilderness that they will give the [English] means and aid . . . to commit whatever evil they wish to put in effect. As a result of these events this kingdom remains fearful and agitated because it is a lamentable thing that the English and the *negros* are united to attack us, the *negros* being so numerous. . . .

To remedy this and avoid the evils that might arise from it, we humbly ask that Your Majesty be served to quickly send to this land relief and defense, the most important we believe are the galleys to patrol the coast, which we have other times asked Your Majesty to send, because if safety comes to the sea so too will it be on the land.

---

1. By "this coast" the Cabildo refers to the Pacific coastline. This claim is likely in error, as during Drake's 1572–73 expedition the English did not establish a base on the Pacific side.

16. Excerpts from "Sir Francis Drake Revived," Drake's Final Attack, April 1573

Source: Nichols, "Sir Francis Drake Revived," 194–202.

In April 1573, the fears of the cabildo came true when Drake's combined force of English, French, and maroons raided Spanish mule trains on the road outside of Nombre de Dios, stealing over eighty thousand pesos of gold, at least eighteen thousand of which were destined for the king. The attack came to fruition after Drake made contact with Guillaume le Testu, a French captain similarly intent on raiding Spanish trade. The two captains quickly formed an alliance, with Testu gifting Drake a pair of pistols and a sword that had once been owned by King Henry II of France. The captains had news that the fleet was preparing to depart Nombre de Dios and that many goods and bullion would soon be arriving at the port. The two companies, along with their maroon allies, agreed to conduct a combined raid assembling their forces at the Río Francisca to the east of Nombre de Dios. The captains left their pinnaces in the care of maroons before setting off.

•   •   •

It is five leagues accounted by sea, between Río Francisco and Nombre de Dios; but that way which we march by land, we found it above seven leagues.[1] We marched as in our former journey to Panama, both for order and silence; to the great wonder of the French Captain and company, who protested they knew not by any means how to recover the pinnaces, if the Cimaroons (to whom what our Captain commanded was a law; though they little regarded the French, as having no trust in them) should leave us: our Captain assured him, "There was no cause of doubt of them, of whom he had had such former trial."[2]

When we were come within an English mile of the way, we stayed all night, refreshing ourselves, in great stillness, in a most convenient place: where we heard the carpenters, being many in number, working upon their ships, as they usually do by reason of the great heat of the day in Nombre de Dios; and might hear the mules coming from Panama, by reason of the advantage of the ground.[3]

The next morning (1st April), upon hearing of that number of bells, the Cimaroons, rejoiced exceedingly, as though there could not have befallen them a more joyful accident chiefly having been disappointed before. Now they all assured us, "We should have more gold and silver than all of us could bear away:" as in truth it fell out. For there came three Recuas, one of 50 mules, the other two, of 70 each, every [one] of which carried 300 lbs. weight of silver; which in all amounted to near thirty tons.[4]

We putting ourselves in readiness, went down near the way to hear the bells; where we stayed not long, but we saw of what metal they were made; and took such hold on the heads of the foremost and hindmost mules, that all the rest stayed and lay down, as their manner is.

These three Recuas were guarded with forty-five soldiers or thereabouts, fifteen to each Recua, which caused some exchange of bullets and arrows for a time; in which conflict the French Captain was sore wounded with hail-shot in the belly, and one Cimaroon was slain: but in the end, these soldiers thought it the best way to leave their mules with us, and to seek for more help abroad.

In which meantime we took some pain to ease some of the mules which were heaviest laden of their carriage. And because we ourselves were somewhat weary, we were contented with a few bars and quoits of gold, as we could well carry: burying about fifteen tons of silver, partly in the burrows which the great land crabs had made in the earth, and partly under old trees which were fallen thereabout, and partly in the sand and gravel of a river, not very deep of water.[5]

The combined party began a retreat to the ships, leaving a mortally wounded Testu behind with some Frenchmen. The French corsairs would eventually be captured and tortured for the location of the buried treasure. After the raid, Spaniards quickly dispatched several ships down the coast. Seeing these, Drake feared that they would discover the hidden pinnaces. Believing that their means of escape had been captured, Drake and a small contingent of men including the maroon leader Pedro built a small raft and ventured onward in the hopes of recapturing their vessels. The Spanish had failed to find the pinnaces, and the crew of the raft found them anchored in a sheltered cove. Drake quickly guided the ships back to the main body of men. Afterward, a detachment of Englishmen and maroons headed by John Oxenham returned to Río Francisca to recover some of the buried loot. They rescued one Frenchman who had escaped capture. After raiding a Spanish merchantman for supplies, they returned to the coast of Panama to bid farewell to the maroons.

Here we stayed about seven nights, trimming and rigging our frigates, boarding and stowing our provisions, tearing abroad and burning our pinnaces, that the Cimaroons might have the iron-work.[6]

About a day or two before our departure, our Captain willed Pedro and three of the chiefest of the Cimaroons to go through both his frigates, to see what they liked; promising to give it them, whatsoever it were, so it were not so necessary as that he could not return into England without it. And for their wives he would himself seek out some silks or linen that might gratify them; which while he was choosing out of his trunks, the scimitar which Captain Testu had given to our Captain, chanced to be taken forth in Pedro's sight: which he seeing grew so much in liking thereof, that he accounted of nothing else in respect of it, and preferred it before all that could be given him. Yet imagining that it was no less esteemed of our Captain, durst not himself open his mouth to crave or commend it; but made one Francis Tucker to be his mean to break his mind, promising to give him a fine quoit of gold, which yet he had in store, if he would but move our Captain for it; and to our Captain himself, he would give four other great quoits which he had hidden, intending to have reserved them until another voyage.

Our Captain being accordingly moved by Francis Tucker, could have been content to have made no such exchange; but yet desirous to content him, that had deserved so well, he gave it him with many good words: who received it with no little joy, affirming that if he should give his wife and children which he loved dearly in lieu of it, he could not sufficient recompense it (for he would present his king with it, who he knew would make him a great man, even for this very gift's sake); yet in gratuity and stead of other requital of this jewel, he desired our Captain to accept these four pieces of gold, as a token of his thankfulness to him, and a pawn of his faithfulness during life.[7]

Our Captain received it in most kind sort, but took it not to his own benefit, but caused it to be cast into the whole Adventure, saying, "If he had not been set forth to that place, he had not attained such a commodity, and therefore it was just that they which bare part with him of his burden in setting him to sea, should enjoy the proportion of his benefit whatsoever at his return."

After this sendoff, Drake and his men left Panama for England. They voyage took them past the western side of Cuba, through the Straits of Florida, and into the Atlantic Ocean. They arrived in Plymouth on August 9, 1573.

---

1. The Spanish called the river "Francisca," not "Francisco." It had been the site proposed by Pedro de Ursúa for the resettlement of Bayano's community.
2. The French feared that the maroons could not be trusted watching their vessels. Drake assured them that the maroons had already demonstrated their trustworthiness.
3. The carpenters were busy repairing and outfitting the fleet that would soon depart with the goods transiting the isthmus from Panama City.
4. *Recua* is Spanish for mule train.
5. "Quoits" refers to flattened disks.
6. The maroons appear to have received no gold or silver from the raids. The iron from the burnt pinnaces represented the more useful prize for the maroons' participation.
7. With this exchange an African maroon in Panama came to own a sword that once belonged to Henry II of France.

17. Cristóbal Monte's Report on Drake's April Raid (1573)

Source: AGI, Patronato 267, R. 72, N. 1.

After capturing the Frenchmen, the Spanish learned of the rendezvous that Drake had planned with his boats. Captain Cristóbal Monte commanded the boats that went down the coast to investigate. These were the Spanish pinnaces spied by Drake. This report summarizes the Spanish expedition.

• • •

I don't have any news to report other than that the English and French, as Your Mercy will have heard, crossed paths with the dispatch boat. The Frenchman took Orozco in an *urca* that had been owned by Albendin and then received word of the Englishman who had been in the Gulf of Acla.[1] He went with the intent to fight him, but after encountering him they became friends. They allied together and went with the *negros cimarrones*. Thirty Frenchmen and English and fifty *negros* waited one league from Nombre de Dios for the mule trains. The Corsican's mule train passed with a certain number of soldiers guarding it—harquebusiers. They did not commit or show themselves. Another day they attacked [a mule train] carrying over two hundred thousand pesos, including thirty thousand pesos of the king. They took and hid all the gold and some bars. A *negro* who spied them, a harquebusier, killed the French captain . . . I mean wounded him mortally and killed an Englishman and a *negro cimarrón*.[2]

The alarm was raised in the town and men left by land encountering the wounded captain and a French gentleman who he had beseeched to stay with him. This one fled and killed the French captain to save the rest and the loot.[3] The one that fled came to the Río del Factor and saw the king's *negros* who work on the dam, these are friends of the *cimarrones*. Believing them to be so, he approached them but was captured and taken [to the authorities]. He was quartered.

Those who left by land sent word to the pueblo that they had captured a *negro* alive that they had tied up with them as they followed the rest. [The captive] told them that the launches [were] in the Río Francisca, three leagues upriver. This news arrived at four in the afternoon and at the *Ave María* I left with seven shallops and eighty-five hand-picked harquebusiers and pikemen with doublets and all the artillery that could be carried by the ships.[4]

That night the wind blew south by southwest. We anchored at midnight between Sardinilla and the river [Río Francisca] so that with the dawn we could enter its mouth, as we then did, even though that night it rained so much that those in the pueblo were astounded at the rainfall. It was such that no powder, match, or food remained, all turned to mud.[5] At the point of the river we unloaded that which remained of masts, sails, resin, food, and drink. We made a large fire and using our doublets quickly dried out the powder and match.[6]

We went upriver to its source but did not find any sign. It turned out that, according to their practice, [they] did not enter through a known [port], fearing [to do so]. They entered by way of Sardinilla, beached their shallops, covered them with branches, and left guards with them. The very night that we slept at the point of the river, they passed to the Cabeza.[7] We learned this from a frigate that they captured. We were told that the Frenchman that died had seen us pass and that unless he killed the captain where he lay no one would have escaped. But God will it to be that I did not gain honor or wealth. Many passengers who had hoped to live well will be left poor.[8]

I believe that these ships that sailed from England likely have returned. If they take Nombre de Dios and Panama [City] the land is theirs as easily as I speak the words. Two thousand *negros* have offered themselves to the Englishman, and there is a shorter road, more populated by *negro* settlements, than from Sevilla to San Lucar.[9] If it is true that they desire to settle, as Your Mercy believes, on the other sea [the Pacific] and build ships outside of Panama [City], it will be necessary to find a solution.[10]

Cristóbal Monte's concerns would prove prescient. Less than four years later, a group led by John Oxenham would traverse the eastern isthmus and build boats on the Pacific side to target ships travelling in the Pacific.

---

1. An *urca* was a wide-hulled ship typically used to transport goods. Here the author appears to refer to the ships by their owners and/or captains.
2. This *negro* was employed by the muleteers to protect the caravan. His legal status is unclear, but he may have been a freeperson.
3. This sentence implies that the Frenchmen killed their own wounded captain to prevent him from being tortured for information.
4. The Ave María, or Hail Mary, is a prayer used frequently in Catholic devotion. Monte suggests that it took several hours to assemble his forces. They left during the evening prayers of either Vespers (sunset or early evening) or Compline (late evening). Nombre de Dios did not have a standing military force. Captain Monte and his men were attached to the fleet waiting to depart Nombre de Dios.

5. A map from Antonio de Herrera y Tordesilla's *Historia general de los hechos de los castellanos en las Islas i Tierra Firme del Mar Oceano* (1601) locates a Río Sardinilla to the east of Nombre de Dios.
6. He uses the verb *"enjugar,"* suggesting they used the doublets to sop up excess moisture and then the large fire to help dry the powder and matches.
7. Punta San Blas, also known as the Punta Cativa during the later colonial period.
8. Likely an allusion to those who lost merchandise or income due to the depredations of the English, French, and maroons.
9. Two cities in Andalucía roughly sixty miles apart.
10. The Spanish recognized that the eastern isthmus could be traversed quickly, especially with the aid of the maroons.

18. The Cabildo of Nombre de Dios to the Crown, May 14, 1573

Source: AGI, Panama 11, fs. 208–9.

In the wake of Drake's second raid, the cabildo of Nombre de Dios quickly wrote to the king to inform him of the raid and seek royal assistance in preventing further damage caused by maroons and foreigners.

• • •

Before now the cabildo of this city of Nombre de Dios has informed your Majesty of the things that have transpired in this kingdom and of what might wait if there is delay in addressing the corsairs and *cimarrones*. The lack of measures has allowed them, with their great industry, to do what they wish by sea or land without our being able to prevent them unless it is with the aid and favor of Your Majesty, for the French and English corsairs have allied and befriended the *negros cimarrones* of the bush, who number over three thousand. . . .

The corsairs have committed great robberies and murders such that in seven years they have killed more than three hundred persons by sea and land and have stolen over two million [pesos] of gold and silver. Now, recently in the month of June, 1572, the English corsairs entered this city, wounded many who came to its defense, and killed nine people. Afterward, they allied with the *negros cimarrones* of the bush. With [maroons'] assistance and guidance, they passed as far as the city of Panama. In March of this year they robbed and burned Venta de Chagres, killing four vecinos and a Dominican friar, and wounding many more.

On April 29, these same corsairs along with some Frenchmen, who later joined, guided and accompanied by the *cimarrones* of the bush attacked the road that comes from the city of Panama to this one of Nombre de Dios. Two leagues from this city they stole over one hundred fifty thousand pesos of gold and silver, among which were twenty thousand pesos of gold from the district of Popayan for Your Majesty.[1]

[A force] left this city quickly as soon as the news arrived, recovering a quantity of silver and gold bars that corsairs could not carry off. [The Spanish force] killed two corsairs and one of the *cimarrones*. Among the dead was the French captain, according to one Frenchmen who was captured wandering the bush. He was executed. Licenciado Diego García carries his confession and additional information along with orders to ask Your Majesty for that which might bring remedy to this land.

---

1. Popayan was a very lucrative gold mining district in southern Colombia. The gold destined for the king came from the "royal fifth," a 20 percent tax on all precious metals.

19. Royal Cedula in Which His Majesty Orders Pedro Menéndez to Wage War, September 3, 1573
Source: AGI, Panama 229, L. 1, fs. 8v–9.

The success of Drake's raid on the interior of Panama prompted a quick royal response authorizing military action against any corsairs and *cimarrones*.

•   •   •

Presidente and *oidores* of our Royal Audiencia that resides in the city of Panama, of the province of Tierra Firme, according to the accounts that you have sent us, and others from the province that arrived in the last fleet, our Council of the Indies understands that the French, the English, and the *negros cimarrones* that wander through the land and coasts have caused damage and robberies to our Royal Treasury, our subjects, and deaths and damages to private persons. In order to castigate and remedy this, as well as prevent future damages and insure that the lands and coasts are guarded, we have resolved that the *Adelantado* Pedro Menéndez[1] with part of his fleet should patrol the coasts, clean them of corsairs, and attend to their defense. Having accomplished those tasks we order that he meet with you to discuss a solution that will be effective in castigating the *negros cimarrones* and waging war against them whenever and wherever convenient. I order that you discuss this issue with the *adelantado* and devise a solution that you are confident will be most suitable. At the appropriate time, you will send companies and squads, united or separate as you see fit, composed of people from the land. As to the crew of the galleons, you may use them if it would be of use in the war against the *negros cimarrones*.[2] Those [*negros*] that you capture alive should be sent to these kingdoms [Castile and Aragon] and not allowed to stay in those parts [Panama], sending them with the warning that even if their masters sell them they may not return to the Indies for they would be known. You will see that merchants, cities, and other persons help support the expenses of this war as it is for their benefit and that of their property. You may spend up to ten thousand *ducados* but no more. . . . Ordered in San Lorenzo el Real, on the third day of September 1573.

1. Pedro Menéndez de Avilés served as the captain general of the Indies Fleet and had been the *adelantado* in the expedition that founded St. Augustine and destroyed the French settlement of Fort Caroline.
2. The king authorized the use of soldiers attached to the fleet but expected that most soldiers be recruited from the vecinos and residents of the territory.

20. Pedro de Ortega Valencia to the Crown, November 1, 1573
Source: AGI, Panama 11, fs. 119–24.

This letter from Pedro de Ortega Valencia, the royal treasurer in Nombre de Dios, offers a glimpse at the immediate efforts made by the Audiencia of Panama to punish the maroons for their alliance with the English. Ortega Valencia recounted that the audiencia held an open session with the residents of Nombre de Dios to determine the best course of action. The assembly favored raising troops and making war on the maroons. The proposal included maintaining two hundred armed men for the defense of Nombre de Dios at an annual cost of forty thousand pesos. This would be in addition to seventeen thousand pesos set aside to support Gonzalo de Palma as *alcalde mayor* (chief magistrate). Ortega Valencia went on to critique the audiencia for attempting to enact two contrasting strategies against the maroons: the continued military incursions favored by the residents and overtures of peace. Part of his animosity lay in not having been named *capitán general* of the military effort against the maroons. Nevertheless, his account offers candid details of the anti-maroon strategy pursued in late 1573.

• • •

The audiencia decided to send a friar from the Order of St. Dominic to talk terms with the *negros cimarrones* and to bring them by peace. Immediately after proposing peace, the audiencia named Luis de Torres captain with fifty men.[1] He left with them a day after the friar to make war on the *cimar-rones*. The audiencia ordered five or six free *negros* to accompany the friar. They were forced to do so against their will, making it known that they were being sent to die. It was well known, even to the *negros cimarrones*, that even though they went to make peace, [others] went to make war at the same time. It happened that the *negros cimarrones* hanged the friar and killed four of those who went with him. Two returned to report the news. Luis de Torres went to a different place and encountered a little settlement of *negros*.[2] He killed three and captured seven or eight. He left toward the north sea and along the coast saw a palisaded fort left by the Englishmen where they had once been and from which they had traversed the coast and communicated with the *cimarrones*.[3] With the news of the friar, the audiencia ordered that the cabildo convene a second time, calling the vecinos of the pueblo to gather. They came to the same decision as before [to make war]. . . . They resolved that no *negro* or *negra* of any age be taken captive, instead all would be put to the sword, giving rationales for this. One of these was to instill fear in the *negros* for the deaths of their wives and children, also holding a *negro* or *negra* captive if they surrendered alive occupies two soldiers. This [policy] would create the necessary effect in the war and avoid the harm that has passed before when *negros* from the *cimarrones* have been brought [back] to the cities—they run away anew and encourage others by taking them in their company. The audiencia was not satisfied with the opinion [of the veci-nos] and after a few days ordered the *alcaldes* to put forth a petition on behalf of the cabildo that the war be undertaken with all speed.[4]

---

1. The audiencia issued a commission to Luis de Torres Guerrero on June 26, 1573, to seek out maroons who had attacked the ranches of Francisco Nuñez de Silva and Alonso Hernández Pacheco and killed a Spaniard. AGI, Patronato 152, R. 4. N. 2, bloque 2.

2. In 1587, Torres Guerrero composed a *probanza de mérito* requesting royal renumera-tion for his service. The witnesses testifying on his behalf noted that he captured a pueblo led by Juan Jolofo and Juan Angola along the northern coastline, near the Río Caracoles. AGI, Patronato, R. 7, N. 1.

3. Torres Guerrero describes these discoveries more fully in a probanza from 1580 not-ing that he recovered some cannons left by Drake in the fort. AGI, Patronato, R. 4, N. 2, bloque 2.

4. The audiencia justified its anti-maroon efforts as a response to complaints and sug-gestions by the subjects of the region. It appears that its members did not agree with the rationales being put forward and solicited a new request from the local magis-trates upon which they might base their decision.

21. Royal Cedula concerning the Peaceful Surrender of *Negros Cimarrones*, June 21, 1574

Source: AGI, Panama 42, N. 21, fs. 622–23. Transcribed in Tardieu, *Cimarrones de Panamá*, 174–76.

Despite the authorization for war against the *cimarrones*, two campaigns organized in the wake of Drake's visit appear to have had negligible effect. Ortega Valencia's letter noted that Luis de Torres had only encountered a small settlement. Following Torres's fifty-man expedition, in November 1573 the audiencia authorized Gabriel de Navarrete to undertake a five-month expedition with over one hundred twenty men.[1] Writing in April 1574, the cabildo of Nombre de Dios lambasted this incursion, noting that no maroons had been captured or killed (despite expenses in excess of fifteen thousand pesos) and criticizing Navarrete as "incapable for such work."[2]

Although word of Navarrete's failure had likely not reached Spain, by mid-1574 the king recognized a new strategy was needed and authorized the audiencia to pursue negotiation in lieu of war. This order lays out a more coherent and extensive process than the audiencia's prior misguided attempt to use a Dominican friar.

* * *

Presidente and *oidores* of our Royal Audiencia, that resides in the city of Panama in the province of Tierra Firme. You know that Lic. Diego García, *el franco*, in the name of this province sent us an account of the many robberies, damages, and deaths that have occurred regularly as a result of the *negros cimarrones* and the little security that our subjects enjoy because of the throng of *negros* as every day they continue to multiply, asking that we order that the necessary remedies are put into effect so that the *negros* are defeated or reduced to the service of God, Our Lord, or our own.[3] Having discussed this with those of our Council of the Indies it appears that the aforementioned can be achieved through one of two means, waging war against them or approaching them in peace in the manner that I now give to you:

First, after you receive this our cedula you shall call and gather the persons that you believe have the knowledge and experience in similar things and discuss with them which of the two means is most appropriate for remedying the [problem]. If after examining and discussing the issue with great understanding and deliberation you agree that it would be best to wage war and conquer them, [then] summon Diego Flores de Valdés to you in this

Audiencia to serve as the *capitán general* of the fleet that guards the lands and coast of these our Indies, and [to serve] in the position of *adelantado*, Pedro Menéndez, or whichever person is brought by the fleet [for this task]. With them and the aforementioned persons you shall deliberate over the form and order that you believe the war against the *negros cimarrones* should take. . . .

If you believe the best route is to bring them to peace, and thereby to our Holy Catholic faith, and to subjugation and obedience, it should be as follows:

- Firstly, you should announce that all the *negros cimarrones* that come in peace within a period that you determine shall be free and that their owners shall not be able to have them as slaves or use them as such.
- That those that come in peace shall be pardoned for all the crimes that they have committed.
- That [the *negros cimarrones*] shall be required to gather and settle pueblos wherever you designate.
- That all those free *negros* and *negras* that are currently in this province or who from this point forward are freed shall go and live in those pueblos within a period that you determine so that none remains [in the bush] under penalty that whoever does not can be taken as a slave and held as a slave and be sold if desired.[4]
- That those who surrender and settle can capture and take as slaves those *negros* who remain in rebellion. When [these slaves] are captured and do not submit to enslavement and sale, they are to have their left foot broken and their right ear cut off.[5]
- That the *negros* who surrender and settle shall be obligated to support the priest who teaches them doctrine and to give him that which is necessary.[6]
- That you shall appoint Spanish magistrates to the pueblos so that they have justice as well as appoint other officials as you see fit.
- That the *negros* who settle shall be obligated to capture *negros* who have fled from their masters within two months of being informed [of their flight] and return the [runaways] to their masters under penalty of paying the price for the slave to their owner, as assessed by the magistrate. A master is obligated to pay ten pesos for every *negro* that he is brought. If the *negro* has been absent more than fifteen days then one foot shall be broken and one ear cut off.[7]

- That the *negros* shall be obliged to keep the roads safe and passable between this city [Panama City], Nombre de Dios and the Casa de Cruzes.
- That similarly they shall be obliged to open roads between the pueblos they settle and this city and Nombre de Dios.
- That they shall keep fields and pastures and all other improvements of the land like our other vassals.

Because you all are aware of these issues, you should understand what would best succeed, and if you believe that changing or ordering something other than what is stated here [would be better] you should do it. Ordered in Madrid on the twenty-first of June of 1574.

1. AGI, Panama, 11, fs. 23–26.
2. AGI, Panama 11, fs. 212–13.
3. Document 18 notes that Diego García departed soon after Drake's April 1573 raid.
4. This clause echoes Panama City's earlier attempt to force all free Africans to live in their own settlement. The resettlement of pardoned maroons offered an ideal moment to concentrate all of the region's free people of color into discrete communities that could be closely monitored and regulated.
5. This incentive sought to create division among the maroons by allowing pardoned maroons to enslave those who rejected the king's offer. No law prevented free Africans from owning slaves; nevertheless, examples of free Africans owning enslaved Africans were rare in the sixteenth century.
6. Most parish priests received their income from the tithes of the community. This clause establishes that the resettled maroons would likewise tithe.
7. This clause mirrors provisions in Panama City's slave code from 1571–72.

22. Act concerning Pardon for *Negros Cimarrones*, February 28, 1575

Source: AGI, Patronato 234, R. 6, fs. 337–41v.

In early 1575, the Audiencia of Panama met to consider the king's suggestion for a peaceful alternative.

• • •

In the city of Panama of the Kingdom of Tierra Firme, on the 28th day of February, 1575, the *señores*, *presidente* and *oidores* of the Royal Audiencia and Chancellery of His Majesty, that there reside, stated that on behalf of the cabildo of this city on the 25th of this month, four cedulas of His Majesty were presented to the *señores*. . . .

In order to put into effect that which the last royal cedula mandated in its chapters pertaining to the issue of peace or war, wherein Your Majesty stipulated that certain persons meet to discuss the issues Your Majesty raised, the *señores, presidente* and *oidores* ordered the following persons to assemble in the chamber of this Royal Audiencia in order to discuss and converse about this problem:

[Here the document listed over thirty participants, royal officials, cabildo officers, and local notables.]

And so, with the declared persons gathered in the Royal Audiencia, the *señores, presidente* and *oidores* stated the reason that they had been gathered. The royal cedulas, previously mentioned, were read word for word. . . . Having been seen and understood by all the aforementioned persons, the *señores, presidente and oidores* discussed and conferred with them over the two options that Your Majesty ordered be taken, that of peace or war. Having been discussed and conferred and being of the same opinion they agreed upon the following:

That the route of peace should be taken because it will be more useful for the benefit of all those of this kingdom and the vassals of His Majesty that there reside.

Having selected the route of peace, they discussed and conferred over the best means to put it into effect and how to notify the *negros cimarrones*. Discussing and conferring, they resolved to do the following:

The peace should be announced shortly in public in this city of Panama by the crier. . . .[1]

The *negros cimarrones* that shall benefit from royal mercy and the pardon of His Majesty, which was conceded by the royal *cedula*, are understood to be those that have been *cimarrones* until today, the twenty-eighth day of February, 1575.

That it is understood that to be a *cimarrón* who can benefit from the mercy and pardon one must have been absent [from their masters] at least one month as of today.

So that the peace be made clear, those soldiers who have gone out in search of *negros cimarrones* shall be called back from their expeditions and ordered to return to this city. The *negros cimarrones* that the soldiers, or other persons, have taken before the publication of this peace shall benefit from this mercy and peace and be freed without regard to having been captured before the publication of the peace.[2]

The time frame that will be given for the *negros cimarrones* to submit and surrender in peace, so as to benefit from this grace and mercy, shall be four months, beginning the day that this peace is proclaimed in this city. To benefit from the mercy and freedom that His Majesty has conceded to those who surrender and accept the peace, within this time frame, the *negros* must submit to the service of His Majesty and present themselves before an *alcalde ordinario* of this city and a scrivener of its cabildo so that they can be entered into a book, which shall be kept, and that the *negros* be given a copy of their letter of liberty without being required to pay the usual fees.

Item, that the *negros cimarrones* that do not come and present themselves within four months will be considered rebels and disobedient, so that war may be waged against them in the manner that His Majesty has decreed. They will be incapable of benefiting from the grace and pardon. Similarly, this will be announced in all the cities, *villas*, and other places of the district of this Royal Audiencia with all necessary solemnity so that it comes to the attention of the *negros cimarrones*, and they cannot feign ignorance.

And so conferred and agreed upon, the *señores, presidente* and *oidores* ordered that this be announced in this court so that it will be done and fulfilled and so that the other parts and places of the district of this Royal Audiencia remit the necessary funds and provisions. They so resolved, ordered, and signed. And that the *negros* who surrender be put into pueblos according to the order [contained in the royal cedulas].

---

1. Networks of trade and communication between maroons and enslaved residents in the cities ensured that such proclamations reached the maroons.
2. The documents do not describe these expeditions, but this clause offered a particularly generous concession to maroons that had been recently captured.

23. The Audiencia to the Crown, May 6, 1575
Source: AGI, Panama 11, fs. 8–12.

Despite the proclamation of pardon for maroons, few Africans came forward to
take up the offer. Halfway through the proscribed period for accepting the pardon,
the audiencia wrote to the king. In two months, only three maroons had come forward. This letter reveals that the authorities placed the blame on the maroons and
put forward stereotypical notions of Africans' limited intelligence to explain the lack
of interest in the peace. Although the audiencia suspected that the maroons might
fear a trap, they did not consider that repeated duplicity on their part might explain
the maroons' reticence.

•   •   •

With the fleet we received a royal cedula from Your Majesty that ordered
this Royal Audiencia to confer and discuss with the *justicia* and *regimiento*
and vecinos [of this kingdom] who may have ideas for how to best reduce
the *negros cimarrones* to obedience and the service of Your Majesty and to
consider choosing the route of peace with them, promising them liberty
and the forgiveness of their crimes. In fulfillment of this, we undertook the
task, and it appeared to all that the most advisable [choice] for your royal service was the route of peace, and so it was chosen and proclaimed publicly.
Four months were given, running from the first of March. It has appeared
to have had little effect because up to now only three *negros* have come forward. Being a bestial people and very suspicious, for they are of little understanding, it appeared appropriate to us to suspend the measures that we
had ordered to help make war, such as the tax that was to be levied on merchandise, because if they thought we were [planning war] they might
believe that the peace that has been offered them was false and meant to
trick them.[1] For the same reason the tax of one mark of silver that Your
Majesty imposed on each free *negro* and *mulato* in this kingdom has been
suspended.[2] These are the mediators through whom the *negros cimarrones*
may be brought to your royal service. Once the term has expired, if they
have not accepted the peace all [these measures] will be enacted.[3]

Although no new alliances between maroons and foreigners emerged during 1574
and 1575, maroons did not cease their normal raids. In April 1575, the cabildo of
Nombre de Dios sent information to the king documenting a series of assaults and
robberies that took place after the proclamation of the royal pardon.[4] Similarly, on

May 7, 1575, the cabildo of Panama noted that maroons had ransacked ships travel-ling up the Río Chagres, taking clothes, "iron for weapons," and wine.[5] They pro-posed abandoning overtures of peace and a return to "crude war."

---

1. This statement reveals the extent to which Spaniards assumed maroons had detailed information about their plans.
2. In 1574, the king ordered that all free persons of African descent pay an annual tribute. AGI, Patronato 275, R. 77. Almost immediately, the free people of color in Panama would appeal the imposition, citing their continued service to the Crown in the defense of the region from "*negros cimarrones* and English and French cor-sairs." AGI, Panama 42, N. 1.
3. Since the measures in question had been ordered by the king, the audiencia wanted to clearly justify the rational and duration of their suspension.
4. AGI, Panama 32, N. 17.
5. AGI, Panama 11, fs. 214–15.

24. Lopez Vaz's Account of John Oxenham's 1576 Expedition (1586)

Source: "The Voyage of John Oxnam of Plimmouth," in Hakluyt, *Principal Navigations*, vol. 10, 77–81.

During the 1580s and 1590s, Richard Hakluyt, a major promotor of English over-seas ventures, gathered travel narratives, explorers' accounts, and other descrip-tions of new lands, peoples, and colonial ventures of foreign powers. This account reached Hakluyt in manuscript form after the Earl of Cumberland, Sir George Clif-ford, captured its author, a Portuguese man named Lopez Vaz, during an expedi-tion to South America in 1586. Although the original manuscript has been lost, Hakluyt's English translation preserves the account.[1]

John Oxenham left England in April 1576 and made directly for the Panama coast where he and Drake had previously formed alliances with maroons. He and his men would spend September 1576 through February 1577 in the maroon com-munity of Ronconcholon. In February, the English and their maroon allies travelled down rivers to the Gulf of San Miguel, where they constructed some small ships to raid Spanish trade ships and estates in the Pearl Islands. These raids precipitated a robust Spanish response that would initially target the English but then expand into a war against the maroons.

• • •

There was another Englishman, who hearing of the spoil that Francis Drake had done upon the coast of Nueva España, and of his good adventure

and safe return home, was thereby provoked to undertake the like enterprise, with a ship of one hundred and forty tons, and seventy men. [He]
came thither, and had also conference with the foresaid Negros.[2] Hearing
that the gold and silver which came upon the mules from Panama to Nombre de Dios was now conducted with soldiers, he determined to do that
which never any man before enterprised, and landed in that place where
Francis Drake before had his conference with the Negros. This man covered his ship after he had brought her aground with boughs of trees and
hid his great ordnance in the ground. Not leaving any man in his ship, he
took two small pieces of ordnance, and his calivers, and good store of victuals, and so went with the Negros about twelve leagues into the mainland
to a river that goes to the south sea.[3] There he cut wood and made a pinnace, which was five and forty foot by the keel. Having made this pinnace,
he went into the south sea carrying six Negros with him to be guides and so
went to the Pearl Islands, which is five and twenty leagues from Panama in
the way that they come from Peru to Panama. There he was ten days without showing himself to any man to see if he might get any ship that came
from Peru. At last there came a small barque, which came from Peru from
a place called Quito, which he took and found in her sixty thousand pesos
of gold and much victuals.[4] But not contenting himself with his prize, he
stayed long without sending away his prize or any of the men, and in the
end, six days after, he took another barque, which came from Lima, in
which he took a hundred thousand pesos of silver in bars, with which he
thought to have gone [decided to leave] and entered the river.[5] But first he
went into the islands to see if he could find any pearls, where he found a
few, and so returned to his pinnace again.[6] Sailing to the river from whence
he came and coming near to the mouth of the said river, he sent away the
two prizes that he took, and with the pinnace he went up river. The Negros
that dwelt in the Pearl Islands, the same night that he went from them,
went in canoes to Panama. The Governor within two days sent four barques,
one hundred men, twenty-five in every one, and Negros to row with the
Captain Juan de Ortega, which went to the Pearl Islands and there had
intelligence which way the English men were gone.[7] Following them he
met by the way the ships which the English men had taken, of whom he
learned, that the English men were gone up river. He going thither, when
he came to the mouth of the river the captain of Panama knew not which to
take, because there were three partitions in the river to go up in.[8] Being

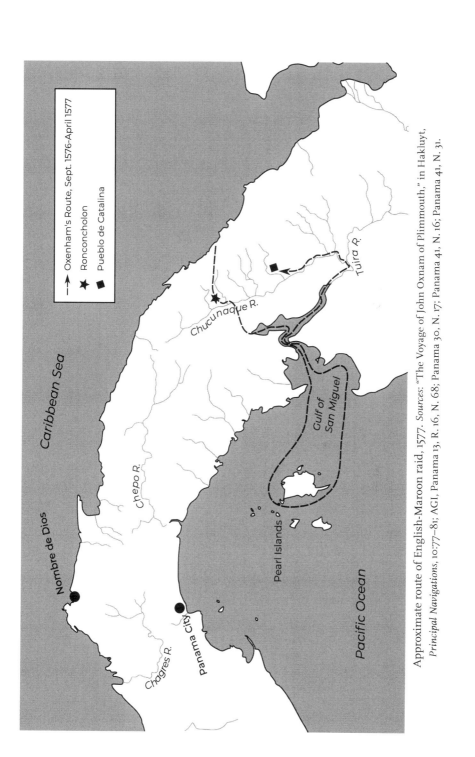

Approximate route of English-Maroon raid, 1577. *Sources:* "The Voyage of John Oxnam of Plimmouth," in Hakluyt, *Principal Navigations*, 10:77–8; AGI, Panama 13, R. 16, N. 68; Panama 30, N. 17; Panama 41, N. 16; Panama 41, N. 31.

Legend:
- → Oxenham's Route, Sept. 1576–April 1577
- ★ Ronconcholon
- ■ Pueblo de Catalina

Map labels: Caribbean Sea; Nombre de Dios; Chagres R.; Panama City; Chepo R.; Chucunaque R.; Tuira R.; Gulf of San Miguel; Pearl Islands; Pacific Ocean determined to go up the greatest of the three rivers, he saw coming down a lesser river many feathers of hens which the Englishmen had pulled to eat. Being glad thereof, he went up that river where he saw the feathers, and after that he had been in that river four days, he descried the Englishmen's pinnace upon the sands. Coming to her there were no more than six Englishmen, whereof they killed one, and five escaped away. In the pinnace he found nothing but victual. This captain of Panama not herewith satisfied, determined to seek out the Englishmen by land, and leaving twenty men in his pinnaces, he with eighty shot went up country. He had not gone half a league, but he found a house made of boughs where they found all the Englishmen's goods and the gold and silver also. Carrying it back to their pinnaces the Spaniards were determined to go away, without following the English men any further.[9]

But at the end of three days, the English captain came to the river with all his men, and above 200 Negros, and set upon the Spaniards with great fury. But the Spaniards having the advantage of trees which they stood behind, did easily prevail, and killed eleven Englishmen and five Negros, and took other seven Englishmen alive, but of the Spaniards two were slain and five sore hurt.

Among other things, the Spaniards enquired of the Englishmen which they took why they went not away in fifteen days of liberty which they had. They answered that their captain had commanded them to carry all the gold and silver which they had to the place where they had left their ship. They had promised him to carry it, although they made three or four journeys of it, for he promised to give them part of it besides their wages, but the mariners would have it by and by.[10] So their captain being angry because they would not take his word, fell out with them and they with him, in so much that one of the company would have killed the captain so that the captain would not have them to carry the treasure, but said he would seek Negros to carry it. So, he went and sought for Negros. Bringing those Negros to carry it, he met with the five Englishmen that he had left in his pinnace, which ran from the Spaniards, and the rest also which ran from the house, and they told him what the Spaniards had done. Then making friendship with all his men, he promised them half of all the treasure if they got it from the Spaniards. The Negros promised to help him with their bows and arrows, and thereupon they came to seek the Spaniards. Now that some of his company were killed and taken, he thought it best to return to his ship, and to pass back for England. The Spanish captain hearing this, having buried the dead bodies, and having gotten all things into his barques, and taking the English men and their pinnace with him, he returned to Panama. So the voyage of that English man did not prosper with him, as he thought it would have done.

Now when the four barques were come to Panama, they sent advice also to Nombre de Dios, and they of Nombre de Dios sent also from them other four barques, which (as the Spaniards say) found the English ship where she was hid, and brought her to Nombre de Dios. The viceroy of Peru not thinking it good to suffer fifty English men to remain in the country, sent a servant of his called Diego de Frees, with a hundred and fifty shot [men armed with harquebuses] into the mountains to seek them out, who found them making certain canoes to go into the north sea, there to take some barque or other.[11] Some of them were sick, and were taken, and the rest fled with the Negros, who in the end betrayed them to the Spaniards, so that they were brought to Panama. The justice of Panama asked the English captain whether he had the Queen's license, or the license of any other prince or lord for his attempt. He answered he had none, whereupon he and all his company were condemned to die, and so were all executed, saving the captain, the master, the pilot, and five boys which were carried to Lima. There the captain was executed with the other two but the boys be yet living.

The King of Spain having intelligence of these matters sent three hundred men of war against those Negros which had assisted those Englishmen, which before were slaves unto the Spaniards and as before is said fled from their masters unto those mountains, and so joined themselves to the Englishmen to the end they might better revenge themselves on the Spaniards.[12]

At the first coming of these three hundred soldiers, they took many of the negros, and executed great justice upon them. But after a season, the Negros grew wise and wary, and prevented the Spaniards so that none of them could be taken.

The Spaniards of that country marveled much at this one thing, to see that since the conquering of this land, there have been many Frenchmen, that have come to those countries, but never saw Englishmen there but only those two of whom I have spoken. Although there have many Frenchmen been on the coast, yet never durst they put foot upon land, only those two Englishmen adventured it, and did such exploits as are before remembered.[13]

All these things coming to the hearing of the king of Spain, he provided two galleys well-appointed to keep those coasts. The first year they took six or seven French ships. After that this was known, there were no more Englishmen or Frenchmen of war that durst adventure to approach the coast until this present year of 1586, that the aforesaid Francis Drake, with a strong fleet of 24 ships arrived there, and made spoil of Santo Domingo, Cartagena, and Saint Augustine, things that are known to all the world. But it is likely that if the king of Spain lives, he will in time provide sufficient remedy, to keep his countries and subjects from the invasion of other nations.

1. Lopez Vaz also described Drake's 1572 expedition, although he appears to have had more accurate sources for Oxenham than Drake.
2. John Oxenham had firsthand knowledge. He had been a member of Drake's earlier expedition and likely had personal connections with the maroons who had offered help. He also knew the location where they had buried the bullion that could not be carried away from their second raid.
3. Probably the Río Chucunaque and Río Tuira.
4. Quito is located high in the Andes and has no port. The author means that the ship came from the port of Guayaquil.
5. Lopez Vaz criticizes Oxenham for not having left immediately after taking the second ship.
6. Oxenham and his men did not dive for pearls. They raided Spanish pearl fisheries for those already collected by enslaved African pearl divers.
7. Lopez Vaz confuses the name of the commanding officer. The expedition was led by Pedro de Ortega Valencia.
8. By the "mouth of the river" Lopez Vaz appears to be describing the Gulf of San Miguel, into which flow several large rivers.
9. Lopez Vaz appears to suggest that the Spanish cared only for the stolen gold and silver.
10. Oxenham's men would likely have signed on to his expedition with set terms for the distribution of spoils. This dispute suggests that the men were attempting to renegotiate the shares that had been initially stipulated.
11. Diego de Frías Trejo. The commissioning of two expeditions by different Spanish administrators led to disputes among the expeditions as each claimed to have sole authority in the region.
12. After his initial 1577 campaign, Pedro de Ortega Valencia returned to Spain and requested a royal commission to lead a larger expedition. This paragraph describes his return in January 1579.
13. Lopez Vaz appears unaware of Guillaume le Testu's participation in Drake's 1572 assaults.

25. The Cabildo of Panama to the Crown, April 26, 1577
Source: AGI, Panama 30, N. 17.

There are no known letters written by royal officials or local cabildos for most of 1576. Although Oxenham's audacious raid appeared to catch the Spanish off guard, they knew of his presence almost as soon as he arrived off the coast. Captain Luis de Torres Guerrero received a commission to go against the English and maroons on August 3, 1576.[1] In September 1576, another expedition captured the ships that Oxenham had anchored off the coast of Acla.[2] As Oxenham would later recount (see document 31), the capture of his ships forced him to rely more heavily on maroon aid and prompted his assaults in the Pacific.

On April 15, the cabildo of Panama wrote a letter urging the king to "make war on the *negros cimarrones*, exterminating them [and] eradicating them" for allying with the English.[3] This letter follows up and praises the successful Spanish response to Oxenham's raids.

· · ·

After having written to Your Majesty about how English allied with the *cimarrones* passed to the south sea and their theft of seventy thousand pesos, what has happened is that Dr. Gabriel de Loarte, your president in this royal Audiencia, among the many precautions that he took, the most important was to dispatch six frigates, brigantines, and vessels under the command of Pedro de Ortega Valencia, factor and inspector of your royal treasury, as we have reported, who, with good fortune, travelled to the Gulf of San Miguel in pursuit of the corsair.

He and his captains, having explored the many rivers that empty into the gulf, found no traces except that in one they found a quantity of nails, oakum, saws, and things of carpentry. Guided by the Divine Majesty they entered into the river, which is named Pedro de Ortega. The ascent of which took eight days, because it travels deep into the land of the Bayano. When the vessels could go no higher because, being summer the rapids of the river were raging, the General and sixty of his men went ashore leaving the rest with their captains to guard the vessels. [Pedro de Ortega] trekked into the wilderness. Encountering the river many times, he found signs of the English who had left pork and biscuit, which they carried, on the banks of the river when they had stopped to eat.

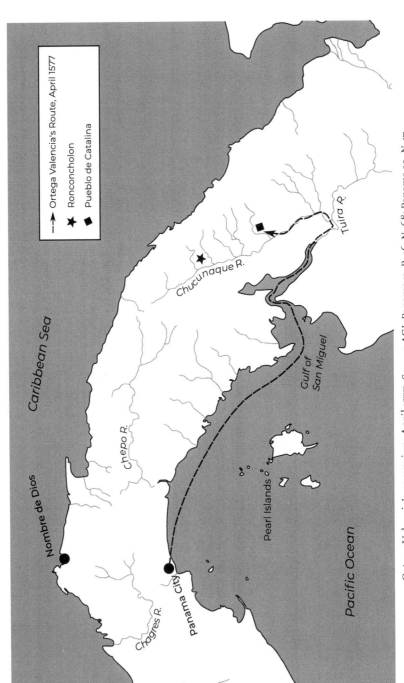

Ortega Valencia's campaign, April 1577. *Sources:* AGI, Panama 13, R. 16, N. 68; Panama 30, N. 17.

After having travelled for four full days, on Tuesday of Holy Week, having halted around ten in the morning, they heard two harquebus shots. The general ordered a soldier to venture into the bush to see what there was. He went and saw that on the banks of the river there were thirty Englishmen and over eighty *negros cimarrones*, [and] a large quantity of pork in kettles. They were all entertaining themselves the ones with the others. They had made an awning under which they had unloaded all the biscuit and everything else that their launch had carried, which because it displaced less than a *palmo*[4] of water had been able to travel so far. [The soldier] returned to report to the general.

Having extorted his soldiers as a pious Christian captain, he ordered them to pray to God, Our Lord. With great silence, so that no one could perceive them, they arrived through the trees and fired the first volley, killing over twenty-five of the English and a number of *negros cimarones*, some of whom fled with the English that had turned to flee.

Later, after having rested that day and a *negro cimarrón* and a English boy having surrendered, [the general] commenced a march to search for the enemy. On Holy Thursday he arrived at the pueblo of the *negros cimarrones* where the English [captain] and those that remained of his company had fortified themselves along with the negros, awaiting in their fort.[5]

The general ordered the attack, invoking the name of our patron and apostle, Santiago [Saint James]. After a long hour of fighting in which many of the enemy were killed and the rest injured with little harm to our side, as they did not have many harquebuses and used mostly arrows, [the enemies] were dislodged from part of the pueblo [that] was set on fire. They fled into the bush where it is believed they died from their wounds, and the *negros* having seen the harm caused by [the English] have likely killed those that remain. The general captured three boys and a man wounded in the leg with a round.

Having achieved victory, the general searched for the booty captured by the enemy but could not find it that day nor the next until the day of Easter when one of the lads that had been captured was pressured and told us he would take us to where they had buried it. Therefore, the *sargento mayor*, Antonio Salcedo with a dozen soldiers went to the place that the lad had indicated where they found twenty-seven bundles or sacks of gold and thirty-three of silver coinage and thirteen bars, which was all that had been taken from the boat coming from Quito, and other gold and silver that had been taken in the robberies committed in the north sea. All of this was brought to the general who worked harder to safeguard it from his friends and soldiers than retake it from his enemies. He brought it to President Gabriel de Loarte who made an inventory of it and the many jewels that were taken by General Pedro de Ortega in addition to the gold and silver. All of this is being returned to those to whom it appears to belong.

The English captives also told Pedro de Ortega where other gold and silver had been buried on the Atlantic coastline and where two launches had been hidden, scuttled in a river, so that they might have a means of escape. The cabildo went on to praise Pedro de Ortega for his service and the great harms it prevented.

We ask that Your Majesty be served in securing this kingdom and all of Peru by sending us the four galleys we have requested along with four hundred men that can found a settlement on the north sea in the Gulf of Acla and another in the south sea in the Gulf of San Miguel, and a force sufficient that through fire and the sword the *negros cimarrones* be dislodged and scattered and the entrance of infidels to this land and [their] passage to the south sea prevented.

1. AGI, Patronato 152, N. 4, R. 2, bloque 2.
2. "Pedro Godinez to the Crown, Veragua, March 22, 1577," in Wright, *English Voyages*, 100–101.
3. AGI, Panama 41, N. 16.
4. A palm is an old unit of measurement roughly twenty centimeters in length, the distance between the tip of the thumb and the end of the little finger when the hand is fully splayed.
5. Later documents suggest this was a settlement called the Pueblo de Catalina.

26. Dr. Loarte to the Crown, April 26, 1577
Source: AGI, Panama 13, R. 16, N. 68.

Before turning to the specific events of Oxenham's expedition, Dr. Loarte, speaking as president of the Audiencia of Panama, informed the king of the series of naval encounters that had alerted authorities of possible attack. Reports suggested that at least sixteen ships appeared to be poised to attack the region. Loarte critiqued the commanding officer of the Atlantic fleet, don Cristóbal de Eraso, for not using his vessels to patrol the coast.

• • •

All these things have given me more work and worry than I can relate here. I can say that given all the corsairs that they say are coming, with far fewer they can take this city. The route to the south sea will be easy for them having, as they do, control of the whole countryside thanks to the alliance with the *negros cimarrones*. That which is most amazing is how long they have waited, because by way of Acla there is not twenty leagues of travel, and only six or seven are by land, the rest by going travelling downriver to the Gulf of San Miguel, which is the route taken by ships from Peru. In the mouth of that river, or others that are nearby, they can make a thousand ships.[1]

The suspicion that they intend to pass to the south sea has been confirmed by the testimony of two *negros cimarrones* that have been captured. Before they were executed, these two declared under torture the alliance that had been made with the corsairs and that they expected their arrival this year.[2] [The *negros cimarrones*] offered to transport the materials and fittings for ships, cordage and tar, and all else that needed to be transported to the river [that empties into the Gulf of San Miguel].

To bolster defenses, Loarte ordered the creation of a forty-man company in Nombre de Dios, paid for equally from city and royal funds. In Panama City, he ordered a muster of male Spanish residents that identified five hundred able-bodied men, three hundred of whom already had their own weapons. These men were organized into a city militia, with fifty men ready to defend against a surprise attack.

I sent a captain and thirty men from this city by land to the coast of Acla to see if any corsairs had made landfall there. The captain could not reach Acla because of the many swamps in the way, being winter. He only brought word that in some of the rivers of that coast they found many signs of *negros* who appeared to be going toward Acla.

By the south sea, I sent a brigantine with a captain and soldiers to the mouths of the rivers from which the corsairs might reach this sea to see if there were signs that they had arrived there or had built a ship or were constructing one. The captain, even though he was diligent, could find no signs.

I also sent a brigantine by the north sea with a captain and soldiers to see if it was true that three ships had anchored at Acla [as had been reported by previous naval encounters]. He found two frigates and a shallop anchored along the coast of Acla in a bay named '*de Piñas.*' Firing several *versos* he saw the people flee to land.[3] He grappled with the frigates and took them. On land nearby, they had begun to build a fort. After taking clothes that he found inside, he returned to the frigates, setting fire to the fort to ensure that he would not be overtaken by more men that could be defended against. He returned with the ships. . . .

With this I was convinced that the corsairs had come ashore and joined the *negros cimarrones* . . . it appears certain that the people that fled the frigates are few and they went to join up with the rest who are on land. . . .

Through the negligence of these officers or because God willed it so, they failed to discover that near the bay of Acla some corsairs had joined with the *negros cimarrones*. It has been learned that they were the owners of the frigates taken by the captain of the brigantine. These men having passed to the south sea in a galliot, twelve oars a side, with the help of the *negros cimarrones* whom they brought with them, landed on the Pearl Islands, twenty leagues from this city, on the first day of February. They robbed Spanish houses there and took seventy *negros*. To prevent warning from reaching this city, they took great care to burn or scuttle all the boats on the island such that there was no news for twenty-two days, after which a man escaped in a canoe and brought word, although not as accurately as could be desired.

The day I was advised [of the robberies] I dispatched a ship to Peru with the news so that the ships that carry silver and gold come prepared. Within six days I sent out six boats, with oars and sails, carrying two hundred men, sailors and soldiers. They went to secure the sea and castigate these corsairs. The same day they left, they encountered a ship coming from Quito that had been robbed of eight thousand pesos of gold. With this capture and news of the fleet that had been sent after them, [the corsairs] returned to land by the rivers that they had previously taken. The fleet followed them and finding signs searched the many inlets and estuaries found there [the Gulf of San Miguel]. At the same time, other investigations were conducted. By land I sent another company of soldiers well accustomed to the terrain in case [the corsairs] fled and escaped the armada they could not leave by the bay of Acla where they had entered or be aided by other corsairs.

Loarte noted that once word of the English attacks became known, don Cristóbal de Eraso brought thirty harquebusiers to Panama City and apologetically offered their services until the fleet departed.

On the eighteenth of this month of April, the fleet I had dispatched against the corsairs appeared at the port of this city with such good news that the whole city and kingdom celebrated. What happened was that having searched the rivers that [the corsairs] had entered, thirty leagues upriver in the Río Balsas they encountered [the corsairs] on the shore. All the gold and silver they had robbed had been sent to a pueblo of *negros cimarrones* five leagues from there. They were collecting everything else they had in order to carry it to the same pueblo. Our soldiers brought battle to them there, killing the larger part of them including many *negros cimarrones* and two *negro* captains. The rest fled to the pueblo where the [English] captain was, and our men pursued them. Another day they found the captain and his men and many *negros* in a fort within the pueblo armed with harquebuses and many bows and arrows. Bringing battle to them, our men captured the fort and some of the English. Other English and the captain fled, leaving behind all their weapons and the captain leaving with two harquebus wounds. With this, our men remained masters of the pueblo.

Another day, our men searched for the gold and silver that they had left buried and found much of it, over one hundred thousand *ducados* in gold and silver, of which forty thousand or so pesos of gold and one thousand nine hundred or so pesos of silver belong to your Majesty. With this victory they returned to this city.

The royal funds were placed in the treasury in Panama City. Ten percent of the remaining recovered gold and silver was given to the soldiers and officers for their service and to several religious institutions in thanks for the success of the venture.

According to the declarations of four prisoners, youths that had been captured from the English, eighteen to twenty English escaped, although without weapons, among them the captain and another five valiant men determined to commit any great feat. In the north sea, where they had come ashore, they had left two launches with sail and cordage and hidden two bronze cannons and four or five thousand pesos buried in the ground.

In order to prevent these men from escaping with the launches and the silver they left buried, returning to England with the news of the alliance they had made with the *cimarrones*, and the ease with which one can pass to the south sea, I have dispatched a captain and soldiers with two of the English prisoners who say they will show where all these things are so that they may be recovered and the captain and the remaining men who have fled can be captured or killed.[4] They are to attack a pueblo of nearby *negros cimarrones* who assisted the English in entering so that they might be punished for their great audacity. I hope that God will see that all goes well. At the very least this is the greatest measure that has availed itself to do, and, since winter comes abruptly, all that can be done for now concerning war. If it were summer, I would order these *negros* punished for aiding the corsairs' entrance.

Your Majesty should be advised that before our victory, the prisoners stated that their captain had said that he wished to go back to England and return later with two thousand men to settle ~~Acla~~ among the *cimarrones* and infest the south sea.[5] I believe that none of those that have fled will arrive there because the *negros* will kill them for having suffered defeat or they will fall into the hands of the captain that I said I sent out.

Loarte proved prescient in his appraisal of the continued English-maroon alliance. The Spanish counterattack would increasingly target maroon settlements and strain the maroons' tenuous alliance with the English.

---

1. The region around the Gulf of San Miguel had many trees. By the early seventeenth century, Spaniards would set up logging camps there, bringing lumber by sea back to Panama City.
2. The English plan had likely been agreed on prior to Drake's departure in 1573.
3. *Versos* were small cannons that shot nine-to-twelve-pound balls.
4. The other two young prisoners had been sent to Seville to be "examined and instructed" by the Holy Office of the Inquisition on matters of the faith. One adult prisoner had been executed in Panama City. AGI, Panama 13, R. 16, N. 71, fs. 6.
5. "Acla" was crossed out, indicating a correction. This slip may be telling, a sign that Spaniards perceived Acla to be vulnerable to foreign settlement.

27. The City of Panama to the Crown, June 7, 1577
Source: AGI, Panama 30, N. 18.

This letter from the city of Panama details the continued expeditions searching for the scattered English and their maroon allies. The city leaders offer various rationales for why a quick and expansive campaign would be most effective.

•   •   •

The president commissioned a captain, named Luis García de Melo, with forty men to go to Nombre de Dios and to embark with two of the young Englishmen that had been taken so that they may show them where in Acla they had hidden the two launches brought by the English in the north sea, as well as the gold and silver. After Captain Melo arrived in Nombre de Dios, don Cristóbal de Eraso, general of the fleet, believing it better that the mission be undertaken by his hand, took the two youths and placed them in his fleet. He sent a Captain Vera with eighty men in search of the launches. Melo left Nombre de Dios after the other [captain], continuing his journey with forty men in search of the launches and Englishmen. It turned out that the two captains reunited in the bay of Acla.[1] While Captain Melo went about searching rivers and estuaries, he found the two launches half sunk in an estuary, hidden under some branches. At this point Captain Vera arrived and they divided the launches, each taking one. They found the sails, oars, two bronze cannons and four iron *versos*. Afterward, the two returned to Nombre de Dios and after two days Captain Vera continued to Cartagena and his general [Cristóbal de Eraso].

As Captain Melo was preparing to leave Nombre de Dios for Acla, General don Crisóbal de Eraso sent the two English boys. Melo continued his journey to the bay of Acla with them in order to have some success. However, few are the men that go with him, around seventy men, having gained twenty more than what he had. We have little hope that he will have success with so few men and the whole bush up in arms. The captains and soldiers that came from there report that it appears that many English remain. They now say that thirty of their most valiant and principal men remain in the bush. It is understood that they will sell their lives dear.[2] We do not know if they subsequently joined with other corsairs that have frequented this coast.

The cabildo lamented that the audiencia had not acted more swiftly or decisively and that it chose not to spend more royal funds to pursue war. The cabildo noted that it would take almost a year for any royal response to reach Panama.

Therefore, we believe that if no resistance is offered now the land will be abandoned by most vecinos who do not wish to live with such uncertainty and risk.

Now it is winter, a very good time to make war because the maize crop and banana groves are yet to be harvested. If they are burned by our men [the *cimarrones*] will be left without food, which is the most effective warfare that we can achieve. Now they cannot hide their food for it is not yet ripe. In the summer, even if it is only twenty thousand bushels of maize, they can hide it in the bush where a thousand men cannot find it. Similarly, with the rains and mud, the *negros* leave signs wherever they go and cannot avoid doing so. They cannot travel by the rivers as they do during summer without a trace because they are swollen. Also, the *negros* and English cannot live unless they are in a shelter because of the great rains. In the summer, they can hide anywhere even if they appear greater in number than they are. Further, they are not as well equipped with weapons as they will be in a year, if war is brought to them as they are now. A thousand other benefits would result from swiftness but a delay will cause the opposite. God willing, a hundred soldiers leaving now from this coast, from among those good ones that can be found, together with the seventy that went down the other coast, would have a great effect.[3]

The cabildo specifically asked that the king authorize the expenditure of royal funds in the pursuit of the war. The cabildo also related several other encounters with corsairs along the Atlantic coastline of Veragua and Nicaragua to the west. The presence of so many foreign ships had reduced the number of ships transporting foodstuffs to Nombre de Dios. In Panama City, the cabildo reported that Spaniards had resorted to using maize and maize flour after an English ship captured a transport ship carrying fifteen hundred bushels of wheat.

1. Despite being commissioned by different officials, the captains agreed to help each other rather than fall into disputes over jurisdiction and authority.
2. In other words, they will protect their lives at all costs.
3. The cabildo is proposing that a second larger expedition be sent from Panama City to assist Captain Melo and his men already operating near Acla.

28. Dr. Loarte to Viceroy Toledo, June 8, 1577
Source: AGI, Panama 13, R. 16, N. 76, bloque 2.

In addition to informing the king of the course of the war, the Audiencia of Panama sent reports to the viceroy of Peru, the highest-ranking official with jurisdiction over the region. In this letter, Dr. Loarte updates the viceroy on events that had transpired. He offered a critique of local interests, such as those of the cabildo of Panama, and General Pedro de Ortega Valencia's command decisions.

• • •

After the good news of our victory abated, everyone here clamored that more troops be sent up the river in which the corsairs had been found because all believed that some more English remained and that they could regroup themselves and attempt to leave by the south sea.

Even though it is true that twenty of the wounded escaped, not thirty as some would suggest, they are unarmed, without a knife, or weapons, or harquebus, or arrows, without supplies, tar, cordage, nails, or tools. All of this was taken, including the medicines they had to heal themselves. Among people of such faithlessness . . . as the *negros*, I do not doubt that they have either died from their wounds or have been killed by the *negros* or have been devoured by the land, of which it is capable. Especially, ours have taken the launches, sails, cordage that they had for making their escape.

Because of this, at this time it has not appeared necessary to me to spend money from His Majesty's treasury on unnecessary sorties.[1] It would be throwing money to the wind, I prefer to save it for spring. If by then, His Majesty has not issued a new order, I believe it will be necessary to protect the pass through which the silver travels on its way to the fleet. For good reason, this is when the corsairs should attempt to leave, not at this time when there are no ships in the south sea nor are any coming, for they have as much knowledge of the fleet's movements as we do.[2]

While it is true that Pedro de Ortega did well in this campaign against the English, he lost the best opportunity that will avail itself in many years, for the pueblo that he took from the *negros* had over eighty large houses as well as smaller ones. They found many supplies. Because of the short time that they had to make their escape, the horde of *negros*, including the young *negros*, could not be more than a league from the pueblo. Within five or six leagues of this one were another three or four pueblos of *negros*. If they had stayed in this pueblo, they could have ranged from there and searched diverse parts with captains and men, an effort that would have done notable damage to the *negros*, for they are largely unprepared and overconfident in their safety. In the instructions I gave to [Ortega Valencia], particularly in one paragraph, I ordered him to do so, and not to return without having done so, even should he achieve a total victory over the enemies.

All this mattered little, for he was desirous of returning to Spain to pursue advancement, and since he had achieved much, I did not see a reason to sadden him by reprimanding him for what he failed to do. Nevertheless, afterword I regretted the damage and lost opportunity. If it please God, at another time it will be regained.

Although Pedro de Ortega Valencia returned to Spain to seek royal favor for his efforts, the overall campaign did not abate. Smaller sorties continued to search for the English. Even as Loarte composed this letter, Viceroy Toledo had commissioned an expedition under the command of Captain Diego de Frías Trejo to travel from Lima to Panama.[3] Frías Trejo's commission called on him to raise a force of over 150 men and to pursue war by land and sea to kill or capture the English and punish the maroons for their assistance.

Trejo's expedition arrived in Panama City on June 20, 1577. His arrival and the terms of his commission rankled the Audiencia of Panama. President Loarte perceived that the viceroy had interfered with his authority as governor by commissioning an independent expedition. The dispute ultimately revolved around whether the viceroy or the president of the audiencia held the authority of *capitán general* for the territory. Trejo would be tied up in legal disputes for over a month before finally being allowed to fulfill the terms of his commission.

---

1. Loarte structured his claims to respond to the cabildo of Panama's complaint that the audiencia was not acting swiftly enough.

2. The maroons likely provided the English with knowledge of fleet movements and the comings and goings of ships. Their connections to enslaved Africans in the cities afforded them an ideal intelligence network.

3. AGI, Panama 41, N. 23. This letter from Diego de Frías Trejo recounts his departure from Lima and critiques the Audiencia of Panama for not recognizing his commission.

29. Dr. Loarte to the Crown, September 5, 1577
Source: AGI, Panama 41, N. 25.

In September 1577, President Loarte updated the king on the campaigns against the maroons. Although Ortega Valencia had returned to Spain, Captain Melo continued his expedition along the Atlantic coast. This letter related Melo's discovery of a maroon community that likely numbered in the hundreds. .

•   •   •

I dispatched a captain with sixty soldiers to prevent [the Englishmen's] flight and capture their launches and artillery, taking with them two young English captives to serve as guides to show where the launches had been hidden. Don Cristóbal de Eraso took the guides and sent them in a galleon to Cartagena. Despite losing them, the captain continued his search and, even without guides, discovered the launches and artillery along with lots of cordage and sails. He could not find the silver.[1]

Afterward don Cristóbal returned the guides, but by that time the English, and the *negros* that helped them, had made off with the silver. [The captain] discovered the stash already open and evidence that it had been removed. As I had ordered, the captain and his party went off to the pueblo of the *negros* in which the English had hidden in order to punish them.[2] Even though he was discovered, and in the journey some of the English and *negros* attacked from advantageous positions, they were always able to overcome the attacks and capture the pueblo, which had already been abandoned.

This pueblo had two hundred seventeen large houses, which for *negros* is large because they live many to a house.[3] He burned the pueblo and razed many fields and fruit trees that they had for their sustenance. He killed two English and some of the most principal *negros*. Later, they learned from some captives that after [Pedro de Ortega Valencia] had defeated them, those that escaped had fled to this pueblo where the king (as the *negros* call him) gave them people to guide them to where they had left the launches hidden. This was during the time that the captain was already searching for them, when they realized that he had found them they removed the silver. They returned downtrodden.

As a last resort, they decided to make canoes out of tree trunks, which are very large in this land, and hollowed out, like a trough can navigate the sea and rivers, and bear sails. Having built eight, which would fit a hundred men, they decided to travel to the south sea and capture a ship that a resident there had and outfit it and commit further robberies. These canoes were burned, and so an expedition like the one raised was unnecessary. Even though the English are few, with the aid of the *negros* they could have caused great damage. The expedition of this captain was of great importance because at the very least it is certain that the [English] cannot return to England and encourage others to come to these parts as they did.

Loarte also reported that the continued presence of corsairs on the Atlantic coast had restricted trade to the mining region of Veragua. The lack of seaborne trade had caused shortage of supplies, including food, and necessitated the creation of an overland route. However, Loarte warned that an overland road would make it easier for the enslaved Africans who worked those mines to escape and join the maroons present elsewhere.

Loarte also criticized the commissioning of Frías Trejo. He informed the king that the expedition had been sent even though the Audiencia of Panama had notified the viceroy that Pedro de Ortega Valencia's success negated the need for reinforcements. Loarte also outlined irregularities with the commission of Frías Trejo. Loarte opined that, although the Audiencia of Panama had been ordered to follow instructions from the viceroy in matters of government, finance, and war, no royal cedula had granted the viceroy of Peru the powers of governor or *capitán general* in Panama. Nevertheless, the audiencia recognized that the need to pursue military campaigns against the English and maroons represented a more immediate problem than their complaints over the viceroy's jurisdictional oversteps and graciously allowed Frías Trejo to undertake his campaign. Yet Loarte feared that Frías Trejo would use his commission to conscript captains and soldiers sent out by the audiencia. The president admitted that he had ordered one captain to delay his departure so that Frías Trejo could not disrupt the expeditions organized by the audiencia.

1. Captain Melo's first expedition to Acla. Here Loarte omits Captain Vera's presence.
2. Captain Melo's second expedition, after Captain Vera had rejoined the fleet. The following events transpired between April and September 1577.
3. Probably the main maroon settlement of Ronconcholon.

30. Diego de Frías Trejo to the Crown, October 21, 1577
Source: AGI, Panama 41, N. 31.

In October 1577, Diego de Frías Trejo summarized his actions since arriving in Panama. He reiterated his critique of the audiencia for holding up his expedition before recounting the events of his campaign. The following excerpt details his efforts from early August through late October 1577.

• • •

I left the port of Perico on August 8 and navigated until the 16th when I arrived at the mouth of the rivers that empty into the south sea, where the English entered. These are the Río de Indios and the Río de Bonbas, they lead to a site known as the Real de San Miguel.[1] I came with the intention of ascending the Río de Indios to the pueblo of Catalina with half my men, which is where Pedro de Ortega reached.[2] This is near the Río de Piñas and is home to the *negros zapes*.[3] The *maestre de campo* would proceed with the other part of the men by the other river to the Real de San Miguel, go ashore, and move to occupy Ronconcholon, which is the fortress of the Bayano, the largest settlement of the *negros*, and from whence I write this letter. This [plan] could not be put into effect because the river was so swollen that I could not navigate it.

I believe Your Majesty has been informed that it was always my intention to begin my campaign before the start of summer as it would best benefit the service of Your Majesty. Recognizing my intention, the President [Dr. Loarte] ordered that the *oidores*, *fiscal*, myself, and captains who had previously gone out against these *negros* come confer together and discuss how best to undertake the expedition. There it was decided to enter by four directions. I would occupy Ronconcholon and the pueblo of Catalina with my men. The President would send two other captains with more men, one by the north sea and the bay of Acla and the other to Portobelo. With luck, we will capture English and the *negros* in the middle and in this way deal with all of them at once. By scouring the land, if they flee from one, they will be run into the others. Like this we can destroy [the English and *negros*] most quickly and with least effort.

Thereafter, I undertook that which had been entrusted to me. To occupy the two places assigned to me, I set out at once on the expedition. With so many days having passed since I left Panama, as I hold this inland position, the President never sent the captain and men to the coast of Acla by the north sea. This [failure] has made this expedition the most tiring and difficult such that it has not had pronounced effect.[4]

I made landfall at the Real de San Miguel on August 20 with all the men I brought. I left thirty men there, including some sick ones, to guard the food that was brought and the site and port that is the key to conveniently supplying all the men in these mountains.[5] From there I left with part of the men to take this site of Ronconcholon. I sent the *maestre de campo* with the other contingent traversing the land to the Río de Piñas and the pueblo of Catalina. These are the two places that were my duty to occupy per the arrangement.

I arrived very quickly and silently at the site of Ronconcholon. I found it deserted and burned, with only two houses in which were three or four *negros* and some English. Being very alert, they perceived me, for only a few days before a Captain Melo—that the President had sent with seventy or eighty men—had traversed from the north sea to this site. The *negros* and English had sallied against him and attack[ed] him at several passes, after which he left the region quickly, arriving in Panama with his men before I had left.

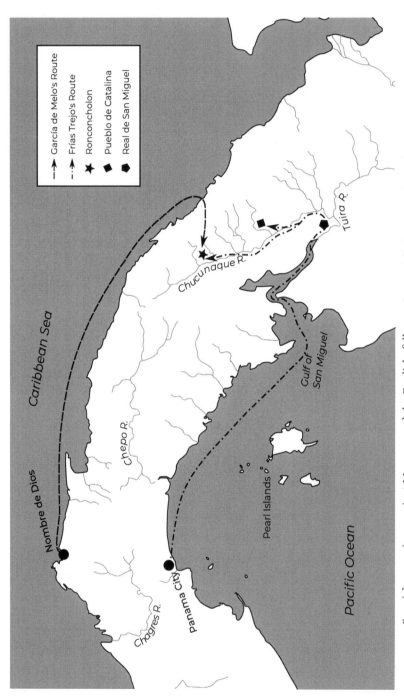

Spanish campaigns against Maroons and the English, fall 1577. *Sources:* AGI, Panama 41, N. 25; Panama 41, N. 31.

Legend:

- García de Melo's Route
- Frías Trejo's Route
- ★ Ronconcholon
- ◼ Pueblo de Catalina
- ⬟ Real de San Miguel

Map labels:

- Caribbean Sea
- Nombre de Dios
- Chagres R.
- Panama City
- Chepo R.
- Chucunaque R.
- Tuira R.
- Gulf of San Miguel
- Pearl Islands
- Pacific Ocean

Believing that [the location of] this pueblo was known and that *españoles* would return, the *negros* burned it and agreed to divide themselves into camps in the mountains, not keeping pueblos so as to not be discovered. Now they are so well hidden with such prudence and vigilance that even though I have captured some, by my great diligence, who have led me to many of the *negros'* camps, their cunning is such that if one of them does not come back at night they assume they have been taken and flee to another place so that the [captive] cannot bring the *españoles* to where they are.[6] Consequently, in no camp nor pueblo have I found a *negro*, all is depopulated and they have fled.

When I arrived at this place, the English who were there fled from me. Although I followed their trail as best I could through the rivers and mountains I could not catch one. But God willed that in fleeing from me, and with my pursuit, they fled to where the *maestre de campo* was, fifteen leagues away. He captured the captain of the English, named Juan Ocsnan, and seven others. I captured the master of the ship in which they arrived, who was very esteemed by them.[7] There are nine that I have in custody, well-guarded. They say there were thirty-four survivors, the best soldiers, not counting another two or three that have died. The men killed or captured by Pedro de Ortega were the servants left with the launch.

According to the captain's confession, which I took, he and twenty-one English were about to go once again to the south sea to a river that he did not know, for the *negros* were to have taken them, where boats come to load lumber—it is believed that this is the Río Chepo—from there capture a boat, remove its fittings, take them to the north sea, and fashion a boat in which to escape and go to their land. They would have done what they intended and carried out their plans, aided by the character and emptiness of the sea and land they would traverse, had the passes not been closed to them. But God willed that the thread be cut, and their design undone by my expedition. Had it been delayed until summer it would likely not have had as good an outcome. These twenty-two English had been wandering near this site and my arrival caused them to flee and disperse, separating one from another by accident. Until now it has not been possible to find or capture more than these nine, two have been spotted but they fled. It is said that the other twelve English have joined with one named Jacome Canoa. They say they want to go to the Río de Chagres, or they say the north sea. With that intent, they separated and divided from the rest, but wander nearby like the others.

With my arrival they fled and hid as Your Majesty can see more fully in the declaration of the captain that accompanies this letter.

I have scoured much land, and having arrived at the north sea where they entered to see if they had reached there, I did not find any sign of them. It is understood that they are hidden in the mountains and only leave to collect bananas, the food and sustenance of the *negros cimarrones* and the English. The banana groves are a thing to be amazed, for they cannot be razed for it is a property of theirs that when one tree is cut four or five children spring up that can bear fruit in a year.[8] I hope to God that I will have all the English in my hands and destroy these *negros*. After all, it is work for His holy service that he should direct, and so I will continue to bring that about even unto losing my life, and many if I had them, in the service of Your Majesty.

Although at the present, I am greatly lacking footwear for my men due to the frequent rains of winter; the swamps and mud have worn out what we brought. I am awaiting a ship travelling from Peru to Panama by which I understand that the viceroy has supplied all that is necessary. Thus, I am confident that Your Majesty will be well served by this expedition.

Frías Trejo concluded by reiterating his frustration that President Loarte did not send a captain to Acla since this had allowed the English more space to flee and forced him to cover more ground in his searches. He also complained that the audiencia's jurisdictional dispute with the viceroy led it to poorly supply his men with guides, porters, and necessary items. In recognition of many years of service, he asked that the king confirm his appointment as *alférez general* in Peru's company of lancers. He further requested that the king consider naming him *alguacil mayor* of the Audiencia of Lima or grant him an *encomienda*.

---

1. This could also be translated as Fort San Miguel. A site previously used by Ortega Valencia.
2. The origin of the name Catalina is unknown.
3. Importantly, the Spanish recognized that the maroons organized their groups using categories like Zape. Unlike most terms from Upper Guinea, Zape represented a catchall that could encompass a variety of smaller groups originating near modern Sierra Leone. Wheat, *Atlantic Africa and the Spanish Caribbean*, 50–51. During the mid-sixteenth century, the various peoples subsumed within the Zape category entered the transatlantic slave trade when the Mane, a Mande-speaking group, expanded into the region and began exporting captives taken there. Between the 1560s and 1620s, continued conflicts in the region led to sizable numbers of Zape captives entering the transatlantic slave trade. Green, *Rise of the Trans-Atlantic Slave Trade*, 234–41.

4. Frías Trejo was aware that the audiencia delayed expeditions. He may have been ignorant that the delay served to prevent him from conscripting those forces. Reports from audiencia officials confirm that expeditions did go out. In a letter dated October 24, 1577, Loarte reported that a captain that he had sent had taken and occupied a different maroon settlement. Two days later, the *fiscal* of the audiencia reported that a captain had been sent to the Bay of Portobelo to prevent maroons there from aiding the English or those in the Bayano. AGI, Panama 13, R. 16, N. 76 and N. 77.

5. Frías Trejo does not exaggerate the importance of the site. The Real de San Miguel would continue to serve as a bastion of Spanish defense in the region until the early seventeenth century.

6. This strategy speaks to maroons' knowledge of Spanish tactics and the history of Spanish campaigns against their predecessors.

7. Oxenham was the captain, or leader, of the expedition. The master of the ship was responsible for the navigation and sailing of the ship while at sea.

8. Bananas are not trees, but perennial herbs that produce fruit. When cut, as described by Frías Trejo, the underground corm (root) sends up new shoots or suckers.

31. Excerpts from the Questioning of John Oxenham, October 20, 1577

Source: AGI, Panama 41, N. 31.

A day before writing the previous letter, Frías Trejo interviewed the recently captured John Oxenham.

• • •

At the site of Ronconcholon, which is in the Bayano, in the kingdom of Tierra Firme in the Indies of the Ocean Sea, on the twentieth day of October 1577, Diego de Frías Trejo . . . having taken prisoner nine Englishmen of those that wandered about, corsairs through this land, and in order to record those things which are convenient to the service of His Majesty and the good of this expedition, ordered that the captain of the English appear before him . . . and asked the following questions through an interpreter, one of the nine Englishmen, named Guillermo Parcar [William Parker] who is moderately fluent in our Castilian tongue.

Asked what his name is, what land and kingdom is his native one, and if he his captain of the corsairs that passed to the south sea and at present are wandering through the forests of the Bayano: He said his name is John Ocsnam and he is an Englishman native of the pueblo of Plymouth. This declarant is captain of the English that passed to the south sea and are at present wandering the forests of the Bayano.

Asked what motivated this declarant and the other English whom he brought to leave their land and kingdom and pass to the south sea and what intent did they have: He said that Captain Francisco [Drake], Englishman who travelled this coast of the Indies with another French captain, returned to England to the pueblo of Plymouth, where he is from, and told this declarant how in the Bayano there were *negros* rich with gold and silver and well acquainted with the land who would trade for whatever goods that he could bring.[1] It was about two years ago more or less that this declarant came with the intent to trade the many goods they brought with them from England with the *negros*, cloths, axes, and other types of things with which to trade for gold and silver before returning to their land. They left England on the ninth of April of last year.

Oxenham then described their arrival on the coast and the capture of a frigate trading between Veragua and Nombre de Dios.

Near Nombre de Dios they spied two *negros cimarrones* spoken of by [Drake] and they told them that they came from England with goods [that] they would trade for gold and silver. The [*negros*] asked if Captain Francisco had come. They responded that he did not come, in his stead this declarant came as captain of these English. The *negros* told them that if they wished to go to their pueblo once there they would trade gold and silver for what they have brought. With this the *negros* took them to a port on a river the negros call Xerenxeren which is on the north sea.[2] They arrived there on the day of San Miguel in September of that year. There they left a launch hidden in the river while several soldiers went in another launch to bring the frigate to the port, it being in another one.

Afterward, this witness left with twelve soldiers and the *negros* to see their pueblos and the land and to trade with them. They brought him to this settlement of Ronconcholon which was previously inhabited by many *negros* and full of many houses. After arriving he saw that the *negros* did not have any gold and silver so he decided to return. He was there fourteen days when he received word that the *españoles* had taken the frigate that carried all his trade goods, supplies, nine pieces of artillery, powder, and the munitions that he had brought. Nothing remained except a barrel of powder that they fled with inland. The *españoles* took twenty harquebuses, on the land his men escaped with another twenty. The *españoles* took the swords and weapons that were in the frigate so that they were disarmed and discomfited.

When this witness learned this and saw that he did not have supplies, weapons, or munitions to return to his land nor trade goods to give to the *negros* as he had promised, he stayed put in the pueblo and sent for his soldiers. The *negros* told this witness that if he stayed they would feed him and his men and advised that he burn the ship that had been brought to the port of the river Xerenxeren and give them the iron, nails, and three hogsheads of salt that it carried along with its other goods. This declarant recognized that he did not have another alternative to sustain himself and that unless the ship was burned the *negros* would not feed him and had told him to leave. But, if he burned the ship, they would give him food and take him to the south sea and help him capture much gold and silver, so long as they could kill all the *españoles* they captured and if they captured *negros* they would be given to them. Compelled by necessity this declarant accepted all the conditions and ordered the ship burned, giving the *negros* all the nails and iron that it had. They hid the other launch in the river near the first and returned to the pueblo of Ronconcholon where they spent the past winter.

During this time, they cut wood for the launch that they took to the south sea using a saw that they set up with great pains and difficulty. They made the launch in the Río de Indios, four or five leagues from this pueblo, which is the river that passes near this pueblo, travelling downstream. Once made, they carried it as best they could downriver, portaging it in the shallows, until they left by the Río Maize, which is navigable. Some *negros* left from here with them and others left by the Río de Piñas. All those that left reunited, they were seven *negros* and an *indio* that went with them. Among them was Juan Vaquero, a *negro*, captain of *negros*, and others who were not captains. They said that these *negros* and their captain went to ensure that they killed any Christians they found. There were fifty English with this declarant, among them many were boys and sailors and sailor apprentices not suited for war. They left England with fifty-seven men total, of whom seven had died.

Like this they travelled to the Pearl Islands. There they captured an *español* and his wife and children, whom were later freed, and other *españoles* on the island of Mançaneda. The soldiers took some clothing, and the *negros* took some other *negros*, this deponent does not know how many nor what the soldiers took. Some pearls and other things made of gold that had been taken were recovered by Pedro de Ortega from the Río de Piñas. They were in the islands for fourteen or fifteen days when they spied the ship coming from

Quito to Panama. They went out and took it, taking all its gold and silver without murdering anyone travelling in it. With haste they returned to the Río de
Piñas, where Pedro de Ortega arrived and defeated them. He took all that they
stole along with their weapons and munitions, and all that they had. He killed
twelve Englishmen and captured two boys and two sailor apprentices. The
twelve men who died were sailors, sailor apprentices, and servants because
the soldiers that were there fled along with the *negros* because they had been
eating along the bank of the river when Pedro de Ortega arrived with his men
and began to shoot harquebuses. With this the soldiers fled along with the
negros, and the twelve men died. At the time, this declarant and some soldiers, six or seven, were farther upriver, five or six leagues from here, at a place
called the pueblo of Catalina, which is a pueblo of *negros*. After defeating
those that were along the river, Pedro de Ortega travelled there and killed
three of the twelve that died. The captain [this declarant] fled with the rest that
were there, and Pedro de Ortega took all the silver, gold, and other things.

Oxenham was asked if they brought women and children to settle the region, which
he denied. They also questioned him about how much artillery he carried and
whether he planned to build a fort, which he also denied. The Spanish asked if the
queen had authorized the expedition or whether they had been able to send word
back to England. Oxenham answered no in each case. By the time of his capture,
Oxenham knew of only twelve other Englishmen at large, led by a man named
Jacob Canoe (Jacome Canoa).

Asked how did the *negros* treat them after they were defeated [by Pedro de
Ortega]: He said that they treated them very poorly and would not give them
food or any other thing. They survived eating bananas that they picked in
the groves. One kindly *negro* gave them some maize, but . . . their leaders
told them not to give anything because they had not killed the *españoles*
they had captured in the islands or in the ship from Quito. This complaint
was made many times, saying that this declarant and his men are the cause
of the [*negros'*] perdition because they did not kill the *españoles*, and had
they done so they would not have followed [the English] or defeated them.
Because of this [the *negros*] do not give them food or clothing, they wander
about hungry, naked, and disarmed.

Asked if he knew where the *negros* and their families could presently be
found: He said that he does not know where they may be at the moment

because they had all abandoned their pueblos and burned them. After they learned that the general had arrived with his men in this land, they spread the word one to another that they should leave their pueblos, burn them, and hide in the bush scattered about. With this, the pueblo of Catalina . . . was abandoned and the *negros* fled.

---

1. Oxenham accompanied Drake on the earlier expedition. His statement likely sought to avoid incriminating himself further.
2. The Río Sardinilla.

32. Diego de Frías Trejo to the Crown, December 7, 1577
Source: AGI, Panama 41, N. 37.

After capturing Oxenham, Frías Trejo's expedition only made slow progress as it undertook the difficult task of searching for dispersed hamlets of maroons and scattered bands of Englishmen.

• • •

About a month ago I wrote to Your Majesty telling of my arrival and this expedition to the Bayano against the English and *negros cimarrones* that inhabit it, as well as of the captures I made of the captain and another eight English and some *negros*. [I also conveyed] the knowledge gained of the remaining English who wander hidden in the bush and of the great difficulty in searching for them because of the harshness of the land, the scarcity of food, and the few *negro* porters that the president of Panama granted me. These are vital and most necessary to this venture as Your Majesty will see by the letter and dispatches that I sent to Panama by special messenger, who is to take them in the first ship sailing by any route.

Since then Your Majesty should be informed that among many sorties and sallies I have made in the bush in search of the English and *negros*, one of these was the longest and most laborious. In it, I traversed the rivers Chongone, Banique, Baño, Gallinazo, and Bogota, along with many streams and ravines, and all other places that on this coastline one might suspect to find them, aided by guides brought for the task. At the end, God willed that, guided by a *negro* who I captured in a banana grove, and another leader, who approached me in peace with his wife, I captured four English who were in a camp and attacked several other *negro* camps. I captured twenty pieces large and small, although others fled. With this capture I returned to the Real de Ronconcholon. Fortunately, at the present I have thirteen English captives and many *negros* and *negras*, boys and girls.

I am informed that in this area there are no more English, but toward the north sea there are another fourteen or fifteen with their leader Jacome Canoa in a river named Bayano. I am traveling there to search for them with guides for the task. I also received word of another two or three English and some other *negro* pueblos. I plan to deal with them with the will and perseverance that I have always had in the service of Your Majesty. I trust that God will bring success in this for the beginning has gone so well, although the soldiers are tired and worn down by the lack of porters, more so since the majority of those given to us by the president have fled to Panama. With those that remained I made this recent capture and will make the trip to the Río Bayano.

Frías Trejo concludes by again complaining that the president of the audiencia has not sent more porters or supplies.

33. Diego de Frías Trejo to the Crown, February 18, 1578
Source: AGI, Panama 41, N. 39.

In early 1578, progress against the English and maroons continued to proceed slowly. Frías Trejo found few signs of either group. This letter updated the king on his successful capture of John Butler, alias "Chalona," and the destruction of two maroon settlements. Although Frías Trejo spoke positively of his successes, his letter betrays the weariness felt by the Spaniards after six months of campaigning.

•   •   •

I have written at length to Your Majesty about the successes of this expedition of the Bayano through the seventh of last December when I wrote my last letters. I believe these have been delayed in Panama due to the lack of a ship and will go forward with this one. What has since happened here is that I scoured the land by many parts, occupying me for many days with great hardship and want. God willed that this was not in vain. In a river named "Indios" we saw six English in a hand-fashioned canoe traveling with supplies upriver. They intended to leave the canoe and pass to the north sea to find a means of escape. The [English] perceived us and, leaving the canoe, fled into the bush without leaving any trace to follow. In this bush, after losing sight of a man one cannot find them or follow with any certainty. We searched for them without hope of finding them. After three days, following a sign we found in a river, I spotted them hidden in the bush ten leagues from where they had fled. Attacking them by night I captured five, one of whom is the most important of those that came here for he is the most astute and wise. He served as pilot and translator, he is very skilled at piloting and fluent in our tongue and others. They call him "Chalona" and by this name he is well-known and famous.[1] By good fortune, I now have eighteen English captives.

Completing this, I set upon a camp of *negros*, guided by a sentinel that I took. I captured some *negros* and *negras*. From there I went to the coast of Acla on the north sea guided by the English pilot to see if any others had arrived of the fifteen English that remain. Arriving there, I found no sign that they had arrived or been present there. I am certain they are in the Isla de Piñas or the [Isla de] Iguanas that are of the coast toward Nombre de Dios for in sight of [the islands] I have recently found traces of a campsite these fifteen used, as I wrote to Your Majesty. Additionally, the pilot Chalona says that Jacome Canoa, the leader of the fifteen English, had previously visited the Isla de Piñas with him. He says there is an abundance of game and fish and other food there. They cannot be anywhere but these islands close to the coast without a boat to take them. They will have gone there in a raft or canoe that they made.

I sent word of this to the Royal Audiencia and the president of Panama so that they can search for them, and [I wrote] to don Miguel Eraso who is with Your Majesty's fleet so that he might take measures as I cannot do so for lack of boat or vessel. I believe that if these tasks are done they will not escape. In the bush none have remained, nor are there any signs.

I later learned from the *negros* I captured that the one who fled when I captured the five was killed by them, for they are now mortal enemies of the English because of the punishments that they have faced on behalf of the [English]. Because of this, I could not find a trace of him despite much searching.

From Acla I returned scouring the land by other paths. I went to the Río de Manta and to the Río de Piñas where I had heard there was a *negro* settlement. I captured a scout who led me to the pueblo where I captured some *piezas* of *negros* and *negras* and *indias* who were with them.[2] The rest fled into the bush. I burned the pueblo and the fields. I spent several days

searching for traces by paths and trails through the bush without finding
any or obtaining news of any other settlement or camp in all of the Bayano.

With this, forty odd days after leaving the site of Ronconcholon, I
returned to the Real de San Miguel four days ago. I am here with all my
men awaiting dispatches from the viceroy, whom I have always informed of
my activities on this expedition, to see what he shall order me to do.

Frías Trejo again criticized the president of Panama for not sending troops to Acla.

I have done all that is possible in Your Majesty's service during this expedition up to now. No Englishman remains in the bush that is not a prisoner,
or a *negro* that is not wandering homeless, hidden, thoroughly punished,
and regretful for having guided the English. I have captive forty odd *piezas*
of *negros* and *negras*, large and small, and killed another eight or ten. The
soldiers are now very tired and sick, unable to continue the expedition, nor
do I believe that any more can be done at present. As I say, I cannot find a
trace, or heard word, of any *negro* pueblo, all those that remain wander
about hidden in the bush without pueblos or a safe place to sleep. If I receive
any news, I will do what I must as I have always done and send word of
everything to Your Majesty.

---

1. Frías Trejo appears unaware that *chalona* simply meant translator and carried the
   same meaning as *lengua*, the word he used to describe Butler's linguistic skills.
   Wheat, *Atlantic Africa and the Spanish Caribbean*, 231.
2. Notably, Frías Trejo does not suggest that the *indias* were captives of the maroons, a
   common Spanish assumption.

34. Dr. Criado de Castilla to the Crown, May 12, 1578
Source: AGI, Panama 13, R. 17, N. 83.

In early 1578, President Loarte died. Following his death, Dr. Criado de Castilla, the
senior *oidor*, took over as interim president. This letter captures the fluid responses
of the maroons to the changing events. While many fled deeper into the wilderness, in some cases maroons switched sides, allying with the Spanish to help capture the remaining English.

•   •   •

About the entrance of the English corsairs to this south sea, which Your
Majesty will have heard from many sources, the last that I wrote to Your

Majesty . . . related that the men that your viceroy of Peru sent to aid this [kingdom] . . . defeated them and captured their captain and eight Englishmen. A few days later, at various times they captured another nine, so that as of now they have captured eighteen and at least forty *negros*.

This has been a costly success, since the first of last August until the beginning of April of this year men have been in the bush searching all routes for the English and *negros cimarrones*. Of the *negros*, so few have been captured of their great number that they have caused no less trouble than the English because they avoid fighting and their defense is to flee and hide in the most remote hidden parts of the mountains, abandoning their pueblos and burning some of them. When they sense the approach of soldiers, they destroy the homes, fields, and fruit trees that might support [our soldiers] hoping to do them harm by any means.[1]

Some of these *negros* have offered peace of their own accord, and with their help and the information they gave about what has happened in the bush the captain and his men have made several captures. There only remain fifteen left to capture of the English, these are from a different bunch that in discord split with the rest. The soldiers in their pursuit followed them to the coast of the north sea.

The audiencia asked that the commander of the fleet, Juan de Velasco de Barrio, send ships to search the coastal islands. Having found no signs, Criado de Castilla opined that the English must have drowned attempting to reach the islands.

In order to ensure that no English remain in the bush, the captain and his men diligently searched the places and parts where they could be and could not find any sign, other than those of the *negros cimarrones*, who fugitive and weary from the pursuit of our men wander from place to place. Unable to capture any and seeing that such work was futile, the captain and his men returned to this city with their prisoners because of the English they believed none remained in the bush except for one who had escaped the last raid.

In Panama City, the prisoners were interrogated and all but four executed. [Those executed] included John Oxenham and John Butler (Chalona) who the Spanish learned had been a participant in Francis Drake's raid on Nombre de Dios and Venta de Chagres and who served as the expedition's primary contact with the *negros*.

Although the punishment that the *negros cimarrones* have received promises that for now there is some safety in thinking that so harried they will not admit other corsairs into the bush, because even those that are currently here have been cast out and disfavored because of the harm they caused [the *negros*], yet despite this the route between the north sea and this one is so well known that we are obliged to continuously care for its defense. Therefore, until Your Majesty orders us otherwise, we will insure that, for the least cost, some soldiers patrol the coasts of the south sea, near the coast and rivers the English used to arrive at the sea, and explore the land so that the *negros* know that we are not inattentive.

The audiencia ordered that the fleet in Nombre de Dios be inspected to ensure that no Englishman attempted to sneak on board one of the ships. Additionally, Criado de Castilla reported that some of the slaves taken from the Pearl Islands had been recovered and were returned to their owners. The "barbarous" *indios* taken by Frías Trejo were sent to Indigenous towns to be "disciplined" and instructed in the Catholic faith.

Until now experience in conquering the *negros* has shown how fruitless waging war on them is unless it is by attempting to settle pueblos among them. Therefore, extirpating them it would require a great amount of time and infinite funds from your royal treasury. This might be avoided for now by the introduction of the galleys that have been requested of Your Majesty, impeding their passage and preventing another union with the *negros*. On their own, they pose no threat, even those that allied with the English, because they inhabit the *montes* of the Bayano content in their nakedness and difficult life, only desiring the solitude of the bush and the good climate of the land, lacking any desire to conquer or anything else. This province has never received on their account alone any damages, nor is there any reason to expect such so long as they do not ally with corsairs.

---

1. Maroons recognized that the Spanish would use their fields and stores for their own supply. Burning them as they fled prevented the Spanish from benefiting from them.

35. Diego de Frías Trejo to the Crown, May 15, 1578
Source: AGI, Panama 41, N. 49.

After seven months of campaigning, Diego de Frías Trejo brought his campaign to a close in April 1578. This final letter, written after returning to the city of Panama, informs the king of his successes and offers his assessment of future dangers. He concurred with Criado de Castilla that while some maroons remained, they no longer presented a danger to the Spanish, nor would they dare to ally with foreigners.

. . .

What has since happened that needs to be reported to Your Majesty is that while I awaited the dispatches of the viceroy I decided to investigate the land toward Old Bayano, which is where Pedro de Ursúa encountered *negros* when he began his campaign. I suspected and conjectured that some may have returned to settle there. I left with forty men, the rest being very sore, sick, and exhausted could not be taken. I proceeded with my accustomed silence, scouring the land in those parts. I arrived where Pedro de Ursúa had been and continued on. Eventually, I encountered a sentinel that the *negros* had sent out. He sensed us and fled with great haste to give word to the pueblo, that they had begun to build when my campaign began. It was well hidden and concealed in a place they believed could not be found or discovered. We went in pursuit of the sentinel with all possible speed. He arrived at the pueblo shouting warnings that they should flee. Even though we arrived almost at the same time, we could not see any other *negro* within a harquebus shot because we later learned that other sentinels had perceived us the day before and warned the pueblo. They left and hid the *negras*, the rabble [children], and some *negros*. Only the most agile remained prepared to flee should we discover the pueblo.

Ours followed them as best as possible through the mountains but could not find a trace except that of [a *negro*] stolen by the English from a resident of Panama.[1] He surrendered to us later and told us that these *negros* had been gathering there bit by bit, believing that they were safe and well hidden in the pueblo they were building. Now they would flee very far and not return to gather or construct the town for many months, according to what he understood from them. Of the English that remain at large, nothing more is known except that they fled from us toward the north sea and the Río de Bayano, which is where I found their trail. It is believed they are dead because they had no food and nothing more than an axe. In such short time they could not use it to build a canoe or raft with which to escape.

Among the *negros* there are great disputes and disagreements, complaints against Antón Mandinga who aided and guided the English.[2] They are determined to kill him and say that because of him the ills and damage have befallen them. The *negros* I have captured say the same as did the one who surrendered. Antón Mandinga had to have known of this because after I discovered his pueblo, destroyed it and burned it, [and] captured his women and children, he became so dismayed that he has not been heard of nor has he attempted to rejoin the rest of the *negros*.

The pueblo was burned like the others. All their lodgings and stores were destroyed so that none could be carried away. The fields and plantings that they had begun to cultivate were destroyed.[3] Seeing that there were no more *negros* to pursue in all the land, I returned to San Miguel and the rest of my men. Once there, nothing remained to be done in this expedition. It is not possible to settle here, nor can anyone sustain themselves here or be sufficiently supplied from outside without spending enormous sums of silver. The purser of the expedition petitions me daily that staying does nothing but spend money from the treasury of Your Majesty since we have already completed the matter of the English and have captured many *negros* and their women and children and punished the rest by harassing them, destroying their banana groves and fields, and scaring them from the land.

I wrote to the Royal Audiencia of Panama informing them everything. They provided me with some boats in which we departed because I determined that in these mountains no more English remained, and as I say to Your Majesty the *negros* fled and hid and are so fearful that it is believed none will return to the land. Consequently, nothing more can be done in Your Majesty's service there. I transported all the men, many sick and sore from the excessive hardships we endured over nine months in the mountains. In all that time, God provided me health so that I could be present at all times in Your Majesty's service to encourage the men, which is necessary due to the terrain and task involved.

Frías Trejo returned with eighteen English captives. The magistrates of Panama executed most of them. A letter from the viceroy ordered Frías Trejo to return to Peru with the leaders. The expedition also posted notices for slave owners to claim the maroons they had captured.

I believe what has been done to the English will be a lesson so that none return to attempt a similar endeavor nor will the *negros* dare to aid or guide them, without such aid I believe it impossible to pass to the [south sea]. It is shocking to see the rough route the English used.

With this goes a description of this mountain range of the Bayano if Your Majesty be pleased to see it, Chalona, the pilot, made it in my presence. It is very accurate.[4]

---

1. One of the slaves stolen from the Pearl Islands.
2. The term "Mandinga" represented an umbrella category that likely incorporated Africans from various groups from the interior of Upper Guinea. During the sixteenth century, a federation of Mande-speaking states known as Kaabu expanded toward neighboring states along the coastal littoral. Mandinga maroons may have been enslaved in Kaabu, for debt or through other judicial measures, or they may have been taken by neighboring groups resisting Mande expansion, such as the Biafada. Wheat, *Atlantic Africa and the Spanish Caribbean*, 34–37; Green, *Rise of the Trans-Atlantic Slave Trade*, 46–52, 201, 242–45.
3. Frías Trejo is unclear as to who did the burning. The maroons probably burned the site to prevent the Spanish from using it or its supplies.
4. The "description" appears to have been separated from the letter. It is unclear if it took the form of a hand drawn map or a narrative description.

Part IV
The Second Bayano War:
Tenuous Negotiations (1579–1582)

36. Royal Cedula Ordering War with *Negros Cimarrones*, May 25, 1578

Source: AGI, Panama 234, R. 6, fs. 345v–47.

Although by May 1578 Alonso Criado de Castilla believed the threat of the *cimarrones* to be minimal, the king and his ministers would not receive his letters for some time. As Frías Trejo's campaign ended in Panama, Pedro de Ortega Valencia, having travelled back to Spain, petitioned the king to authorize continued military action. The king acceded to his requests and named Ortega Valencia *capitán general*. Ortega Valencia and his officers would spend the fall of 1578 recruiting men in Spain for his new campaign. This order, one of the several issued in late May on behalf of the new campaign, established penalties designed to punish free persons of color for assisting maroons.

• • •

Whereas, having understood the many damages, robberies, and deaths that the *negros cimarrones* have committed, and that they wander about the province in rebellion with corsairs against our royal service, and in order to prevent the damages and root out and castigate the *negros* and corsairs we have resolved to make war against them . . . having discussed and debated this with those of our Council of the Indies, it was agreed that we should order the following:

Firstly, we order that no person, regardless of *calidad*, dare to shelter any soldier [of the enemy] that in this war wander about, or keep them in their home or hidden on their property. . . . [1]

Similarly, we order that no *español*, [neither] *mulato* nor *mestizo*, *negro* nor *zambaigo*, be without an employer in the province of Tierra Firme, nor shall any person dare to give food to such persons. . . .

Item, that no free *negro*, *mestizo*, *mulato*, or *zambaigo* carry harquebuses or crossbows, swords, or daggers unless they are serving in the war.

Item, we order that no *español*, free *negro*, or any other person of any *calidad*, shall shelter any *negro* or *negra* who has been in the bush [i.e., has been a *cimarrón*] or who has fled from the fear of war. He that does shall incur a

fine of 100 pesos, for the first violation . . . for the second violation the penalty is doubled, and for the third violation they shall be exiled from the
Indies. And those *negros* and *negras* that are found shall be remitted to our
capitán general . . . so that they may be prosecuted for any crimes they have
committed. . . .

All of the above, we order be kept and fulfilled so that the contrary does not
come to pass. . . . In order that the aforementioned is well known and no
one can feign ignorance this our royal cedula shall be announced publicly
in the cities and pueblos of the province of Tierra Firme. . . . Ordered in San
Lorenzo el Real, on the twenty-eighth of May, 1578.

---

1. The term *calidad* (quality) referred to status along various modes of difference. It
   could distinguish racial differences. *Españoles* had greater *calidad* than *indios*, but
   the term could also map onto socio-economic difference. A wealthy merchant who
   could use the title *don* had greater *calidad* than a simple farmer.

37. Deposition of Antón *Criollo*, June 24, 1578
Source: AGI, Patronato 234, R. 6, fs. 376v–80.

Between May 1578 and January 1579, the Spanish war effort entered a lull. No major
Spanish campaigns went out against the maroons or English. Nevertheless,
maroons did not cease their periodic raids for supplies or new members. In early
June, maroons killed a Spanish traveler on the way from Nombre de Dios to Panama City and raided Nombre de Dios, capturing at least one enslaved woman.[1]
Later, on June 24, the *alcade mayor* and *capitán general* of Nombre de Dios interviewed an African slave who had been recently captured by maroons. This testimony offers a brief glimpse into a firsthand encounter with maroons by an enslaved
African who chose to return to the Spanish.

•   •   •

The *alcalde mayor* ordered that a *negro*, who said his name was Antón *criollo*
from São Tomé,[2] slave of Pedro Juan de Ribera, to appear before him. The
following questions were asked of him. . . .

Asked, when did you come to this pueblo and from where? He said that just
now not quite being eight o'clock in the morning, more or less, he arrived
in this pueblo. He came from among the *cimarrones* where he has been for
fifteen days more or less.

Asked, who took you to the *cimarrones* and what places have you been during the aforementioned time? He said that while traveling from this city to that of Panama leading a horse owned by Pedro Juan de Ribera, his master, two *negros cimarrones* came upon him near the Treasurer's Gully, about one league from Panama.[3] They threatened him with their bows and arrows, calling out to him and saying that he should go with them. He responded that he had a good master and did not wish to go with them. With that they took him, tied up, traveling through the bush. He was tied up with another two *negros* who had been captured. He does not know whose they were. Passing [illegible], another man, whom this witness did not know, came travelling on horseback toward Panama. Seeing the two *negros*, he galloped past them. Later the two said that if they were followed, they could easily be taken. As they walked, the *negros* whistled and another two *negros cimarrones* came out, this was about half a league from the Treasurer's Gully. Altogether, the four *negros cimarrones* walked to the Rio de la Puente where they joined more, sixteen *negros cimarrones* with bows and arrows who were keeping watch in the countryside ready to rob someone.[4] They travelled into the bush until they reached the Río Pequeni and from the Río Pequeni to the headwaters of the Río del Factor, where there were twelve more *negros* camped and situated with their bows and arrows.[5] According to what they said, they were watching who arrived in this city of Nombre de Dios. From the headwaters of the river they walked until they arrived at the pueblo of Pedro de Ursúa, which is where they have settled and wish to greatly expand.[6] This witness stayed there four days.

Asked, what *negros* were in this pueblo and who was their captain? He said that there were many *negros* and that the company holds Andrés, a *criollo* from Santo Domingo, as their captain.

Asked, if there were any English or French among the *negros* and what had he learned or gathered from the *negros*? He said that what happened was that one morning, about seven days before, he saw two English came to the pueblo, one tall and skinny, the other rotund. This witness heard that the tall one was the English captain. The two took a long narrow canoe that the *negros* gave them. They put two small bronze cannons and four muskets and a barrel of powder into it. This witness heard the English tell the *negros* that they went to find their companions and to capture a ship. He heard the English tell the *cimarrones* that they knew that they killed their companions and they would not miss having English in their lands.[7] The witness saw the English place [in the canoe] lots of food, lard and meat, given to them by the *negros*. They placed a sail on the canoe and left going down river the same day they arrived.

Asked, how many English boarded the canoe and who embarked with them? He said that he did not see anyone other than the two English that he already declared and two *indios* who came with them to the pueblo. The [*indios*] entered the canoe against their will, and he does not know if other English joined later. He saw them load seven pigs and lots of maize and bananas. This witness believed that they loaded so much food because they would take on more people. From what this witness saw, the canoe travelled to this city to attempt to take a ship to get back to their land.

Asked, what other people did the witness see in the company of these men? He said that the day the English arrived at the pueblo he saw seven [men], like *mestizos*, with their harquebuses, they appeared to be *zambaigos*.

Asked, if he heard how many the negros number? He said he heard them saying among themselves that fifty *negros* would come to this city to search for people to gather and settle the pueblo.[8]

Asked, what other camps did the witness see in the countryside before arriving at the pueblo? He said when they had him tied up while travelling, they found signs that many people had been there shortly before but the *negros cimarrones* did not know whose they could be until they followed the trail farther and came upon a camp. In the camp, harquebuses were hanging, clean and well maintained with their matches. The *negros cimarrones* said that all that we had found belonged to the people from inland.[9] The route where they found the signs is well used, and the trail led them for over six leagues.

Asked, if he learned from the *negros* if a new gathering of English, or French, had come, or if some ship had stayed in Acla, Cabeza, or another port? He said he doesn't know.

Asked, how this witness came [to this city], and how he came to escape from the *negros cimarrones*, and why did no other *negro* come with him? He said that while they were travelling, he being tied up, as they went farther and they believed he did not know the way . . . they let him go. They did not keep such a close eye on him, and he fled. He took three and a half days travelling by night and day. He came by a different path than the one they took, following the sun and beach.[10]

Asked, if following the path, he had encountered any *negros* or camps? He said that he had not. . . .

1. AGI, Patronato 234, R. 6 fs. 381–84.

2. In Spanish America, *criollo* (creole) denoted an individual of African descent born in the Americas. Eventually, it would also be applied to individuals of wholly European descent born in the Americas. López de Velasco, *Geografía y descripción universal*, 37–38; Arrom, "Criollo." However, in this case the term *criollo* indicated birth and upbringing within the Luso-African society on the island of São Tomé. Wheat, *Atlantic Africa and the Spanish Caribbean*, 125–27.

3. Quebrada del Tesorero.

4. The Río de la Puente, probably the Río Gallinero (modern Río Abajo). The bridge over this river marked the northeastern edge of Panama City. The maroons' ambush appears to have been set only yards from the Spanish city.

5. This describes a journey north paralleling the road between Nombre de Dios and Panama. The Río del Factor emptied into the bay of Nombre de Dios.

6. Over twenty years after his campaign, the maroons remembered both Ursúa and the site of his camp.

7. The use of multiple third-person verbs confuses the interpretation of this encounter. The English appear to be accusing the maroons of killing some of their number. The exchange between the English and the maroons suggests that the maroons offered the English one last bit of aid before breaking off ties.

8. Despite the danger, the hinterland of Spanish cities represented a place for disparate maroons to rendezvous before establishing settlements farther afield.

9. Given their location near to Nombre de Dios, "the people from inland" probably referred to the main maroon settlements of the Bayano, such as Ronconcholon and Catalina.

10. He likely knew he was somewhere to the east of Nombre de Dios and found his way back by following the coastline west. This conforms to Aguado's description of Pedro de Ursúa's camp.

38. Pedro de Ortega Valencia to the Crown, June 14, 1579

Source: AGI, Panama 42, N. 6. An earlier, more hopeful letter from March 20, 1579, appears in Jopling, *Indios y negros en Panamá*, 358–60; original in AGI, Patronato 234, R. 5, fs. 83–92.

The nature of the Spanish-maroon conflict changed quickly in January 1579. In that month, the fleet arrived in Nombre de Dios, bringing Pedro de Ortega Valencia and the men he had recruited in Spain. The audiencia began the preparations for the campaign authorized by the king, including plans for founding two or three settlements in the region. Using several "faithful" Africans as intermediaries, the audiencia publicized that the maroons would be welcomed in peace if they surrendered.[1] In the face of these changes, the maroons decided to entreat with the Spanish for peace. This letter from Pedro de Ortega Valencia describes the maroons' overture and the initial negotiations.

· · ·

A few days after arriving in this kingdom, two captains from the Bayano with another eight *negros*, among them principal leaders, entered into Nombre de Dios in search of me. They told me that they would await me at the Venta de Chagres, to whence I travelled despite poor health as I was very sick. On the journey there, they let it be known that they had always been friends to me. When Navarrete went out against them, they asked if he was I or my son because they would come in peace to one of us. When the captain from Peru came to go out against them, they did not attempt to hurt him because of their love for me. They did not harm people they encountered on the road from Nombre de Dios but instead helped them because of my friendship. They only ventured out to see if I had arrived.[2] They said they were the flesh and I the knife that cuts where it wishes. Their king, Domingo Congo, and all the captains of the kingdom of the Bayano, have said they want to offer the same as these.[3] I thanked them for their desires, gave them gifts, and said that by my supplication Your Majesty ordered that if they came in peace and recognized Your Majesty as their sovereign lord they would be pardoned of the crimes they had committed, such as the murders on the royal roads, the robberies, and the alliance with the English. I gave them a royal seal that this Royal Audiencia had given me as a token of safety.

We came to this city [of Panama] and they offered the same, first on their behalf and then for the rest. The audiencia gifted them and gave them clothes, and ordered that I go with them alone. I wish to God that it had been so. Later it was decided to send some men, up to thirty persons. I arrived at the Real de San Miguel, where I was to meet the primary captain, who in our tongue is called Antón Mandinga. After several days, he arrived and brought the king and many captains. They gave themselves as vassals of Your Majesty. By my order, the king summoned Juan Jolofo,[4] another captain who was the one who was with the English that I captured, and brought him and other captains of the Congos and Biafaras.[5] All of them, with great signs of happiness, gave themselves as vassals of Your Majesty. Taking the royal seal that had been given as a token of safety for their pardon, in the name of Your Majesty I gave it [to them], in doing so kissing it and putting it over my head, they did the same.[6] In addition to liberty and pardon, I offered that Your Majesty would give them land on the Río de Chepo, fertile land to settle. They were also offered maize to eat for one year and to sow, tools to make their fields, [and] five hundred cows and one hundred sows, all pregnant. They would have to pay for the rest, but not up front, only once they had reaped. But this could only happen if they left these lands where they are and come among us. I infinitely hoped to bring this about by travelling over land to Chepo. Yet there was no lack of someone protesting, saying that it would be better to go by sea. I feared that they could become suspicious that by going by sea they might be taken to a different place. In the end, because of their maliciousness—if it had been planned—or because someone encouraged them, the choice was left to the Royal Audiencia to decide. They ordered me to come by sea.

With things in this state and all the *negros* very happy and content, the Royal Audiencia informed me that Captain Francisco [Drake], English corsair, had entered the south sea through the Straits of Magellan and committed many robberies. He came confident in the friendship of these *negros* in order to enter the Bayano. The one who brought me the message kept the secret, but those who accompanied him told others at the landing. As luck would have it, as soon as I knew, the king and his *negros* also knew, either from those that brought the news or because within days they know everything that happens in these cities. They acted fearful that I would attempt some deception, asking that I tell them what I had received from the messenger. To remove their suspicion, I had to tell them the truth—even though they knew it—and remind them of the benefit and mercy that they had received from Your Majesty and that they should not lose it or their souls. If they wished to try and trick the devil and hold this thieving corsair in greater friendship than the benefits and friendship they had sought from me, they would dishearten me. I would rescind their vassalage in the name of Your Majesty and hold them as my declared enemies. To this they responded with immense faith, happiness, and determination that they would die in the service of Your Majesty and mine such that I could not respond. They spoke of the evils and damage that the English had brought upon them and that I had discovered their pueblos, hidden from all the world, and killed their brothers. The captain from Peru had killed people, but for my friendship they had not done damage. Ingratiating themselves with me they said that becoming vassals of Your Majesty had brought less good to them than simply my friendship. They would die with me in the service of Your Majesty. In this way, they supposed they gave their reasons, but with great hypocrisy did they show their Christianity and holiness. In their confessions, they deceived the dean, who had come with me, and did likewise in all else.

They left to get their women and children, setting a date when they would return. This having passed, and many more, I sent a very trustworthy *negro* of mine, a great friend of the king and other *negros*, along with another free *negro* and *negro* of the *cimarrones* who had stayed with me, a leader of theirs, to see if illness had detained the king or some other cause. They have not returned, nor have I dared to make war because the Royal Audiencia ordered me to remain at the Real de San Miguel to whence the English comes. The viceroy of Peru and the president of the Royal Audiencia ordered the same. Even though he has not arrived and though I may wish to make war, I do not have the necessary men, munitions, porters. Without these one cannot attempt an expedition. . . .

I said above that I wish to God I had come alone because if it had been so they might have tricked me or detained me, as they have my *negro*, but I would not lose time in making war. Because of the delay, I deal with people in whom I have no confidence they wish peace. Some of them wish to benefit from the income offered by Your Majesty.[7] I also have little faith that enslaved *negros* won't sway [the *negros cimarrones*] away from what has been offered so as not to lose the refuge of the bush in the future. I am losing my mind over this. I keep thinking that if this evil was agreed to among them, it is not in human nature for such leaders to keep it so secret. For barbarous people, exceptionally vile, to keep it for so long, as I gave gifts to all of them and they showed such friendship, it cannot be understood. If it was treachery by one of ours, it is for God, Our Lord, and he will discover it so that it may be punished accordingly in this life, or in the next, if they do not make confession and restitution of what is owed.

General Ortega Valencia went on to lament the youth and inexperience of his captains. He also informed the king that he had not granted commissions for every military position authorized by his commission because to do so would have only cost the royal treasury more in salaries. By having fewer officers, he could run a more cost-effective campaign.

The *negros* of Portobelo have also come looking for me and say they will come here shortly.

1. AGI, Panama 13, R. 18, N. 89; and AGI, Patronato 266, N. 20.
2. These statements may be flattery but suggest that the maroons had some knowledge of or interaction with Ortega Valencia before his expedition in 1577.
3. The term "Congo" identified individuals who entered the transatlantic trade through commerce with the Kingdom of Kongo. Like other terms denoting origins in West Central Africa, "Congo" served as broad geographic catchall rather than a specific ethnolinguistic marker. Maroons bearing these ethnonyms likely began their transatlantic passage at the Portuguese entrepôt of São Tomé, having been enslaved on the mainland in wars involving the African Kingdom of Kongo and its neighbors. Wheat, *Atlantic Africa and the Spanish Caribbean*, 73–77.
4. Individuals identified as Jolofos originated in Upper Guinea. During the fifteenth century a Jolof empire had ruled over several states along the Senegambian coastline. Although the region contained various ethnic groups, the ethnonym "Jolofo" likely referred to ethnic Wolofs. Wheat, *Atlantic Africa and the Spanish Caribbean*, 30–31, 56–58. The prevalence of Jolofos in early Spanish America resulted from warfare following the breakdown of the empire as former subject groups, such as the Serer, raided the traditional Wolof heartland. Green, *Rise of the Trans-Atlantic Slave Trade*, 91–92. In 1521, enslaved Wolofs on Hispaniola led the first major rebellion of Africans in the Americas. In the decades that followed, the Crown prohibited the importation of Jolofos out of fears that similar events might transpire in other regions. The presence of Jolofos in Panama suggests a relaxing of those earlier fears. Stone, "America's First Slave Revolt," 209; Eagle, "Early Slave Trade," 144–45.
5. "Biafara" marked individuals from Biafada states in Upper Guinea. These states engaged in frequent trade with Iberian merchants, including the export of enslaved peoples. Biafada peoples maintained trade connections with both Nalu and Zape groups to the south. Wheat, *Atlantic Africa and the Spanish Caribbean*, 41–43. It is likely that many Biafara maroons had been enslaved as Mande groups raided the region during the middle decades of the sixteenth century. Green, *Rise of the Trans-Atlantic Slave Trade*, 202, 242.
6. The reverence paid to the royal seal by Ortega Valencia illustrated to the maroons his deference and fidelity to the king.
7. Ortega Valencia suggests that the soldiers and officers have no interest in peace because it would mean an end to their salaries.

39. Testimony of Rodrigo Hernández,
Dean of the Cathedral, August 30, 1580

Source: AGI, Panama 234, R. 5, fs. 95–109. A transcription
appears in Jopling, *Indios y negros en Panamá*, 360–64.

In August 1580, the audiencia moved to document the breakdown of negotiations with the Bayano maroons. To this end, they collected testimony from those
who had accompanied Ortega Valencia on his mission. One of the most detailed
accounts was provided by don Rodrigo Hernández, the dean of the cathedral of
Panama City. A resident of Panama for over twenty years, Hernández knew of
the long history of conflict against maroons and that there were two large
groups, those from Bayano and Portobelo. He opened his testimony by relating
that in January 1579 fourteen leaders from Bayano came to offer peace to the
audiencia.

•   •   •

The *negros* told this Royal Audiencia, and the vecinos of this city, that they
had been sent from the Bayano by Domingo, and the other captains of the
Bayano, to manifest and attest to His Majesty, and this Royal Audiencia,
that they wished to surrender and serve God and His Majesty. They were
tired of living in the bush. They saw clearly that the devil had bound them.
This witness heard these formal words spoken multiple times in this city
and the Bayano.

Believing this a good proposition, the judges of the Royal Audiencia
ordered Pedro de Ortega, who His Majesty had sent as general in the conquest of these *negros*, and this witness, because he has resided in this kingdom long and is dean of this holy church, a person that the *negros* hold in
some respect and devotion because in this city he has always interceded on
their behalf so that their owners don't mistreat or punish them, to accompany the fourteen to the Real de San Miguel, a site suitable for the [others]
to come. According to what had been promised, King Domingo and the
other captains would come there and come to an agreement over the peace.

So this witness went with General Pedro de Ortega to the Real de San
Miguel and the *negros*. After they arrived, Pedro de Ortega, with the agree-
ment of the fourteen *negros*, dispatched one of them named Captain Antón
Mandinga, a brave man of sound understanding, to send word to King
Domingo, who the *negros* said was in a pueblo named Ronconcholon, eigh-

teen leagues from the camp, informing him that Pedro de Ortega together with the *negro* captains and this witness awaited him. After telling this to Domingo, he was to go to the other pueblos of the Bayano in which reside many *negro* captains in their pueblos with their soldiers and families.

After some time, a messenger came from King Domingo along with a number of *negro* soldiers with their bows, arrows, lances, and machetes. They said that Antón Mandinga had told the leader Domingo of what had transpired. Afterward, Domingo ordered that he go to all of the Bayano and inform all the pueblos, the captains and soldiers, and the other people, to come to the Real de San Miguel to await the rest. The ambassador said that King Domingo would come later. He also related to Pedro Ortega, this witness, and all those present, that King Domingo was very content knowing that the fourteen captains and leaders he had sent to this city to negotiate surrender and peace had done so. A few days after this, Domingo arrived at the Real de San Miguel with many people and well-equipped soldiers. A messenger came before him to bring word that he was coming. This witness and the rest saw that he spoke truth because they saw a great quantity of *negros* coming from a long way off, one in front of the next, well-formed, and understood that King Domingo was coming. Like this, Domingo and the rest arrived at the camp. Pedro de Ortega, this witness, and the rest came out a good stone's throw to receive Domingo and those with whom he travelled. Recognizing Pedro de Ortega, Domingo bowed his head. Pedro Ortega made a sign indicating that this witness was of the Church and had come to do well for him and that he should be treated well. After he said this, Pedro de Ortega embraced [Domingo], lifting him off the ground with much love. This witness did the same. Placing [Domingo] between them, they escorted him into the camp and sat down with Pedro de Ortega and this witness on each side, [and] the other leaders that came with him sat when he commanded.

After a few moments, Domingo rose and removed the hat he wore, saying sweet words explaining that he was very happy to see this fine day come to pass and that for a long time he had desired to return to the service of God and His Majesty. He implored that by the love of God could he be absolved before going further because he knew that he had been excommunicated from the flock of God and his king. After this, what he wished was done for him and his captains. This witness stood along with the rest, and taking Domingo between him and Pedro de Ortega they went to the chapel, where Domingo knelt down. This witness absolved him of the excommunication that he had incurred for having left the flock of the Holy Catholic Church, for having committed evils in the bush, according to what he explained with apparent anguish, and for having received and promised to aid the thieving Lutheran English who had arrived. This witness absolved him, after which Domingo blessed himself with holy water and still kneeling stayed for a long while with hands set [in prayer] and his eyes fixed on a cross set upon an altar. This witness requested that he pray something to see if he knew the prayers.[1] He said these very well.[2] He then stood, crossed himself, and said to this witness, for the love of God may all his captains and people enjoy from the same benefit, and so it was done. They knelt down and this witness absolved them of the same censures. Before absolving them, Domingo and the rest held hands with this witness and promised to be subject and obedient to the Catholic Church and to do what is asked of them. With this commandment, they were all absolved.

Everyone returned to the place where they had previously been, the general's hut. At his command they sat again, and Pedro de Ortega received them on behalf of the Royal Audiencia and noted that His Majesty was well served and would be pleased with their surrender. Domingo, who always spoke very little, made known his great pleasure in what had been said and responded with very pleasing and reasonable words. He was always understood to be a man of good understanding. Later, Pedro de Ortega asked for a chest, opened it, and removed a wax seal from this Royal Audiencia bearing the royal arms. Taking it in his hands, Pedro de Ortega knelt down, kissed it, and placed it above his head. This witness, who was kneeling with the rest, took the seal, kissed it, and placed it above his head. Afterward, King Domingo, likewise kneeling, took the seal, removed his hat and placed it on the floor, kissed the seal, hugged it, and placed it above his head. Then he told all his captains and soldiers to do the same as he had done. With this ceremony completed, Pedro de Ortega told Domingo that the seal was of His Majesty and had been given by the Royal Audiencia to be given to them. It was brought as a sign of safety for him and his people so that what is discussed will be firm and valid and that he should take the seal so that what the judges ordered can be effected. King Domingo clasped hands with Pedro de Ortega, showing his understanding of the seal's significance. Wrapping it in a piece of silk, Domingo placed it on his chest and said that by the love of God [might] they rest for a bit as they had

arrived very tired. Pedro de Ortega, this witness, and the rest led Domingo
to a well-appointed hut nearby where he stayed resting for a bit.

Later, Pedro de Ortega ordered that food be brought for [Domingo] and
all the rest. Very late, as the sun set, Domingo left the hut with his people
and sat in the doorway. He turned to one of his subordinates, the one who
had first come as ambassador, and said that he would like permission for
his people to celebrate. Pedro de Ortega replied that Domingo should order
it so, for he too wished it. Afterward, all the soldiers and leaders gathered to
one side, and the ambassador went out in a little plaza in sight of the camp's
huts. Standing before Domingo holding a large blade mounted on a lance
he freely performed many acts of war and using a bow fired many arrows at
a lance placed in sight of Pedro de Ortega and this witness. Having done
this, he went to King Domingo, knelt, and the king made a certain sign. He
stood and returned to where Pedro de Ortega and this witness sat. He knelt
with all his weapons in his hands and then returned to the side of King
Domingo. Another *negro*, called *alguacil mayor*, a leader among them, came
to the ambassador, knelt down, and using an *alfanje*[3] hanging from his belt
made a sign three or four times that he wanted to cut off a head. With this
the game ended. This witness asked the *negro* captains what this meant.
One of them replied that the king wanted it known that anyone who made
war on the *españoles* would have his head cut off. Consequently, through
these games and signs, this witness came to understand clearly that the
peace was firm and true.

From that day forward, this witness taught them doctrine in the morning and afternoon. It seemed to this witness that the *negros* came to the
chapel of the camp with great willingness and love. At other times of day,
many of them came to this witness's quarters and knelt down pleading to
be taught doctrine.[4] Because it was Lent, this witness enjoined those who
attended mass to confess, for it was time.[5] From that day forward, many
negros cimarrones made Christian signs, coming to confess with this witness. They showed signs of great sadness for the time that they had been
without doctrine and confession. Some of these did so with many tears.

After several days, more maroon leaders arrived at the fort. Domingo instructed each
leader to kiss the royal seal and place it above their heads as the others had done.

From that day, many times it has been discussed whether they should go
via the Río de Chepo or by sea. One of the *negros* who discussed this favored

going by land and others by sea to a certain place that the Royal Audiencia
had designated for them to settle. This was along the Río de Chepo near the
passes, eight leagues from this city, a wide and spacious place, pleasant and
fruitful for the *negros* and their fields. From there they can travel the Río de
Chepo with their boats and canoes to this city of Panama to trade. They can
[reach there] easily by sea. They agreed with their king, Domingo, that they
should travel by sea to the site. If they could not all make it in one trip they
should make two or three, because travelling by land was very difficult for
children and old men as well as pregnant and nursing women and old
women. With this decision made, Domingo asked that a ship be sent to
Panama for boats to carry the women. He repeatedly pleaded with Pedro de
Ortega not to send soldiers [with the women] so they would not be mis-
treated, sending only this witness as their priest. Later, an order was given
that the captains, leaders, and Domingo send for their families from their
pueblos, bringing all the men, women, and rabble, who they say are a large
number. All agreed that Antón Mandinga should be the messenger to the
pueblos, one of the first fourteen *negros* to come to this city, a man respected
and obeyed by all *negros*.

With this completed, other soldiers would go out pueblo by pueblo. It
was promised that all the Bayano would return within a month. At the
time he went out, this witness confessed him because he asked. After he
left, all the captains stopped [to do the same]. [This witness] said that
doing so wasted much time, of which there was none. Each one wished to
collect their people. The king said he wished to go in person, and so it was
agreed. Before each set out on their journey they confessed with this
witness because they had asked many times with signs of contrition, devotion, some of them crying, others mortifying themselves in hidden places.
This witness knows this because he wandered among them very carefully,
visiting with them and watching them by night and day. This witness
found some kneeling in the chapel crying and hitting themselves across
the chest.[6] With this the *negro* captains left with some of their soldiers to
go to their pueblos. Within four or six days, all those going had left, this
was six or eight *negro* captains. King Domingo Congo stayed with the general and this witness in the camp, intending to send for his people during
this time.

Before the six or eight captains left the camp for their pueblos, Captain
Antonio de Salcedo arrived with warnings from the Royal Audiencia for

Pedro de Ortega. Later word spread in the camp that Captain Francisco [Drake] wandered in the south sea. Seeing that the news had spread, Pedro de Ortega called a meeting with this witness, Domingo, and the *negro* captains in his hut, being the most secure place in the camp. He related to them the news that Antonio Salcedo had brought. In communicating and discussing they showed great excitement, and Domingo and the captains wished to use all of their forces to help [defend] against the English, especially a captain named Antón Tigre who wished to go to his pueblo and befriend Captain Francisco, to warn his people, for he is very able, and give orders to his people that if [Francis Drake] goes there intending to enter the land they should befriend him, giving gifts and embracing, having each of his soldiers embrace him and each of his men. He hoped that God allowed only his men to kill and destroy [the English].[7] They were thanked for their support, and it was quickly determined that all should go for their people and return to the fort on the appointed day, which was very soon. King Domingo offered many times to stay with Pedro de Ortega and only send for his people and household. Pedro de Ortega did not allow it, wanting [Domingo] to go in good time, so he went with his captains within four or six days. All of them went to their pueblo, intending to return shortly with all their people.

One night, before King Domingo left, he told Pedro de Ortega, publicly and in the presence of everyone in the fort, that he did not want to go but instead stay and die for his king in his service. He said this many times, insisting he wished to stay. Pedro de Ortega told him to go with God and to come back as planned. When King Domingo went, no other *negros cimarrones* remained other than a Juan Lucumí and another *negro* who said he was Lucumí's godson, but he later left.[8] With this, Pedro de Ortega, this witness, and the rest waited many days for the return of Domingo and the others, including Antón Mandinga. It appeared to this witness that King Domingo should have stayed in the fort as he wished while the other captains and *negros* of the Bayano returned to the fort during the appointed time, because all of them, especially the captains and leaders, demonstrated great love and obedience to King Domingo. He treated them with much love and friendship, and they obeyed him, which this witness understood from some of them.

Unfortunately for the peace, the maroons did not return. Hernández described several attempts to send messengers, including Ortega Valencia's trusted slave

Baltasar. Hernández offered to go entreat with Domingo, but Ortega Valencia refused. As the Spanish grew frustrated, several young captains also offered to go in search of the maroons, but Ortega Valencia likewise denied their request. Shortly after, Hernández left the camp after becoming ill.

1. The standard prayers of the faithful included the Lord's Prayer, the Apostles' Creed, the Hail Mary, and the Gloria.
2. This is glowing praise. Not all Spaniards could say these prayers well.
3. A type of cutlass typical of Mozarabic Spain.
4. At the end of the document, the notary certified that when Rodrigo Hernández related confessing and preaching to the *negros*, he "spoke through tears, weeping because such a good work had been lost after only just beginning."
5. In the early modern period, most lay Catholics confessed once a year during Lent.
6. During various Catholic prayers, including the Mass, this motion was a sign of penitence.
7. Tigre proposed to double-cross the English.
8. The term "Lucumí" pertained to the Yoruba-speaking region of Lower Guinea. During the sixteenth century, Lucumí captives likely originated in the Kingdom of Benin and entered the transatlantic trade via Portuguese entrepôts in São Tomé and São Jorge da Mina (Gold Coast). Law, "Ethnicity and the Slave Trade."; Lovejoy and Ojo, "Origins of the Yoruba Nation."

40. *Negros* of Portobelo Approach the Audiencia, March 11, 1579

Source: AGI, Patronato 234, R. 3, fs. 70. Also AGI,
Panama 42, N. 35, fs. 1102.

While Pedro de Ortega worked to secure the surrender of the maroons of the Bayano, the audiencia sent word to other maroon groups that they would be welcomed in peace. Even as the negotiations at the Real de San Miguel began to stall, the maroons of Portobelo ventured to Panama City in the hopes of securing their own pardon and peace.

•   •   •

In the city of Panama, on the eleventh day of March, 1579, around midday more or less, a *negro* who called himself Antón Biafara, a young man who was between a *boçal* and a *ladino*[1] but who talked in such manner as to be well understood, carrying a bow with three iron-tipped arrows and dressed in a cotton shirt in the manner of a *cimarrón*, appeared before the illustrious *señor* Dr. Alonso Criado de Castilla, most senior *oidor* that presides in this Royal Audiencia of Panama, . . . accompanied by a *negro ladino* that called himself Antón Bañol,[2] a slave of Francisco Pacho, a citizen of this city. [Antón Biafara] said that the *señor* doctor had sent him to encourage the *negros cimarrones* of Portobelo, the [*cimarrones*] that have caused the most damage [to this land],[3] to come in peace and meet with the *señor* doctor at a place of their choosing. Having given them the message, his *capitán mayor*, named Antón Moçanga Congo,[4] sent him to return [with this message]: The *señor* doctor is the knife and they the flesh that can be cut at will, and if [the doctor] wishes, he might kill him to demonstrate that he represents the king. They [the *cimarrones*] do not wish to go to Nombre de Dios, nor [to] have any other person come to them. He comes in the name of the *capitán mayor* and of all the other *negros* that reside with him at Portobelo [to say that] should the *señor oidor* come to see them [in Portobelo] they would come in peace and serve the king as Christians, but if it is not the *señor oidor* they will not come with anyone else. As such, I came to ask that the *señor oidor* come to the bush; afterwards the *capitán mayor* and *negros cimarrones* will come to meet with him and accept the peace. The *señor oidor*, having seen [Antón Biafara] and heard what he said, stated that an account be made of what was presented so that which is most appropriate for the service of His Majesty can be resolved. . . .

1. Spaniards differentiated between Africans who had acculturated to Spanish language and customs, *ladinos*, and those who had not, *boçales*.
2. The term "Bañol" identified individuals from Bañon states in Upper Guinea. Judicial enslavement and conflicts with neighboring groups including the Mande-controlled state of Casa, the Floups, and the Brames drove captive Bañons into the transatlantic trade. Wheat, *Atlantic Africa and the Spanish Caribbean*, 38–40.
3. These maroons had aided both Drake and Oxenham. Their settlement's location on the Atlantic Coast near Nombre de Dios made them an ideal ally for pirates.
4. Like "Congo," "Moçanga" (and "Maçanga") indicated West Central African origins associated with trade in slaves originating in the Kingdom of Kongo and its vassals. Wheat, *Atlantic Africa and the Spanish Caribbean*, 73–77.

41. Act Relating to the *Negros* of the Cerro de Cabra, April 27, 1579
Source: AGI, Patronato 234, R. 6, fs. 322.

As the possibility of a negotiated settlement became more likely, the audiencia worked to inspire trust in the maroons, even when that meant preventing Spanish slave owners from hunting down runaway slaves.

• • •

In the city of Panama, on the twenty-seventh day of April, 1579, the *señores*, *presidente* and *oidores* of the Royal Audiencia and Chancellery of His Majesty, that there reside, stated that some *negros cimarrones* have their settlements on the Cerro de Cabra, near this city. Through messengers sent to this Royal Audiencia, we have reason to hope that these [*negros*] and others nearby with whom they have dealings will come to make peace. Recently, [the audiencia] has received word that Gonzalo Peçero, a *vecino* of this city, has gone against the *negros*, saying that a *negro* of his is among their company, taking with him manacles so that finding [the enslaved man] he might bind him. At the moment there is a promise of safety that has been given to the *negros* so that they might come in peace and be returned to the service of His Majesty, and it is understood that they are currently appeased, if Gonzalo Peçero arrives to achieve his goal it might be cause for the *negros* to revolt and cause a scandal should they believe he was attempting to capture them. To avoid this, and to resolve that which [is] most appropriate for the service of His Majesty, [the *presidente* and *oidores*] order that an *alguazil* be named and sent to where Gonzalo Peçero is believed to be in order to arrest him and bring him to this court. So it was resolved, ordered, and signed. And if [Gonzalo Peçero] has taken any *negro*, [the *negro*] is to be freed and the *alguazil* is to allow him to go wherever he should wish.

42. Arrival of *Negros* from the Cerro de Cabra to Surrender to Royal Authority, May 2, 1579

Source: AGI, Panama, 42, N. 35, fs. 1100v–1101; AGI,
Patronato 234, R. 3, fs. 68.

The efforts of the audiencia bore fruit, despite the lingering fears of a betrayal like that of Ursúa, and the maroons of Cerro de Cabra soon began to appear, hoping to benefit from the audiencia's promise of freedom. Despite the period of war that occurred during Oxenham's incursion, the methods used to arrive at peace mirror those laid out in 1574 and 1575 (see documents 21 and 22).

• • •

In the city of Panama, on the second of May, 1579, before the illustrious *señor* Dr. Alonso Criado de Castilla, *señor oidor* in this Royal Audiencia of Panama, around midday there appeared Pedro de Tapia, *español*, foreman of the estates of the *señor oidor*, located on the Cerro de Cabra near this city, with four *negros* and one *negra cimarrones*.[1] They carried bows, arrows, and spears in the manner that *negros cimarrones* are accustomed. They said that they were called Francisco Berbesi,[2] the capitan of the group, Hernando Bran,[3] Pedro Congo, Antón Congo, and María Biafara, the wife of Francisco Berbesi. Pedro de Tapia said that the *señor oidor* had ordered him to negotiate with the *negros cimarrones* that move about in rebellion on Cerro de Cabra so that they might come in peace and surrender to the service of His Majesty, be pardoned of their crimes, and [be] given their liberty. Having done what the *señor oidor* ordered, the [*negros*] understood what was being offered and said that they wanted to come in peace to talk with the *señor oidor* in order to enjoy the mercy that His Majesty offers. Having come with [Pedro de Tapia] . . . , the *negros* knelt and said that they came in peace and the *señor oidor* ordered that I, the secretary, attest to what they had done so that being made known to the *señores*, *presidente* and *oidores* of the Royal Audiencia they might determine that which is just, so it was resolved and ordered. . . .

---

1. To secure peace, Criado de Castilla sent his own employee to seek out the maroons. During this same time, the *oidor*'s brother Manuel Criado de Castilla helped with the preliminary entreaties to the maroons of Portobelo.

2. The term "Berbesi" derived from the Wolof title "*Bur ba Siin*" meaning "ruler of Siin," Siin being a constituent state of the Jolof empire in Upper Guinea. Individuals identified as Berbesi were likely members of the Serer ethnic group from Senegambia. Wheat, *Atlantic Africa and the Spanish Caribbean*, 31–34, 56–57. Ongoing Wolof-Serer warfare during the mid-sixteenth century fueled the trade in Serer slaves to Portuguese merchants in Cabo Verde. Green, *Rise of the Trans-Atlantic Slave Trade*, 205–7.

3. "Bran" referred to individuals from Brame people of Upper Guinea. From their central location in the region, Brames played a key role as traders linking Biafada networks in the south to Bañun networks to the north. Captives exported by the Brame could include persons sentenced to captivity through judicial enslavement, captives traded from neighboring Floup and Balanta groups, or those captured in Brame raids on the Biafada, Nalu, and Balanta. More Brame captives arrived in Spanish America during the late sixteenth and early seventeenth centuries than from any other region in Upper Guinea. Wheat, *Atlantic Africa and the Spanish Caribbean*, 44–48.

43. Concession of Liberty to Certain *Negros* and *Negras* from Cerro de Cabra, May 16, 1579

Source: AGI, Patronato 234, R. 6, fs. 323.

By conceding freedom to the relatively small band of maroons from Cerro de Cabra, the audiencia likely hoped that word of the trustworthiness would spread to other, larger communities like those of the Bayano and Portobelo.

• • •

In the city of Panama, on the sixteenth day of May, 1579, the *señores, presidente* and *oidores* of the Royal Audiencia and Chancellery of His Majesty that there resides, stated that, by virtue of a royal cedula, *negros cimarrones* who wander the *montes* of this kingdom in rebellion who come in peace to this Royal Audiencia can be pardoned for the crimes they have committed and granted freedom from captivity and subjugation, as is stipulated at length in the royal cedula. . . . Francisco Berbesi, slave formerly of Juan Pérez Castaño, Antón Congo, slave who said he had been of Juan Gómez, and María Biafara, slave who said she had been of Francisco Gómez, have been *cimarrones* in the bush for over eight years. In order to receive the favor [promised by the cedula] they have come and presented themselves in peace in this Royal Audiencia. They have asked that they be granted their liberty and freedom in the name of His Majesty by virtue of his royal cedula. [The *presidente* and *oidores*] declare that each one is now free of all captivity and servitude, removing any right that a person may have toward them who claims that they were once their slave, and granting them the right, as free persons, to travel to all parts and places that they would wish, to engage in trade and commerce, to make their wills and testaments, and to do all other judicial and extrajudicial acts that free persons may. [The *presidente* and *oidores*] order that all magistrates and judges of His Majesty in the district of this audiencia protect and defend their liberty and not allow their liberty to be disturbed or removed at any time by any means, nor shall any one of [the *negros*] be tried for any crime that they have committed before today by virtue of the pardon that was granted by the royal cedula of His Majesty. They shall receive proof of this act. So it was resolved, ordered, and signed.

44. Arrival of Don Luis Maçanbique in Panama City, June 19, 1579

Source: AGI, Patronato 234, R. 6, fs. 288v–90.

The audiencia's strategy succeeded, and, shortly after the maroons of Cerra de Cabra surrendered, those from Portobelo appeared before the audiencia asking for a similar peace agreement. This document preserves don Luis Maçanbique's written request to be pardoned and recognized as a vassal of the king.

• • •

Very Illustrious Lord

I, Luis, king of the soldiers of Portobelo, in fulfillment of the vow that I made on behalf of my soldiers before your lordship, present myself to your lordship with all of the soldiers who accompanied me under the promise that was given by your lordship in the name of the King, don Philip, Our Lord, that if we came in peace to obey the mandate of His Majesty, you would grant us our liberty, for me and for all my soldiers. That being accepted, I present myself before your lordship so that you may tell us where we might serve His Majesty, and reside together, wherever your lordship orders we will go. This written on paper so that your lordship understands that I want to serve His Majesty, may he live many years, and your lordship as you have given us a life more prosperous than it currently is. Your humble servant.

In the city of Panama on the nineteenth day of June of 1579, before the very illustrious Lord, Lic. Juan de Zepeda, of the council of His Majesty, *presidente* of the Royal Audiencia of His Majesty that in this city resides, a *negro* named don Luis Maçanbique presented this letter and petition.[1] Andrés Sánchez, a soldier, attested to the letter and petition and having been read before his lordship, the *presidente* asked [don Luis] if he understood what it said. [Don Luis] responded that he did understand. He then presented a royal seal, impressed in red wax on white paper, which this Royal Audiencia had given him as a sign of peace and safety for his person and for those of the subject soldiers that travelled with him and for those who still remain in the bush in their settlements. His lordship received the seal in his hands, kissed it, and placed it above his head saying that he obeyed that which it represented with all due reverence. [The *presidente*] said that he was ready to complete his vow of peace and to stipulate what must be done for the service of His Majesty, and for the good and tranquility of [don Luis] and the people in his company. In the meantime, [the *presidente*] ordered that the royal *alguacil* disarm them and escort them to the house of the *alcaldes ordinarios* of this city to rest. So it was resolved, ordered, and enacted.

---

1. The ethnonym "Maçanbique" indicates an East African origin near modern-day Mozambique. Although most Africans transported to the Americas originated in Atlantic Africa, Portuguese trade routes in East Africa and the Indian Ocean funneled enslaved people from East Africa into the Atlantic from the sixteenth century onward.

45. Rendition of Don Luis Maçanbique and the *Cimarrones* of Puertobelo, June 30, 1579

Source: AGI, Panama 42, N. 35, fs. 1093–94. Transcribed in Jopling, *Indios y negros en Panamá*, 372–74.

The process of negotiation involved many steps. Just as with those from the Cerro de Cabra, after submitting to royal authority the maroons of Portobelo needed to be formally pardoned of their crimes and received as vassals of the king.

• • •

In the city of Panama, in the Kingdom of Tierra Firme, on the thirtieth day of June of 1579, before the *señores*, *presidente* and *oidores* of the Audiencia and Chancellery of His Majesty . . . there appeared a *moreno*[1] who called himself don Luis Maçanbique, who has been and currently is the leader and the principal caudillo of the rebellious *negros* in the bush and settlements of Puertobelo. . . . [He] stated that it had come to his attention, and that of his *maestre de campo*, captains, officers of war, and other *negros* and *negras* subject to him, that His Majesty by his royal cedula mandated that all *negros cimarrones* who come in peace will be made free from slavery. [Don Luis] came with some of his people so that, in his name and on their behalf, they be made subject to the service of God, Our Lord, and His Majesty, that they might enjoy the mercy, liberty, and pardon for their crimes that have been offered. To that effect, he asks and petitions that the *señores* receive his surrender so that from today forward they will be held as loyal vassals of His Majesty and to that effect in his name, and especially and particularly in the name of all his subjects, men and women, [all] those subjugated from diverse nations, and those that have been born and raised among them, he offers [their surrender] in the following manner:[2]

I, don Luis Maçanbique, of my own spontaneous volition offer, promise, and obligate myself and all those that are present or absent, in each of their names, offering to hold ourselves to perpetual obedient subjugation with total fidelity to the Catholic Majesty of the King, don Philip, Our Lord, and his Royal Crown, his justices and minsters. In his royal name [and] as his loyal and good vassals we obey his royal orders until death. We will leave to populate whatever site [is designated] whenever we receive the order with the hope that we will be maintained in justice with security. We place ourselves before your royal dignity and liberty asking and supplicating pardon for those crimes which we have until now committed. We [ask] that you grant us the freedom of our persons, wives, and children, which at the moment we enjoy, and that in the future, God, Our Lord, would be served by granting us [freedom]. As such we ask, supplicate, and promise that we will keep and fulfill [that which has been agreed to]. I ask all this for myself and in the name of those of us that are here present. We are the following:

- don Luis Maçanbique, principal caudillo, and doña Francisca his wife, María his servant, and another [woman] María
- Antón Congo, his captain, without wife or children
- Rodrigo, from the land of San Tomé, his *mayoral*, without wife or children
- Matheo Congo, his *mayoral*, and Francisca his wife, one son named Blas, two daughters named María and Dominga, aged from seven to twelve
- Pedro Congo, his *mayoral*, and Leonor his wife
- Diego Congo, his *mayoral*, and Ana Zape his wife, no children
- Cristóbal Zape, his *mayoral*, and Elena his wife, no children
- Sebastián Congo, his *mayoral*, and his wife Ana Jelofa, no children
- Pedro Yolongo and Isabel Zape his wife, no children
- Sebastián Congo and Leonor Terra Nova his wife, no children
- Gaspar Calanga and María *criolla* his wife, no children
- Sebastián Maçanbique and Agustina his wife, no children
- Pedro Maçanbique and Pasquala his wife, a son named Francisco of five years and a daughter named Polonia of a year and a half
- Francisco Zape and Elena his wife, two daughters named Dominga and Isabel, both infants
- Marcos Mandinga and Catalina Biafara his wife, no children
- Juan Congo and María Conga his wife, no children

- Juan Congo, single
- Baltasar Boiho, single
- Pedro Herinba, single
- Gaspar Bran, single
- Pedro Mandinga, single
- Baltasar Bran, single
- Alexo *criollo*, single
- Francisco from Terranova, single
- Miguel Biafara and Catalina Bran his wife, Juan his son of four-teen years
- Marcos Zape, single
- Juan Biafara, single
- Francisco Cubo, relative of the [former] *maestre de campo*, currently serving as the *maestre de campo*, single
- Antón Biafara, from the Bayano, single

These *negros* are present [for the surrender] except for the women and children, who are absent.

The *señores, presidente* and *oidores* having seen the aforementioned stated they accept the surrender, in the name of His Majesty and by virtue of his royal cedulas and the instructions contained in his royal letters, and receive don Luis and all of his people as vassals of His Majesty . . . and given their surrender and vassalage from this point forward they are to be held as vassals of His Majesty and subjects of his royal crown, maintained in justice, and [are to] enjoy the full liberty that His Majesty has offered and mandated be given to those *negros cimarrones* that surrender to his royal service. In the name of His Majesty, [the *señores*] grant liberty and pardon, as the case requires, that [the *negros*] may be protected, defended, and maintained in justice as vassals of his Majesty. So that [the *negros*] can enjoy all of the mercies, freedoms and privileges due to vassals of His Majesty, and that they be returned to his royal service, with all necessary solemnity, they grant the necessary assurances based in the authority of the royal decree. Subsequently, they designated the site of Chilibre, located between Cruces and Venta de Chagres six or seven leagues from this city, with its rivers, pastures, and streams, so that [the *negros*] can go and settle, and once settled [the *señores*] will give ordinances for them to keep as well as *capitulaciones* within thirty days of their being settled.[3] The settlement will be made within three months, commencing today.

Within that time [the *negros*] are ordered to present all of their people and subjects without hiding a single person, men and women, with men over the age of seventeen appearing in this Royal Audiencia to be given their letters of liberty and pardon as it has been ordered by this act . . . it is so resolved, mandated and signed, being present Dr. Diego de Villanueva Zapata, Dr. Alonso Criado de Castilla, Licenciado Gonzalo Nuñez de la Cerda

Being present, don Luis and the *negros* accepted that which is contained in this act and promised to complete the settlement within the specified period of three months. . . .

1. When used as a racial label, *moreno* served as a more respectful term equivalent to *negro*.
2. In this context, "nations" referred to the various African groups with which his people identified.
3. The Spanish appear to have chosen this initial site for two reasons. First, it lay adjacent to the overland transisthmian route and could increase the security of transport and trade. Second, it would keep the maroons far from the coast where they might have been tempted to reestablish ties to foreign corsairs.

46. Treaty with Don Luis Maçanbique and Ordinances for Santiago del Príncipe, September 20, 1579

Source: AGI, Panama 46, N. 1, fs. 8–13. Transcription in Jopling, *Indios y negros en Panamá*, 375–78.

As the previous order for pardon and liberty stated, don Luis Maçanbique was required to establish a settlement within three months. Unfortunately, the site of Chilibre was not amenable. This document records the problems that arose and the designation of a new site close to Nombre de Dios. Additionally, this treaty contains the ordinances that the audiencia established to govern this new community, named Santiago del Príncipe. Importantly, while the ordinances clearly attempt to closely regulate the free-black community, they also provide ample authority to its own leaders to govern themselves.

• • •

In the city of Panama in the kingdom of Tierra Firme that is in the islands of the Ocean Sea on the twentieth day of the month of September of 1579, the *señores*, *presidente* and *oidores* of the Royal Audiencia and Chancellery of His Majesty, that there reside, state it is notorious that don Luis Maçanbique, *negro*, the leader and principal caudillo of the fugitive slaves that move about in open rebellion in this kingdom in the *montes* of Portobelo, has come to this Royal Audiencia with some of the *negros* subject to him and, in the name of all of the *negros* and *negras* and other subjects, has promised to submit to the service of Our Lord God and His Majesty and render the obedience owed to His Majesty as loyal vassals. Because they offer and have promised that from this point forward, asking for pardon for their crimes and offenses, ... they be conceded their liberty ... promising that [don Luis] will take all of the people that have remained in the bush to settle the site of Chilibre, that is between Cruzes and the Venta de Chagres, and will keep and follow the ordinances and all [else] that is mandated in the name of His Majesty by the Royal Audiencia in accordance with the act of surrender signed on the thirtieth day of the month of June, of this present year [1579] by the *señores*. In fulfillment of which don Luis Maçanbique with the afore-mentioned people taking in their company the Capitán Antonio de Salcedo, who was named by the *señores* to accompany don Luis and view all the land, settlements, bush, rivers, and ports to see where the *negros* [will] settle ... went out to that effect and [then] returned to the city of Nombre de Dios. Travelling with them [were] don Luis and don Pedro Zape, his *maestre de campo*, with their wives, children, and people.

Don Pedro Zape, *maestre de campo*, along with several *negros*, captains and soldiers, have come to the Royal Audiencia with Capitán Antonio de Salcedo to report on what they have done and how the *negros* have come to establish the settlement in fulfillment of what they have promised, as can be seen in the report that was submitted in writing that tells of all that Antonio de Salcedo did during the time that he was with [the *negros*] in their villages and settlements and which is currently before the scribe of this chamber. Because the site of Chilibre is not amenable to the health and sustenance of the *negros* as it marshy without any countryside necessary for their fields and plantings ... they ask the *señores* that they be granted a site to make their settlement near the city of Nombre de Dios and the Rio de Francisca because that site has good plains, lands, and rivers for their fields [and for their] health and growth, and will be close to the city where they can travel for trade and supplies and live in peace and concord with the veci-nos and *españoles* that reside there as the Christians that they are. They wish to demonstrate by their deeds that which they have promised, to be loyal vassals of His Majesty and of the general welfare of this kingdom.

They promise to be always faithful and to oppose the English and French corsairs, fugitive *negros*, and those that act contrary to the service of His Majesty, and that they and their descendants [will] live and die in faithful vassalage. In order to see that what they have promised is completed they ask that an *español* holding the position of *capitán general y justicia mayor* be ordered to live in their settlement with soldiers to guard and care for the lands.[1] And they ask that they be given a priest to catechize the community and administer the sacraments. [The *negros*] offer to pay for and support [these positions] for as long as the Royal Audiencia so orders. . . .

The *señores, presidente, oidores,* [and] *fiscal* met and deliberated with captains and esteemed residents of this kingdom, with whom they have conferred and discussed this issue. They are in agreement and concede the request that the settlement be established at the site [proposed by the negros] with the aforementioned promises made by the negros. To put in effect that which was agreed upon . . . in the name of his Majesty they order that don Luis Maçanbique with don Pedro Zape, his *maestre de campo,* and the captains, soldiers, people, women and children settle near the Río de Francisca in the place that has been assigned [and establish] a pueblo complete with its plaza, streets, and church. The pueblo will be named the *villa* of Santiago del Príncipe . . . which will have the qualities and prerogatives of all other cities and *villas* of *españoles* found in this kingdom. . . .[2] Don Luis Maçanbique will serve as governor of the *negros* all the days of his life, and don Pedro Zape will serve as his lieutenant.[3] There will be a priest in the villa to administer the sacraments and there will be a presidio with a complement of thirty soldiers and a *capitán general,* who will also serve as the *justicia mayor.*[4] The presidio will guard and defend the villa and its environs and will be paid for by His Majesty. Captain Antonio de Salcedo will serve as the [first] *capitán general* and *justicia mayor* at the pleasure of His Majesty and the Royal Audiencia. . . .

The audiencia set the jurisdiction of the *villa* and of its military and judicial officers to three leagues on all sides except the side closest to Nombre de Dios, where it was to only extend half a league from the villa. The audiencia further enumerated the duties and responsibilities of the *capitán general.*

[The audiencia] mandated that the following orders be observed in the foundation of the *villa* and in those things that were most convenient and necessary for the service of Our Lord God, His Majesty, the administration of justice, and the welfare, increase, conservation, public order, and cate-chism of the *negros* and other people who so populate and reside in the [*villa* and] presidio. . . .

- First, that the *villa* is to be settled at a location near the Río de Fran-cisca that Captain Antonio de Salcedo deems the best and most convenient for the health, prosperity, and preservation of the *negros* and settlers, keeping in mind that the settlement be made on high ground with good air circulation, that it be free of stands of trees, separated from marshes, so that the *villa* can benefit from good waters and good soil for planting their crops and fields and pas-tures for their livestock.
- Item, that the Audiencia insures that the pueblo is established with its plaza and church dedicated to the Virgin, Mother of God, Our Lady, and that the principal feast that is celebrated every year is that of the Feast of the Purification of the Virgin, on the second of February, and that they should name the church Our Lady of the Candelaria.[5] The *negros* should build houses of government in which will live the *capitan* and *justicia mayor*, they should build a jail, pillory, and gallows in the plaza for the execution of justice. The streets should be wide and good, the blocks and houses should be well made, and each *negro* should build a home for himself and his wife, children, and family . . . so that each *negro* has their own home and each of the them and other settlers have their own plots. Captain Antonio de Salcedo should take care that his soldiers are well garrisoned and work to keep the plaza and streets clean, and they should clear the lands around the *villa* so that it can benefit from the fresh airs.[6]
- [A priest was named to preach and catechize the residents. His sal-ary and food was to be supplied by the community.]
- Item, don Luis Maçanbique will be governor of the *negros* of the *villa*. He, and whoever serves as his successor, shall take special care that on Sundays and feast days all the *negros* and *negras*, boys and girls, go to the church to hear Mass, holy doctrine, and the Gospels. Those boys who are seven to ten years old should go to the church every day to be catechized and instructed in the service of the divine cult.[7] There should be an *alguacil* of the *negros* who

shall take care to insure that all go to the church, and if someone hides or is absent they should be arrested and the governor should order them punished, excepting any *negro* or *negra* that has just impediment, such as illness. . . .

- Item, that those *negros* who are married live in separate houses or rooms each with their wife, and that single *negros* should not live with married couples unless they are children, nephews, or cousins so that dangers and inconveniences [not] ensue and that all live honestly and orderly.[8] Those that live badly, causing harm to the rest, should be arrested and punished by the governor, except in those cases that would result in a sentence of death or dismemberment because those should be heard by the *justicia mayor* of the *villa*.
- Item, that the governor should take special care that male *negros* who can work, not having any impeding illness, should sow their fields on good lands at the proper times and that none go about as wastrels or vagabonds. Those that do should be castigated, as their cases require.
- [A field was to be planted for the king to supply food and income to support the garrison. The community was exempted from supporting the garrison and priest for one year.]
- Item, the governor should take special care that in the *villa* there is no public drunkenness among the *negros* and those who get drunk are arrested and punished.
- Item, that the governor should take special care in the good treatment of the *negros*, and that they should not leave the *villa* or its jurisdiction without his license except those that are going to the fields, hunting, and fishing. . . .
- Item, that the governor take care that the *negros* have and raise fowl from Castile and turkeys from Nicaragua and other domesticated turkeys and fowl so that the *negros* have them . . . and that in their corrals and house [plots] they plant oranges, limes, lemons, and other fruit trees and that they maintain their orchards for their sustenance and income so that they are occupied and do not become wastrels and vagabonds.
- Item, that pigs are not allowed to wander through the streets and that those that are present are kept in corrals or pens . . . where they cannot cause damage or bad odors in the *villa*. . . .

- Item, that the fields and orchards that they will make are not set apart from the *villa* more than a half-league so that the remaining land out to the three-league jurisdiction be kept as pasture for the livestock that are common to these parts of the Indies.
- Item, that the governor serve as the *capitán general* of the *negros*, always recognizing that the Spanish *capitán general y justicia mayor* remains superior, don Pedro Zape, who had served as *maestre de campo* in Portobelo, will serve as the *maeste de campo* for the *villa*. Three times a year, every four months, or when ordered by the *justicia mayor*, a *negro* captain, named by the governor, shall be obligated to leave with a sufficient number of *negros* to traverse the *monte* and lands of Portobelo and the other areas surrounding the *villa* to look for *negros cimarrones*, recently fled or long absent, they should arrest and transport them to the *villa* so that justice be served.
- Item, when the *capitán general y justicia mayor* traverses the land and visits its ports, similarly the governor shall take special care to give *negros* to accompany [the expedition] with their weapons and that they be ordered to obey and comply with all that they are ordered. . . .
- Item, that there should be no trade and commerce or communication with corsairs or with *negros cimarrones*, they are always to be held as capital enemies of our Holy Catholic Faith and His Royal Majesty under penalty that a *negro* who violates this order be held as a traitor to the royal crown and as such be punished as the law allows.
- Item, if the *negros* or any person captures a *negro* or *negra* from the *cimarrones* of the Bayano and does not present them to the *justicia mayor y capitán general* of the *villa*, so that he can administer the [punishment] required by the war that has been fought against them, they will incur the penalty of the previous order. Proclamations [of this policy] shall be made, and those that capture [*cimarrones*] shall be rewarded.
- Item, no *negro* from the *villa* shall hide or shelter any *negro* or *negra* that has fled from the city of Nombre de Dios or any other part, and if a *negro* or *negra* from the *villa* or its jurisdiction captures and presents [a runaway slave] to the *justicia mayor* so that the owner can be

contacted to retrieve [their slave], the *negro* who captured the slave shall be paid ten silver pesos by the owner, and the *negro* or *negra* who welcomes, shelters, or hides a [runaway slave] in their home or elsewhere without reporting it incurs a penalty of one hundred lashes, to be publicly administered in the plaza of the *villa*.

The *señores*, *presidente* and *oidores* of the Royal Audiencia order that each and every one of these ordinances be kept, followed, and executed in the *villa* of Santiago del Príncipe . . . with the reservation that the *señores* [of the audiencia] may add or remove [ordinances] to better serve Our Lord, God, and His Majesty, the administration of justice, [and] the well-being, growth, conservation, and good governance of the *villa*. In order that the [ordinances] shall be known it will be proclaimed publicly in this court, in the city of Nombre de Dios, and in the *villa* of Santiago del Príncipe by the crier. . . . it is so resolved, mandated, and signed.

---

1. This clause established a small military garrison within the community and granted its Spanish commander military and judicial powers.
2. In 1573, the crown enacted a wide-ranging set of ordinances, "The New Ordinances of Discovery and Settlement." These established specific rules for how settlements should be established as well as what rights and prerogatives they enjoyed depending on their administrative designation. In general, *villas* had more rights than pueblos, and *ciudades* had more rights than *villas*.
3. The title of governor granted Maçanbique civic and judicial authority over the community. The Spanish commander assigned to the garrison had oversight over Maçanbique's judicial role.
4. A presidio is a military garrison, often established in a fortified location.
5. The advocation of the Virgin of the Candelaria was typically associated with the Feast of the Purification (February 2).
6. Early modern medical theory posited that miasmas (stagnant, moist air) could sicken people. Consequently, settlements were to be placed where they could enjoy fresh air.
7. "Divine cult" [*culto divino*] referred to the liturgies of the Catholic Church.
8. These clauses implied a fear of sexual licentiousness among maroons and mandated a more European mode of residence based around the nuclear family.

47. Account of Captain Antonio de Salcedo in Portobelo, September 28, 1579

Source: AGI, Patronato 234, R. 4, fs. 3–4. Transcribed in Jopling, *Indios y negros en Panamá*, 374–75.

The formal treaties and agreements made between the audiencia and don Luis Maçanbique present a smooth process. This account presented by Captain Antonio de Salcedo provides a more candid picture of the difficulty faced in securing the peace between the *cimarrones* and the Spanish. The audiencia commissioned Salcedo to oversee the resettlement of don Luis Maçanbique's community. Notably, in a situation demanding trust on both sides, Captain Salcedo successfully used deceit to achieve his desired ends.

. . .

I ordered a soldier who accompanied me, named Pedro de Alba, to meet with a *negro* named Antón Bañol who had come with the *negros cimarrones*. The two exchanged words that were very heated. I, the captain, was about a crossbow shot away from them and consequently did not know what was going on or that they had exchanged angry words. I entered carefully into the house of the *maestre de campo* don Pedro Zape where the soldier and the *negro* had exchanged words. [In the house] were don Luis Maçanbique, captain and headman of the *cimarrones*, the *maestre de campo*, and about twenty-three or twenty-four *negros*. When the soldier saw me enter he complained to me that Antón Bañol had berated him. I told him that I did not believe him, but then considering what the soldier had said I stated that the blame should not lie with him but with don Luis and the *maestre de campo*. He should not complain to me about Antón Bañol but rather to don Luis or the *maestre de campo*. He had aggravated me greatly by raising this issue with me, as I had not been present. I [stated] that I wanted to return to Nombre de Dios and that I had fulfilled the word I had given in Nombre de Dios [to come to Portobelo], where I had argued with a *negro* [of Don Luis] that I did not want to come to Portobelo but he told me it would cost my life if I returned to Nombre de Dios, and having fulfilled my word I wanted to leave and not be with them [the *negros*].[1]

Don Luis pleaded with me that by the one God I not go as it would mean the loss of everything [that had been agreed to] but insisted that if I wished to go he would order it so. I called to the *maestre de campo* and requested that he grant me four *negros* to return with me to Nombre de Dios as guides. He told me that I should ignore the words of Antón Bañol and think about what would happen if this whole pueblo was lost, how Our Lord and His Majesty would not be served nor would [the *negros*] gain their liberty. Should I leave the pueblo they would burn it to the ground, take their women and children, and go where they would never be found. By the one God I should not permit such a thing as it would mean their total destruction. In response to his plea, I said I would leave without their *negros* or anything else. I would go to the beach from which I came, and from there I would follow the coast surviving off the sea until I came to Nombre de Dios even if it took me twenty days to arrive. The *maestre de campo* having seen my great anger and that I was determined to leave did not reply and went directly to don Luis and told him all that had been said. This altercation happened about six or seven in the evening. Don Luis asked that I stay the night and not discuss the matter further so that in the morning the anger would have left and pleaded that I not leave.

With the dawning of the next day God passed me on the road and I remembered all the anger I felt about the encounter between the soldier and the *negro*, and seeing the *maestre de campo*, after spending the night in his home, my determination to leave returned so I went to talk to don Luis. I told him that I was determined to leave and at the point of setting out. Later, don Luis came to me while I was smoking a pipe of tobacco. As he entered, he said "Good day, your Grace."[2] I responded "Good day to you too, your Grace. I have asked that you grant me a guide to take me to Nombre de Dios, and it appears to me that you do not want to do so. I have determined to leave by way of the *monte*, and if I get lost or die at least I have served God and His Majesty." Don Luis pleaded that I not do such a thing, that in the matter between Antón Bañol and the soldier the blame lay with Antón Bañol and that they all should not lose the favor that His Majesty had granted them. I persisted, saying that I needed to go and gave my word that I would return for them, as surely as if I would my father. In response [don Luis] said, "If you go to before Real Audiencia and its president your lie will be believed as truth and our truth will be taken as a lie. Surely you see that we are not to blame, don't prevent our children from being baptized and prevent these people from becoming Christians over such a small issue. We see now that we are guilty of letting it happen, in the future we will look after your interests as if they were those of our children." I responded, "I want to go but you should stay. I would not allow such a travesty to occur." Later the *maestre de campo* with all of the armed *negros*, with their bows, arrows, and lances, together asked and pleaded that by the one God I should not go and that they had written to the Royal Audiencia to send a boat to collect me and that it would come in three days so I could leave by sea. [They said] it would be far easier than going by land as the lands are the worst, the most mountainous and marshy, that there are in the world.

I responded, "There is nothing to be done except for me to go as I want and that you should not order me otherwise, unless you, don Luis, and you, *maestre de campo*, and all you that are here present, do what I command down to the letter." Then don Luis, the *maestre de campo*, and the rest said, "Sir, all that you order we will do." I saw that they were so obedient to the service of Our Lord and His Majesty, [with] hands clasped and eyes to the heavens. I said "Blessed are you, Sir, what favor you have done me in having people so willing to serve you and His Majesty. Therefore call Antón Bañol and the soldier of my company and make them reconcile." I then told the *negros* that all this was done and orchestrated so as to see if the peace made with His Majesty was firm. With this the *negros* rejoiced and acted jubilant and said, "The *españoles* are devils trying to trick us to see if we are trust-worthy or not."[3]

Later, as the *negros* held council in order to leave to where the Royal Audi-encia ordered that they settle, the *maestre de campo* presiding along with king don Luis said, "There is no other king here but the King, Philip, Our Lord." He repeated this over six times, after which he said, "I swear to God that should I hear 'King don Luis' whoever said such a thing will be beaten even though I feel they should be broken into two thousand pieces. There is no more 'King don Luis Maçanbique, captain and leader of the *cimarrones*.' We have no other king than the King, don Philip, Our Lord." With that they all took off their hats, crossed their arms and said that he was correct, they would not repeat what he had ordered them not to, and that they did not know any king other than the King, don Philip, Our Lord. They would serve him very loyally as his vassals. Since then no one has heard any other king named other than the King, don Philip, Our Lord. This occurred on a mountain before me and one other *español* in the service of His Majesty.

On September 28, 1579, Antonio de Salcedo presented this account to the mem-bers of the audiencia. In the months that followed he would return to Portobelo to oversee the community's move to a site near Nombre de Dios. On April 15, 1580, Salcedo reported that the move had been completed.[4]

---

1. Salcedo claims to have had an argument with a *negro* in Nombre de Dios in which he claimed to not want to go to Portobelo. Although the exact context is unclear, Salcedo clearly felt that the *cimarrones* were demanding more of him than his com-mission required. Here Salcedo brings up the earlier disagreement as a pretext for abandoning the endeavor.
2. He used *vuestra merced*, the precursor to the modern, formal *usted*.

3. Luckily, the community found some humor in Salcedo's feigned anger and deception. Given the earlier treachery by Ursúa, such a reception was certainly not guaranteed.

4. AGI, Panama 42, N. 35, fs. 1099.

48. Dr. Villanueva Zapata to the Crown, October 2, 1579
Source: AGI, Panama 13, R. 18, N. 105.

Although peace had been achieved with the maroons of Portobelo, the new strategy of negotiation was not as successful with those of the Bayano. Even as the maroons of Portobelo and Cerro de Cabra agreed to peace, by May 1579 those in the Bayano had retreated to their remote hideouts without finalizing a peace agreement. This letter by *oidor* Villanueva illustrates how the willingness to negotiate influenced the perception of maroon communities by Spanish authorities.

• • •

The *negros* of Portobelo, who negotiated for peace after those of the Bayano, have shown themselves to be most truthful, thankfully. A site has already been selected for their pueblo, a league and a half from the Río de Francisca, I mean from Nombre de Dios on the Río de Francisca, where soldiers and a *justicia mayor* will be placed to maintain order. They have made signs of fidelity and have been very well treated. A *negro* of those who live in Nombre de Dios was going about trying to persuade other [*negros*] owned by the vecinos to flee with him, and he was able to make off with two stolen *negras*. Don Luis Maçanbique, their head and captain, later sent them back to Nombre de Dios asking that justice be served on the *negro* for disturbing the peace, or that he be allowed to punish [the *negro*]. He was quartered, and everyone was content. They have been given their letters of freedom and clothing. All that is left is to bring their maize and other small things by the sea, and to bring their women, all of which will be done quickly.

The *negros* of the Bayano, having given signs of peace, humility, and Christianity, have backtracked and revolted. There are many opinions about this, each blaming some other person, especially the head and principal leaders of the [*negros*]. At the time of the peace, their leaders wished to come to this city by sea, their followers coming by land, but the general, Pedro de Ortega, did not wish it. Later because of other childishness, being a people of little trust, changeable and without reason, they withdrew to their lands. . . . Since they

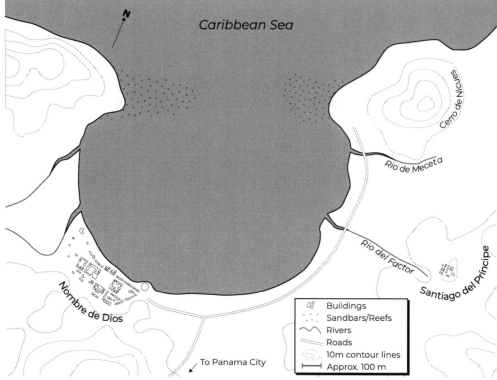

Possible location of Santiago del Príncipe, ca. 1590. *Sources*: AGI, Panama 13,
R. 18, N.105; Panama 14, R. 12, N. 68.

did not complete the agreement, they were called by criers and granted [more]
time, and ultimately troops were sent against them. . . .

Despite a return to war, Spanish sorties made little headway against the maroons
of the Bayano. However, on October 31, 1579, Spanish patrols captured eight more
Englishmen, members of Oxenham's expedition, while several others fled. Alonso
Criado de Castilla estimated that twenty-four remained at large, "wandering in dis-
array without food or weapons and abandoned by the *negros*."[1]

During the remainder of 1579 and 1580, few reports offer details of the conflict.
Spanish forces continued to patrol the Bayano from the fort in the Gulf of San
Miguel. For their part, maroons retreated to ever more remote sites.

---

1. AGI, Panama 13, N. 18, N. 107.

49. Census of the Residents of Santiago del Príncipe, October 6, 1580

Source: AGI, Panama 234, R. 6, fs. 297–304.

After having formally settled Santiago del Príncipe, the authorities conducted a census of the population. Unusually, this document provides some of physical descriptions of the residents. The census accounted for ninety-seven total people, not including others who were in Panama City or aiding the Spanish in the Bayano.

• • •

[. . .] sixth day of October, 1580, before me Juan Alonso de Reinoso, *escribano* of the *villa* [of Santiago de Príncipe], the Señor Antonio Suarez de la Concha, *alcalde mayor* of Nombre de Dios . . . for the support of the residents of this pueblo . . . made a record of the people, of the *negros* and *negras* and children who are present and reside in the pueblo and who came from Portobelo. They are the following:

- don Luis Maçanbique, *caudillo* and leader of the people
- don Pedro Zape, *maestre de campo*, and lieutenant of don Luis
- Juan, from the land of Casanga, *alguazil mayor* of don Luis, man of good stature, who appears to be forty years old[1]
- Antón, from the land of Moconbo, who appears to be forty years old, medium stature with a small face
- Mateo Congo, medium stature and thin, who appears to be over forty-five years old
- Antón, from the land of Angola,[2] good stature, bearded, wide-faced, who appears to be over forty years old
- Simón, from the land of Zape, medium stature, lightly bearded, who appears to be over thirty years old
- Diego Congo, medium stature, stout, bearded, who appears to be over thirty years old
- Francisco, from the land of Enxico,[3] good stature, bearded, who appears to be over thirty-five years old
- Sebastián, from the land of Congo, good stature, slightly fat, bearded, who appears to be over forty years old
- Baltasar, from the land of Zape, tall, medium stature, with a small face, strong arms, who appears to be over forty years old

- Cristóbal Mozo, from the land of Zape, medium stature, small face, has some signs on his face, who appears to be over thirty years old[4]
- Gonzalo, from the land of Bran, medium stature, thin, his right ear has been cut off, who appears to be over thirty years old[5]
- Pedro, from the land of Gilonga, good stature, stout, with some marks on his front, who appears to be over forty years old, lightly bearded
- Diego, from the land of Zape, medium stature, small face, lightly bearded, who appears to be over fifty years old
- Pedro, from the land of Maçanbique, good stature, lightly bearded, who appears to be over forty-five years old
- Gaspar, from the land of Casanga, medium stature, bearded, has a burn mark on his front, who appears to be over thirty-five years old[6]
- Antón, from the land of Angola, medium stature, bearded, who appears to be over twenty-five years old
- Diego, from the land of Zape, medium stature, strong, lightly bearded, who appears to be over thirty years old
- Sebastián, from the land of Moconbo, good stature, lightly bearded, who appears to be over forty years old
- Juan, from the land of Bañon, medium stature, thin, lightly, bearded, who appears to be twenty-five years old
- Gaspar, from the land of Zape, medium stature, bearded, who appears to be twenty-five years old
- Melchior, from the land of Biafara, good stature, lightly bearded, his right ear cut off, who appears to be over thirty years old
- Baltasar, from the land of Zape, small stature, who appears to be thirty years old
- Marcos, from the land of Mandiga, tall, thin, lightly bearded, has a lame hand, who appears to be forty years old
- Domingo, from the land of Biafara, well-built and handsome, who appears to be over thirty years old, has a burn mark on his right arm
- Francisco, from the land of Zape, brother of the *maestre de campo*, don Pedro, who appears to be thirty years old
- Francisco, from the land of Zape, medium stature, lightly bearded, who appears to be thirty years old

- Diego, from the land of Biocho,[7] tall, handsome, who appears to be over twenty-five, one ear slightly cut
- Juan, from the land of Biafara, good stature, lightly bearded, who appears to be over thirty years old
- Domingo, from the land of Bran, tall, lightly bearded, who appears to be over thirty years old, with a burn on his right arm
- Pedro, from the land of Zape, medium stature, stout, lightly bearded, who appears to be thirty years old
- Cristóbal, from the land of Casanga, tall, thin face, lightly bearded, who appears to be over thirty years old
- Marcos, from the land of Zape, small stature, stout, bearded, who appears to be thirty years old
- Francisco, from the land of Zape, tall, *loro* in color, lightly bearded, who appears to be over twenty-five years old[8]
- Juan, from the land of Carabalí,[9] good stature, lightly bearded, a scar on his front, who appears to be over thirty years old
- Pedro, from the land of Zape, medium stature, missing some teeth, who appears to be forty years old
- Juan, from the land of Angola, good stature, bearded, who appears to be thirty years old
- Domingo, from the land of Zape, good stature, stout, trained in gold panning, who appears to be over forty-five years old
- Gaspar, from the land of Zape, good stature, medium and small face, lightly bearded, who appears to be thirty-five years old
- Diego, from the land of Zape, I mean Casanga, good stature, lightly bearded, who appears to be over twenty-five years old
- Antonio, from the land of Biafara, good stature, lightly bearded, his right ear cut off, who appears to be twenty-five years old
- Gaspar, from the land of Zape, good statue, lightly bearded, small face, who appears to be twenty-five years old
- Diego, from the land of Bran, tall, bearded, who appears more than twenty-five years old
- Jusepe, from the land of Zape, good stature, lightly bearded, who appears to be twenty-three years old
- Juan, from the land of Biafara, tall, lightly bearded, who appears to be twenty-five years old

- Antonio, from the land of Jolofo, short and small, not bearded, who appears to be twenty-five years old
- Baltasar, from the land of Biocho, good stature, lightly bearded, who appears to be over twenty-five years old
- Martín, from the land of Bran, small stature, his right ear broken, who appears to be more than 40 years old
- Miguel, from the land of Biafara, tall, blind in one eye, who appears to be thirty years old
- Pedro, from the land of Maçanga, medium build, bearded, with a scar on his face, who appears to be over thirty-five years old
- Sebastián, from the land of Zape, good stature, with pox marks on his hands, who appears to be over twenty-five years old
- Gaspar, from the land of Gilonga, good stature, bearded, who appears to be more than twenty-five years old.

Boys

- Salvador, Blas, Juan, Francisco, Domingo, Sebastián, boys, *criollos* from the *monte* of Portobelo all of whom appear to be over four years old.
- Alexos, *criollo* from São Tomé, tall, declared . . . that for two months he has resided in the pueblo and had been given food by the captain [Salcedo] who has gone to Panama.

Women

- Doña María, from the land of Bran, wife of don Luis Maçanbique, a woman tall, handsome face, who is thirty years old
- Doña María *criolla*, de San Lucar, wife of don Pedro, handsome face and of good stature, who appears to be thirty years old
- Catalina, native of the land of Congo, wife of Juan Caçinga, *alguazil mayor* of the people, small stature, who appears to be forty years old
- Elena, from the land of Zapes, wife of Cristóbal Maça, tall, medium-sized teeth, who appears to be forty-five years old
- Francisca, from the land of Casanga, wife of Mateo Congo, tall, who appears to be more than thirty years old
- Ana, from the land of Zape, wife of Diego Congo, medium stature, *lora* in color, who appears to be over twenty-five years old

- Isabel, from the land of Zape, wife of Pedro Gilongo, small stature, medium face, who appears to be more than thirty years old
- Ana, from the land of Jolofa, wife of Sebastián Congo, tall, thin with a mark on her front, who appears to over thirty years old
- Melgarida, from the land of Cucava, wife of Antonio Jolofo, who appears to be more than twenty-five years old
- Catalina, from the land of Zape, wife of Antonio Angola, small stature, who appears to be over twenty-five years old
- María, from the land of Angola, wife of Domingo Bran, good stature, who appears to be over twenty-five years old
- Polonía, *criolla* from São Tomé, wife of Francisco Enxico, small stature, who appears to be over thirty years old
- María Biafara, servant of Francisco de Enxico, good stature, who appears to be thirty years old
- María, from the land of Biafara, servant of Gonzalo Bran, good stature, who appears to be twenty-five years old
- Catalina, from the land of Biafara, wife of Marcos Mandinga, good stature, thin, who appears to be thirty years old
- Elena, from the land of Zape, wife of Francisco Zape, small stature, who appears to be thirty years old
- Francisca, from the land of Biafara, good stature, who appears to be forty years old, servant of Melchior Biafara
- Lucía Zape, wife of Gonzalo Bran, good stature, with a scar on her chin, who appears to be more than thirty years old
- Juana Zape, wife of Sebastián Zape, good stature, with some marks on her chest, twenty-five years old
- Leonor, from the land of Arada, wife of Sebastián Congo, who is in the Bayano, small stature, with lines on her face, who appears to be over thirty years old[10]
- Agustina, from the land of Zape, servant of don Luis, tall, strong, who appears to be twenty-five years old
- Catalina, from the land of Bran, wife of Domingo Biafara, tall, thin face, who appears to be more than thirty years old
- Leonor Gilonga, wife of Pedro Monçanga, who is in Panama, strong, who appears to be over thirty years old
- Catalina Bran, wife of Pedro Zape, good stature, who appears to be over thirty years old

- Polonía, from the land of Biafara, servant of don Pedro, *maestre de campo*, thin, good stature, who appears to be over thirty years old
- Isabel, from the land of Biafara, servant of don Pedro, good stature, who appears to be over twenty-five years old
- Guiomar Biafara, servant of don Pedro, *maestre de campo*, small stature, who appears to be twenty-five years old
- Pascuala, from the land of Biafara, wife of Pedro Maçanbique, good stature, who appears to be twenty-five years old
- María, *criolla* from Santo Domingo, wife of Gaspar Casanga, good stature, over twenty-five years old
- Leonor Biafara, tall, who appears to be over thirty-five years old
- María Biafara, tall, who appears to be fifty years old
- María Jilonga, wife of Diego Biocho, good stature, thin, who appears to be over twenty-five years old.

Girls

Dominga, María, sisters
another Dominga, Isabel, sisters
Juanilla, girls all of whom are over four years old, *criollas* from Portobelo.

In settling the maroons of Portobelo in their new town of Santiago del Príncipe, the treasury spent almost four thousand pesos on salaries for the Spanish soldiers and officials and for the transportation and subsistence of the maroons. Additionally, in its first year, the Crown agreed to monthly expenses of one cow in addition to olive oil and a bushel of maize per maroon.[11]

---

1. The term "Casanga" applied to enslaved people associated with the state of Casa, located in Upper Guinea along the Casamance River. Wheat, *Atlantic Africa and the Spanish Caribbean*, 37–38.
2. The category "Angola" denoted origins in West Central Africa, frequently those enslaved in regions south of the Kingdom of Kongo. Maroons in Panama identifying as Angola likely passed to the Americas via the Portuguese entrepôt of São Tomé, having been enslaved in wars fought between states on the mainland. In 1575, the Portuguese established a colony at the port of Luanda to the south of the Kingdom of Kongo. By the early seventeenth century, Luanda would supplant São Tomé as the supplier of enslaved "Angolas" to the Spanish Caribbean. Wheat, *Atlantic Africa and the Spanish Caribbean*, 73–81.
3. "Enxico" marked origins in the West Central Africa Kingdom of Ansiku that bordered the Kingdom of Kongo to the north. Wheat, *Atlantic Africa and the Spanish Caribbean*, 132–34.

4. The "signs on his face" were probably ritual scarification or tattoos. His surname was likely a nickname given when he was young since it means "youth" in Spanish.
5. The loss of an ear was a typical punishment for slave disobedience.
6. The burn mark was likely a scar rather than a brand.
7. Individuals identified as Biocho (sometimes Bioho) originated among the Bijagos who inhabited coastal islands opposite the Gêba and Grande Rivers of Upper Guinea. The Bijagos frequently raided the mainland, capturing Floups, Nalus, Brames, Balantas, and Biafadas for sale to Iberian merchants. Retaliatory raids led to the sale of captive Bijagos at the Biafada port of Guinala. Wheat, *Atlantic Africa and the Spanish Caribbean*, 43–44.
8. *Loro* translates as "laurel." This color reference (ostensibly a greenish-tan) was used to describe lighter-skinned Africans. In Iberia, enslaved people from North African could be ascribed this color.
9. Carabalí denoted Lower Guinea origins in the Bight of Biafra. The name derived from the Ijaw port of Kalabari. In later centuries, the Efik people would establish a major slave port called Old Calabar. King, "Descriptive Data on Negro Slaves," 217; Behrendt, Latham, and Northrup, eds., *Diary of Antera Duke*, 47–48.
10. The original reads, "rayada de rostro," suggesting regular lines on her face, possibly scarification.
11. Tardieu, *Cimarrones de Panamá*, 195.

50. Juan de Vivero, Treasurer, to the Crown, February 28, 1581

Source: AGI, Panama 42, N. 24, fs. 826–29. Transcribed in Jopling, *Indios y negros en Panamá*, 385–86.

Juan de Vivero, the royal treasurer, felt that the expenses of war exceeded the utility of the current strategy. In a letter written in May 1580, he reported that expenditures had surpassed three hundred thousand pesos of assayed silver.[1] After ten more months of conflict, Vivero's concerns had intensified. This letter by the treasurer expresses his continued frustration with the cost of war and with the use of former maroons as allies.

•   •   •

[. . .] The war against those of the Bayano continues, and up until 1580 they have spent 136,000 pesos of assayed silver in addition to some money that is owed in salaries and other supplies that have been brought from the province of Quito. . . . This war was undertaken by the president, and everything is being done with the agreement of the other *oidores*, in order to best serve Your Majesty. Hoping to reduce the expenditures of the war, I have tried to do what I can, because I am certain they are and will continue to be fruitless, considering that the location that the *negros* have is mountainous and wooded, known only by them, and throughout they can find food to sustain them. [Their location] is large and expansive, over one hundred fifty leagues, and, even with the large number of people we have, it is impossible to make a difference because of the ease with which they escape when seen or discovered and because of their agility.

The treasurer suggested curtailing military operations and focusing on establishing two or three pueblos in the region settling free *negros* from Panama and Peru alongside *españoles* and *indios*.

As time has shown . . . it is impossible to conquer them through war, their resistance is to flee. They have a great advantage with their agility and the wide expanse in which to hide.

Of the two groups of *negros* that were in this kingdom, one is called that of Portobelo. These came of their own volition to surrender, as they have, even though the cost of this to the royal treasury of Your Majesty is more than if the land had been purchased. They have spent around twenty thousand pesos on roughly one hundred persons give or take, because they have given them in abundance everything they need to eat for over a year and a half, spending between two and a half to three and a half reales per *negro* per day. Having reviewed the accounts and believing this to be excessive, I have undertaken an investigation to see what has truly been spent. . . . Considering the amount that these *negros* are spending and their condition and the manner of life that they kept for so many years, unrestrained murderers and thieves as well as other vices known to barbarous people, and the difficulty we will have in appeasing and collecting them, we can have little surety in what to expect from such a variable people. . . .

As someone familiar with the situation, I believe that it is convenient that Your Majesty be served to order that these *negros* of Portobelo be captured and exiled from this kingdom along with the others that have surrendered, as in one hour they all could be arrested and in another embarked such that the grave threat of their returning to the bush would cease. . . . It is very troublesome to have a pueblo of only *negros* who have previously been in rebellion because in this kingdom it appears to me that there are three times as many slaves as *españoles*, as they do all the labor given the lack of *indios*. Acting as a united people, armed as I have heard they are, the slaves might plot and attempt an uprising in the hopes of liberty for all, which would cause great confusion and place this kingdom in danger more easily than did that of the *moriscos* in Granada.[2] Being such a grave case of such importance, I have tried to present it so that Your Majesty might resolve what might best be done.

1. AGI, Panama 13, R. 19, N. 111.
2. Between 1568 and 1571, *moriscos*, descendants of Muslims, rebelled in the mountains near Granada.

51. President Cepeda to the Crown, February 25, 1581
Source: AGI, Panama 13, R. 20, N. 123.

During 1580, official sources offered few details of successful engagements against the Bayano maroons. The number of maroons captured did not exceed fifty.[1] Yet Spanish patrols continued to range from the Real de San Miguel and a garrison newly established on the Bay of Acla. In February 1581, a patrol led by Juan de Magán encountered an Indigenous community near the Gulf of San Miguel. This letter relates their discovery and their decision to ally with the Spanish against the maroons.

• • •

Sealing the letter with which I send this to Your Majesty, today, the date of this letter, the ship arrived in the port of Panama that in my letter I mentioned I had sent to collect *indios* wandering in the bush.[2] The captain that went to collect them left them at the Real de San Miguel entrusted to Pedro de Ortega Valencia, general of those men, so he might carry out that which touches on their resettlement, where they are to reside and make their fields, their number is recounted in the statement of Diego de Sotomayor, which accompanies this letter.[3] He was in charge of collecting them and bringing them [here].

Along with Captain Sotomayor, Pedro de Ortega sent me a soldier named Juan de Magán with his recommendation. He says that the expanse of the Bayano mountains, in which the *negros cimarrones* wander, is divided by a mountain range and rivers. Some flow into the north sea and others the south sea. Along this range toward the north sea, the soldiers that make war on the *negros* found a pueblo of *indios salvajes* [wild *indios*], which had three *caneys* or balconies that they call their houses and in which they live together to better defend themselves from the continuous war they fight against the *negros* and the *españoles*. They made it understood that they went out to kill *negros* and defend against them. They came showing signs of goodwill, [numbering] seventy-two, forty men of war that fight with bows and arrows and clubs called *macanas*. The rest are women and children. This nation of *indios* has for their name and surname *cueva* and by others *taregras*. Because of the capital enmity they hold for the *negros*, they showed signs of goodwill toward our company and desired to help us castigate [the *negros*] as I have been led to believe. With many good works I will bring this about, God willing, by giving gifts to one and all. This should be done quickly with few resources and less cost because they are simple people, [and it is] easy to win their devotion and friendship.

We have understood from some *negros* that when we spot them they are pursued and harried. They also say that the king's war will not end until they are finished. Some [*negros*] have come with their women and children to the Real de San Miguel. Among them a *negro* named Juan Angola, a leader called a captain who came to this city when peace was discussed. He arrived with twenty-four *piezas*, some of his company having been killed. Additionally, some single *negros* have come forward asking for clemency, and the general has done so. I sent for them and will place them where I can, although it will not be as advantageous as was done for those of Portobelo, settled in the new *villa* of Santiago del Príncipe.[4]

They tell us that a *negro* leader has been killed. He had accompanied their chief to the peace agreement. [The chief] died of anger because his subjects did not return in peace.[5] This [leader], named Antón Marchena, was the one who encouraged them to not return as promised. Everyone blamed him for this, and they killed him. According to the accounts given by these *negros*, General Pedro de Ortega is not at fault for the peace failing, as some have wanted to impute. Instead, the [*negros*] as a fickle, evil people, idlers, are enemies of submission. Being inconstant they did not follow through.

---

1. Reports from May 1580 enumerated twenty-two captives, and a report from June mentioned an unspecified "several." AGI Panama 13, R. 19, N. 112 and 118.
2. This letter has not been located.
3. Sotomayor stated that he travelled to the Puerto de Piñas and Churuca, seventy leagues from Panama City (beyond the Gulf of San Miguel) to "conquer, search, and pacify" *indios*. Having done so, he delivered forty-six to the Real de San Miguel.
4. Cepeda implies that the recalcitrance of the Bayano maroons will result in less favorable terms in the future.
5. These statements reveal that the peace offer sparked a complex, and likely heated, debate among maroons.

52. President Cepeda to the Crown, May 22, 1581
Source: AGI, Panama 13, R. 20, N. 126.

By mid-1581, the tide of war appeared to have shifted. This letter from President Cepeda conveys his sense that reports from the Bayano indicated that the maroons could not hide any longer. Spanish patrols had grown accustomed to the region and were better able to identify possible hideouts. Nevertheless, Cepeda cautioned that the maroons could flee as far as Tolú (modern Colombia). Only Spanish settlements in the region could secure the region from future maroons. After almost thirty years, a plan for settlement had begun to take shape.

.   .   .

The punishment and war undertaken against the *negros cimarrones* continues to improve every day because [our soldiers] capture or kill a good number of them. Those charged with this task, who know this business, gain knowledge of their hideouts from their daily patrols and can more easily find them. As I have said in my other accounts, the elderly that are taken in the bush are executed, those convenient for service in the galleys are sentenced to the oars, the remaining rabble, women and children, are sold outside of this kingdom. The *negro* who has been found with the most people and strength has fled to the land and province of Cartagena. Should he settle there it will cause much damage. To prevent this, I have sent reinforcements. They carry the grandson of the most important cacique of that land. He has never wavered in his obedience to Your Majesty. In this way, and through some gifts that he received with a letter I wrote, I believe he will continue in his devotion and friendship. For they are a bellicose people and great enemies of the *negros* [so] they will help me extirpate them. This was done quickly, fearing that the *negros'* malice might lead them to mislead the *indios* to prevail against them.[1] But as I have said, I have not given them the chance to do so. Nor do I think they will be enticed due to the great harm that [the *indios*] have always received from [the *negros*].

When this business comes to an end, with divine favor I believe it will be soon, it will be necessary to settle the land in two places to insure that this case is firmly concluded and the bad weed does not return. It is divided by a mountain range, tall and harsh, the rivers drain to the north sea, the ocean, others flow to the south sea, which stretches between the provinces of Peru and New Spain and extends to the East Indies. These two pueblos should have fifty *vecinos*. In addition to securing the land so that this evil seed does not return, these [pueblos] once cultivated will provide this province with subsistence for a good part of the year, being fertile and abundant. . . . In addition to its fertility, it is known to be abundant in gold, for this reason the first settlers called it Nueva Castilla de Oro. . . . These pueblos should be constructed with the help and assistance of the [slave] gangs that extract gold for many vecinos because these new settlements will safeguard the slaves who work those mines. The [slave owners] will benefit from the fruits of this labor. Every day the farmers and the miners will see great increase in their yields and other fruits of their labor.[2] I have asked Your Majesty, in my other letters, that the settlers be Portuguese, because of what I have heard about them while I served for Your Majesty in the Canary Islands where I saw that they are hardworking, humble people, who need little to survive, and are marvelous cultivators.[3]

I have started these settlements by noting where they should be located on the northern coast, in a port named Acla, forty leagues more or less from the port and city of Nombre de Dios. They say this used to be a hideout and country for corsairs. There are many other nearby ports that from [the site] can be patrolled and secured with few men, for it is a land easy to defend from the many enemies that wish to infest it. It is where Captain Francisco [Drake], English, entered ten years ago, more or less. In his expedition, [he] explored the land to the other sea and later committed the robberies of which you have been informed. In the company of the *negros cimarrones*, he murdered and robbed along the road from here to Nombre de Dios, many people and a great sum of gold. I have learned that the *negros* conspired with the English so they might return to the land, but having fallen out because [the *negros*] have been killed and punished, I believe that they will not fulfill the agreement. . . . The other settlement, on the south sea, has been established in the Real de San Miguel because I have already established a storehouse there to support the soldiers who currently pursue the *negros*.

The account of *cimarrones* that remain to this day in the province of Bayano and its *montes*, according to the investigations made by the general and his officers of war, accompanies this, signed by the general. Those who surrendered from Portobelo are firm in the fealty they swore and are settled, quiet and subdued, aware of the favor that they have received from Your Majesty's hand.

1. Cepeda implies that the maroons might try to convince the *indios* to switch allegiance.
2. In other words, slave owners would see greater profit from the fruits of their enslaved workers because the proposed cities would protect the investments they made in enslaved Africans.
3. Portuguese were the most numerous foreign residents in the Americas, although sometimes fears over their loyalty led to calls for their expulsion. In most cases, their cultural affinity to Castilians led to positive views such as these. Hamm, "Between Acceptance and Exclusion."

53. Account and List of *Negros Cimarrones*, May 20, 1581
Source: AGI, Panama 13, R. 20, N. 126, bloque 3.

The following list names all the maroons presumed to be at large in the Bayano as of May 20, 1581. Pedro de Ortega Valencia assembled it from information gathered from captured maroons, possibly under torture, as well as those who had come in peace. The list offers clues to the importance of diasporic ethnonyms to maroon social organization. It also reveals that most maroon groups had a relatively large gender imbalance and few younger members.

• • •

Account and list of the *negros cimarrones*, men and women, large and small, in this war in the Bayano according to what I, General Pedro de Ortega, have been able determine from the *negros* who have been captured to be given to his lordship, the President. They are the following:

Diego Congo, captain of the Congo people who is believed to be between the Río Gallinazas and the Río Bane

Diego Congo
Pedro Congo, youth[1]
Lorenzo Bran
Pedro Bonba Bran
Manuel Bañol
Martín Bran
Manuel Biafara
Francisco Biocho

Antón, *criollo* from Santo Domingo
Juan Biafara
Juanico Bran
Antón Zape Mangavela
Cristobal Maçanbique

Women of this pueblo

Juana Mandinga
Isabel Bran
Ana, *criolla* from Panama
Marequella, youth

The *piezas* of this pueblo number seventeen.

People of Pedro Totola who are on the Río Chongone

Pedro Totola
Juanico Bran
Antón Bran
Juan Bran
Pedro Bran
Juan Bran
Andrés Bran
Juan Yalonga[2]
Pedro Hihagua
Francisco Bran
Juan Biafara
Hernando, *zambaigo*
Pedro Congo

Women of this pueblo

Juana Conga
María Calanga
Anica Bañol
Leonor Biafara

They number seventeen *piezas*

Nalu[3] and Biafara people under Captain Juan Nalu who are on the Río Bagre

Juan Nalu
Antón Nalu
Manuel Nalu
Hernando Biafara
Antonico Nalu
Domingo Biafara
Amador Biafara
Gaspar Biafara
Melchior Biafara
Antón, *indio*
Hernando Nalu
Antón Biafara
Felipe Biafara

Women of this pueblo

Vitoria, *zambaiga*
Juanica, *zambaiga*
Leonor, *zambaiga*
Elvira, *india*
María Zape
Vitoria Carabalí
Catalina Biafara
Isabelica, *india*
Catalina, youth
Perico, boy
Andrés, *zambiago*
Juanico, *zambaigo*

They number twenty-seven *piezas*

Captain Antón Mandinga who is on the north sea

Antón Mandinga
Martín Mandinga
Diego Mandinga
Francisco Mandinga
Martín Mandinga, *criollo*[4]
Antón Mandinga

Francisco Yalonga
Alonso Yalonga
Diego Yalonga
Diego, *mulato* from the islands[5]
Pedro Zape
Francisco Zape
Juan Zape
another Juan Zape
Vicente Zape
Andrés Zape
Baltasar Zape
another Baltasar Zape
Hernando Zape
Melchior Zape
Gaspar Zape
Pedro Zape
Miguel, *criollo* from the islands
Pedro Casanga
Juan Casanga
Felipe Casanga
Francisco Casanga
Antón Bañol
Hernando Bañol
Alonso Bañol
Gaspar Bañol
Antón Zape
Juanico Malagueta, *indio*
another Juan, *indio*
Pedro, *indio*

Women of this pueblo and children

María Biafara
another María Biafara
María Bran
Juanica, *criolla*
Beatriz, *criolla*
Felipa, *criolla*

Catalina, *criolla*
Gracia Mandinga
Marequilla Mandinga
Juana Mandinga
Isabelica, girl
Francisca Zape
Catalina Zape
Marequilla, *criolla*
Catalina Zape
Marta Zape
Leonorica Zape
Vitoria Bañol
Juana Bañol
Marequilla Bañol
Polonia Zape
Isabel Conga
María Bran
Elena, *criolla* from Santo Domingo
María Bran
María Conga
Lucía, *india*
Elvira, *india*
Francisco, boy *mulato*
Antonico, *zambaigo* boy
Hernando, boy *negrito*
Francisco, boy *negrito*
Dieguito, boy *negro*
Francisco, boy *indio*

Those of this pueblo number sixty-nine *piezas*, it is the largest

Captain Antón Tigre[6] y Maçatanba,[7] who are together

Antón Tigre
Antonico Anbo
Pedro Zape
Antón Masanga[8]
Juan Casanga

Andrés, *indio*
Francisco Maçanbique
Maçatanba
Antón Casanga
another Antón Casanga
Baltasar Zape
Antón Zape
Luis Zape
Felipe, *zambaigo*
Manuel, *zambaigo*
Pedro Enxico
Pedro Zape Congo

Women of this pueblo

Catalina Conga
Isabel Bran
Felipa Angola
Juliana Angola
Catalina Bran
Elvira, youth
María Bran
Isabelica Bran
Ines Zape
Marequilla, *criolla*
Vitoria, *india*
Francisca, *zambaiga*
Ana, *india*

They are thirty-one.

Felipe Congo Captain of the people of Martín Zape

Felipe Congo
Gaspar Masanga
Antón Masanga
Rodrigo Masanga
Cristobal Masanga
Pedro Masanga
Antón Masanga

Gaspar Maçanbique
Francisco, *criollo*
Hernando Maçanbique
Juan Bala
Blas Congo Maçanbique[9]
Salvador Maçanbique
Pedro de Terranova[10]
Domingo, *zambaigo*
Vicente, *zambaigo*
Juan Congo Cargalanza[11]
Pedro Angola
Francisco Angola
Juan Congo
Francisco, *mulato*

Women

Lucía Zape
Juana Zape
Leonor, *india*
Marquesa, *criolla*
María, *india*
Leonor, *criolla*
Francisca Zape
Guiomarica, *criolla*

Those of this pueblo are thirty *piezas*

Together the pueblos noted here have one hundred ninety-two *piezas*

Missing are Captain Juan Jolofo and the Biafara and Bartolomé Mandinga who according to verifications number seventy-six *piezas*.

All told, the *negros* that are in the *monte*, large and small, number two hundred sixty-eight according to what has been determined from the *negros* captured up to today, May 20, 1581

[signed Pedro de Ortega Valencia]

One hundred seventy-seven *piezas* have been taken alive, fifty have been killed, and seventeen have come in peace, I mean to say those killed number forty-six.

Together, the *negros* taken, killed, and who came in peace number two hundred forty *piezas*. Of these, I have freed ten *negros* because it has been necessary for the good prosecution of the war. They serve and have been of great benefit.

Sixteen *indios* have been taken from the *negros*, who had them in their service as captives. They are in this camp.

Another sixty-two *indios* have been taken from a pueblo in the mountains.[12] They came in peace and are settled at this Real de San Miguel. This is what has occurred in the war up to today.

---

1. The younger captives were differentiated between youths, *muchachos* and *muchachas*, and children, *niños* and *niñas*.

2. "Yalonga" designated individuals from the Susu/Yalunka of Upper Guinea. Yalongas likely entered the transatlantic trade after being captured during conflicts with the expanding Mane. Wheat, *Atlantic Africa and the Spanish Caribbean*, 50–51.

3. The "Nalu" ethnonym corresponded to the Nalu ethnic group of Upper Guinea. During the sixteenth century, the Nalus did not directly trade with Iberians; instead, Biafada merchants served as intermediaries between Nalu markets and European merchants. The close association between Nalu and Biafara maroons reflects the maintenance of preexisting cultural affinities. Wheat, *Atlantic Africa and the Spanish Caribbean*, 42–43, 57–60.

4. In most sixteenth-century contexts, Africans identified as *criollos* did not also identify with an African ethnic category. This entry suggests that despite being born in the Americas, Martín as an individual identified with the Mandinga.

5. As with *criollo* Miguel below, this probably refers to the Caribbean but could also refer to the Pearl Islands or the Atlantic islands of Africa.

6. In Spanish, *tigre* means tiger. Its use here may have been a moniker or honorific. It may also represent a Hispanicized ethnonym.

7. During this period (1570s) a ruler named Maçatanba (Masatamba) ruled the state of Casa located in Upper Guinea along the Casamance River. The ruler Masatamba oversaw a major expansion of Casa against their Bañun neighbors. The man listed here was also known as Alonso Casanga. Given his age in 1582, approximately seventy, Alonso Casanga was a contemporary of the African ruler and may have had firsthand experience in Casa under Masatamba's rule. Alonso's adoption of Masatamba's name reinforced his own position of leadership and military prowess among the maroons. Wheat, *Atlantic Africa and the Spanish Caribbean*, 37–39, 62–63; Green, *Rise of the Trans-Atlantic Slave Trade*, 244.

8. The ethnonym "Masanga" denoted individuals originating from West Central Africa, although it is less well attested than other terms from the region.

9. The pairing of these two ethnonyms ("Congo" and "Maçanbique") suggests that Blas fashioned unique identity based on his place of origin, experience, and social network.

10. Like "Lucumí," the ethnonym "Terranova" identified individuals from Lower Guinea. "Terranova" translates as "new land" in Portuguese and likely referred to captives acquired from "new" entrepôts to the west of Benin in the region that would later be termed the Slave Coast. Lovejoy and Ojo, "Origins of the Yoruba Nation," 356.
11. "Cargalanza" translates as "lance or spear carrier," a possible reference to his marital abilities.
12. The community brought by Juan de Magán in February 1581.

54. The Audiencia to the Crown, December 24, 1581
Source: AGI, Panama 13, R. 20, N. 130.

During the second half of 1581, Spanish successes continued to mount. This letter from the audiencia noted that only one maroon captain remained at large, and Spanish forces had begun to encircle him. Hemmed in between Spanish troops and *indios de guerra*, they expected a speedy conclusion to the war.

•   •   •

We wrote to Your Majesty concerning the state of the war against the *negros cimarrones* of the Bayano and how several notable captures had occurred, especially of some among them who were esteemed leaders, some were defeated by force of arms and others came in peace. This has continued until now according to the *capitán general* and his soldiers' report; the [*negros*] have been put in such a tight space that in short order the desired end will be achieved. For only one leader remains with those who follow him. He has fled from the pursuit and persecution of our soldiers and retreated inland to where they have him very harried and surrounded. It is certain that he cannot escape, especially because the place he hopes to find security and toward which he retreats is settled by *indios de guerra*, well-known enemies of the *negros*, such that we trust in God that this business will be ended shortly.

The audiencia reiterated Cepeda's plan to establish two settlements to guard the region from future maroons and corsairs. The audiencia could not have hoped for a quicker resolution. The following day they received a letter from Pedro González de Meceta informing them that Antón Mandinga had surrendered.

55. Pedro González de Meceta to Dr. Criado de Castilla, December 22, 1581

Source: AGI, Panama 13, R. 20, N. 132, bloque 3.

On December 25, 1581, Alonso Criado de Castilla received this letter from the *maestre de campo* informing him that Antón Mandinga had surrendered. Short and direct, it confirmed the audiencia's expectation that the campaign was near its end.

• • •

I arrived in this city today, Friday, having left Acla the previous Sunday to bring Your Mercy the news that Antón Mandinga had come in peace with all his people on the third [of this month]. Juanico, *indio*, had gone to call on the Zapes, where he knew that they had been to bring them in peace because they too desired it.[1] Two soldiers brought this news to the presidio at Acla, sent by Alvaro Méndez as he stood in the fields of Antón Mandinga, he is one of the three captains that was sent from this presidio with the squads of men.[2]

In the wake of the rendition, the audiencia made plans for peace. Alonso Criado de Castilla would lead this effort, taking charge after President Cepeda left to take up the presidency of the audiencia of Charcas (modern Bolivia).

---

1. Juanico may have been the cacique's grandson mentioned by Cepeda in his May letter.
2. In a later *probanza de mérito*, Meceta noted that Mandinga had fled as far as the rivers of the Darién. AGI, Patronato 152, N. 5, R. 1.

Part V
Spanish-Maroon Peace and Its Aftermath (1581–1620s)

56. Act in Which the *Negros* of the Bayano Were Welcomed in Peace, December 29, 1581

Source: AGI, Panama 42, N. 21, fs. 626–27. The document gives the year as 1582; however, the events occurred in 1581, and subsequent documents correct this mistake.

In the days following the news that the maroons of the Bayano had surrendered, the audiencia moved quickly to secure a formal peace. This act served to justify their pursuit of a negotiated peace and authorized Alonso Criado de Castilla, as senior *oidor*, to oversee the process.

• • •

In the city of Panama, on the twenty-ninth day of December, 1582, the *señores*, *presidente* and *oidores* of the Royal Audiencia and chancellery of His Majesty, that there resides, in the presence of the *señor* Dr. Diego de Villanueva Zapata, *fiscal* of His Majesty in this Royal Audiencia, state that Antón Mandinga, principal caudillo of the *negros cimarrones* from the *montes* of the Bayano, has come in peace with many [of his people] of diverse nations. They are at the Real of San Miguel waiting to hear what this Royal Audiencia orders and mandates. And the *señores* having discussed and conferred, consider it convenient to the service of Our Lord, God, and to His Majesty, that the peace being offered by the *negros* be accepted because of the well-being, universal security, and increase in the royal treasury that will follow and the damages and inconveniences that will be avoided. Additionally, the strategy of war has been a long and difficult process, one that was not capable of being won because of the harshness and altitude of the land and bush in which [the *negros*] moved. They could sustain themselves off wild fruits such that it was impossible to remove them. The undertaking of the war cost a great quantity of pesos from the royal treasury as it has lasted three years up until this point. With this peace, it will be possible to end the danger and risk that this kingdom, and that of Peru, has faced from the corsairs that have been able to arrive and enter by making alliances with the *negros*, who once entrenched are difficult to expel, fortified as they are in the ruggedness of the land. As a result, the road between this city and Nombre de Dios, which is the route to the provinces of Peru and many others, could not be travelled safely for fear of one's life and property, and it was necessary to travel with an armed guard and even so there were many robberies of royal income as well as private property, large quantities of silver and gold. It appears to the *señores, presidente* and *oidores*, in conformity with the royal cedulas His Majesty has sent to this province, that the peace be accepted and maintained, and to that effect it is convenient that the *negros* be relocated to a settlement located in a convenient part of the kingdom. Since the experience of relocating the *negros* that were around Portobelo, near Nombre de Dios, and the Cerro de Cabra, has been very appropriate and so that these *negros* come to live in peace, tranquility, and civic order, and because it is convenient that with all brevity that which will best serve God, Our Lord, His Majesty, [and establish] peace and tranquility be put into effect, [the *presidente* and *oidores*] order that Dr. Alonso Criado de Castilla, the most senior *oidor* who presides in this Royal Audiencia, go to confer with and communicate all the aforementioned with the *cabildo*, justices, and government of this city and to call persons of confidence and experience in this kingdom to converse and deliberate. With his report this Royal Audiencia will resolve that which will best serve God, His Majesty, [and] the peace, tranquility, and security of this kingdom.

On December 31, 1581, Dr. Alonso Criado de Castilla met with the cabildo of Panama City and numerous prominent citizens and officials. They agreed with the audiencia's assessment of the situation and suggested that the *negros* of the Bayano be sent to a site near Panama's Río Grande.

57. Account of the Foundation of Santa Cruz la Real, January–February, 1582

Source: AGI, Panama 42, N. 21, fs. 630–31v.

The audiencia quickly moved to have the maroons of the Bayano relocated to a site near Panama City. On January 1, 1582, five ships left the port of Panama City to collect over two hundred maroons from the Gulf of San Miguel.[1] Spanning almost a month, this document provides a very clear account of how their new settlement of Santa Cruz la Real was formed and how its residents came to live there.

In the city of Panama of the kingdom of Tierra Firme, known as Castilla de Oro, Wednesday the tenth of January, 1582, the illustrious *señor* Dr. Alonso Criado de Castilla, as the most senior *oidor* presiding in the Royal Audien-

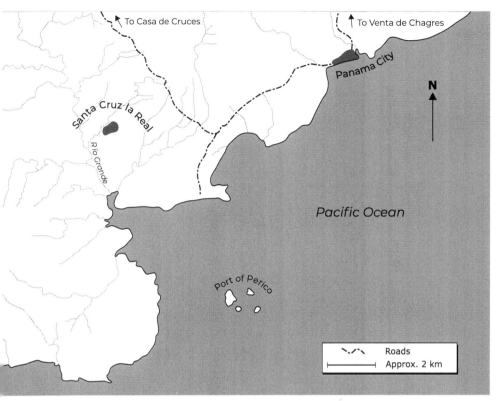

Possible location of Santa Cruz la Real. *Source*: AGI, Panama 42, N. 21, fs. 630–631v.

cia and Chancellery of His Majesty, that in this city resides, by commission and agreement of the audiencia, left the city to search for a site with ports, rivers, streams, and lands, where the *negros cimarrones* of the Bayano can be settled and brought to the service of God, Our Lord, and of His Majesty; Pedro Ortega Valencia, *capitán general* of the war of the Bayano, having already gone to the Real of San Miguel where [the *negros*] are waiting in accordance with the orders of the Royal Audiencia. The *señor* doctor travelled and saw the land, traversing rivers, bush, plains, and old settlements of natives within three to four leagues of this city, taking in his company: Captain Francisco de Neva Céspedes, *alcalde ordinario* of the city, Juan Rodríguez Bautista, *alguacil mayor* and *regidor* of the city; Captain Antonio de Salcedo, *gobernador* of the pueblo of Santiago del Príncipe of the *negros* of Portobelo; Captain Baltasar Pérez; Francisco de Corella; Hernándo de

Mayorga, *alguacil de corte*, and other persons long-resident in the kingdom with much experience and knowledge of its places and lands, and with Francisco Berbesi, *negro*, one of those who surrendered from the Cerro de Cabra, who having been a *cimarrón* in the lands near this city has great knowledge, information, and guidance about suitable locations. The *señor* doctor, having seen the lands, selected a site for the *negros* to establish [their settlement], near the Río Grande, three leagues from the city of Panama on a plain atop a spacious and flat rise . . . fair land with good airs, with room for over three hundred homes to be built. The site is flanked on both sides by streams that provide abundant water, and it is one eighth of a league from the Río Grande. Using small ships and boats they can descend to the Pacific Sea to travel to the city of Panama to trade provisions and fruits, which they can harvest from the land with ease. From the site can be reached a large mountain stretching over fifteen leagues, good land suitable for fields, hunting grounds, and fishing in the rivers that are found in the mountains. The banks of the Río Grande are especially good for planting fruit trees, the flat lands for tending livestock, and nearby groves for other types of animals. The site is located in the interior almost equidistant between the Pacific Ocean and the Atlantic Ocean where the Río Chagres empties into the Atlantic Ocean. From the site to where the *negros cimarrones* used to reside it is eighty to one hundred leagues to the *montes* of the Bayano, and in the middle lies the city of Panama so that the *negros* are further separated and removed from where they used to live.[2]

While at the said site, the *señor* doctor believed it would be a good place to settle and reside, so in the name of His Majesty took possession of it, naming it Santa Cruz la Real.[3] To demonstrate this [the *señor* doctor] ordered two crosses to be made of wood. The larger to be placed on an elevated hill so that it can be seen from the roads that pass from the city of Panama to the ranches and cottages of the countryside, the other to be placed where the holy church of the pueblo will be built. The *señor* doctor indicated the locations with his hand. In the presence of many persons, including free and enslaved *negros* and other residents of the countryside, the captains and those who accompanied the [*señor* doctor] with great devotion and humility, on bended knee reverenced the raised crosses.

Subsequently, it was ordered that houses of wood be built so that later the *negros*, recently arrived, would have shelter. To construct them it was ordered that all the necessary free *negros* of the city of Panama be sent to quickly complete the work. The care of the site was given to Captain Baltasar Pérez and Hernando Mayorga, *alguacil* of the court, who were there present.

Having laid out the town, its church and hospital, its streets and plaza, in the form they should take, and having given the order to begin building the houses, the *señor* doctor returned to this Royal Audiencia to await the arrival, or news, of the *negros*.

After the aforementioned, Thursday the eighteenth day of January 1582, General Pedro de Ortega returned from the Bayano by sea with five ships loaded with all the *negros cimarrones* that could be carried. When they came into view of this city and its port the Royal Audiencia was informed of their arrival. Later, the *señor* doctor left to receive the *negros* where they had been disembarked, two and a half leagues from the city near the banks of the Rio Grande, in order to be taken to the site of their new settlement. There, having disembarked, near a ranch owned by Martín Sánchez, next to the river, the general presented the people and soldiers of the *negros* to the *señor* doctor. He received them in the name of His Majesty. The following are the captains that the *negros* brought with them:

- Captain Juan Jolofo
- Captain Antón Mandinga
- Captain Pedro Ubala[4]
- Captain Juan Angola
- Captain Bartolomé Mandinga
- Captain Juan Casanga
- Captain Pedro Zape

Later, the *señor* doctor asked that the general give an account and list of those *negros* who had surrendered and been brought with the above captains, those that remained at the fort, and those that remained in rebellion in the bush. Before me, the present scrivener, the general gave the *señor* doctor a report and list. . . . The report and list follows these acts.

The general arrayed the *negro* captains and their people along with the *españoles*, captains and soldiers, in a formation of war with drums, trumpets, and the royal standard, and having arrived before the *señor* doctor, the *negros* removed their weapons, prostrated themselves on the ground, and in the name of His Majesty, with great humility and happiness, were received as his vassals. The *señor* doctor addressed them with friendship and thanked them for offering peace.

Then the *señor* doctor ordered the general to shelter the people and see that they were fed and allowed to rest as they had come very tired from travelling. The next day they would be taken to the site that for their benefit had already been established so that they might populate it. The *negros* were about a league from the estancia of Martín Sánchez.

The people were sheltered that day as had been ordered by the *señor* doctor near a small river that was nearby. That night as a sign of the contentment that the *negros* felt for the grace that God, Our Lord, and His Majesty, had given them in keeping and confirming their word, and for granting them pardon . . . they had a great party that lasted all night long, with dancing and drums according to their customs, in the presence of the *señor* doctor, general, captains, and soldiers.

Later, the next day in the morning, Friday the nineteenth of the month of January, the *señor* doctor and the general led the people from where they were to the site that would be their settlement, and, having arrived, they were sheltered near the Río Grande and given food. In the afternoon of that Friday, the *señor* doctor showed the general, *negro* captains, and other principal *cimarrones* the lands, rivers, and bush that were available for their fields and hunting grounds. At this the *negro* captains and their people demonstrated their satisfaction. In the evening, of this day, the *negros* and *negras* celebrated, showing great contentment with their games and dances.

Later, the next day, Saturday, the feast of Saint Sebastian, the twentieth day of January, the *señor* doctor ordered that the *negro* captains and all their people assemble in one of the ravines, and before me, the current scrivener, they came one by one to be listed, distinguishing between men and women, *indios* and *indias*, and *zambaigos* who were in the company of the *negros* and who had surrendered with them. This was done in the following form:

- Cristóbal Jolofo
- Francisco Jolofo
- Juan Jolofo
- Sebastián de Silba
- Pedro Casanga
- Pablo Berbesi

- Sebastián Berbesi
- Melchor Biafara
- Manuel Biocho
- Antón Biafara
- Francisco Casanga
- Domingo Jolofo
- Bartolomé Zape
- Cristóbal Biafara
- Francisco, *criollo* from the *monte*
- Manuel Biafara
- Juan Biafara
- Diego Mandinga
- Vicente Zape
- Melchior Biafara
- Juan Enxico
- Gaspar Biafara
- Mateo Biafara
- Diego Biafara
- Gaspar Biafara
- Antón Biafara
- Andrés Zape
- Juan Congo
- Pedro Zape
- Julián Berbesi
- Diego Biafara
- Amador Biafara
- Baltasar Biafara
- Juan Zape
- Francisco Biafara
- Antón Zape
- Adan Zape
- Pedro Zape
- Antón Biafara Beragua[5]
- Hernando Nalu
- Alonso Zape
- Julián Biafara
- Fernando Bañol

- Pedro Zape
- Gaspar Zape
- Manuel Nalu, *criollo* from the *monte*
- Pedro Zape
- Francisco Zape
- Hernando Biafara
- Felipe Biafara
- Francisco Biafara
- Domingo Yalonga
- Gaspar Zape
- Gaspar Zape
- Antonio Zape
- Antón Mandinga
- Melchior Mandinga
- Juan, *criollo*
- Francisco Biafara
- Juan, *criollo* from the *monte*
- Baltasar Biafara
- Martín, *criollo* from the *monte*
- Antón Congo, *criollo* from the *monte*
- Diego, *mulato*
- Antón Nalu
- Gaspar Berbesi
- Pedro Congo, *criollo* from the *monte*
- Antón Mandinga
- Domingo Biafara
- Gaspar Biafara
- Sebastián Angola
- Juan de Mestança
- Francisco Ubana
- Juan Biafara
- Domingo Congo
- Cristobal Biafara
- Ximon Mandinga
- Francisco Mandinga
- Alonso Jolonga
- Francisco Berbesi, *criollo*

- Antón, *criollo* from the *monte*
- Alonso Angola
- Hernando Casanga
- Francisco Angola
- Canpillo Angola
- Luis Congo
- Francisco Mandinga, *zambaigo*
- Andrés, criollo *zambaigo*
- Juanico Biafara
- Canpillo Zape
- Pedro de Ortega
- María Biafara
- Ysabel, her daughter
- María Biafara
- Leonor Mandinga
- Pedro, her son
- María Jolofa
- Francisca, *zambaigo*, her daughter
- Catalina Berbesi
- Juana Mandinga, *criolla* from the *monte*
- Barbola, *criolla* from the *monte*
- Gracia, *criolla* from the *monte*
- Felipa, *criolla* from the *monte*
- María, *criolla* from the *monte*
- Juanica, *criolla* from the *monte*
- Ysabel Conga
- Antona Zape
- Antonilla, *criolla* from the *monte*
- Leonor Zape
- Beatriz, *criolla* from the *monte*
- Marta Zape
- Catalina Zape
- Monica her daughter
- Mariquilla, *criolla* from the *monte*
- Catalina, *criolla*
- Ynes, *criolla* from the *monte*
- Ana, *criolla* from the *monte*

Negras and their children

- Polonia Zape
- Mari Zape
- Catalina Biafara
- Justas, her daughter from the *monte*
- Francisca Monica Zape
- Brianda Terranova
- Catalina Zape
- María Bran
- Juana Nalu
- Vitoria Carabalí
- María Zape
- Lucía Bran
- María Berbesi, *criolla* from the *monte*
- María Zape
- Francisca Zape
- María Zape
- Juana Zape
- Ysabel, *criolla* from the *monte*
- Catalina Conga
- Catalina Biafara
- Catalina Zape
- Beatriz Berbesi
- María, *criolla* from the *monte*
- María Bran
- Catalina Biafara
- Ynes, her daughter from the *monte*
- Agustina Biafara
- Catalina, *criolla* from the *monte*
- Antón, *zambaigo criollo* from the *monte*
- Juana, *zambaiga criolla* from the *monte*
- Manuel, her son
- Leonor, *zambaiga criolla* from the *monte*
- Vitoria, *zambaigo*
- Juana, *zambaiga criolla* from the *monte*
- Francisca, *india*
- Andrés, her son, *zambaigo*

Zambaigos men and women

Indias and *Zambaigos*

- Lucía, *india*
- Francisca, *india*
- Elvira, *india*
- Juana, *zambaigo*, her daughter
- Leonor, *india*
- Marta, *india*
- Felipa, *india*
- María, her daughter, *zambaiga* from the *monte*
- Isabel, *india*
- Julián, her son, *zambaigo*
- Isabel, *india*
- María, her daughter, *zambaiga* from the *monte*
- Luis, *indio*
- Antón, *indio*
- Catalina, his daughter
- Jorge, *indio*
- Antonico, *indio*
- Francisco, *indio*
- Toque, *indio*
- Francisquillo, *indio*
- Agustin, *indio*

Indias

Afterward, the next day, Sunday the twenty-first of January, the *señor* doctor ordered the *negros* to congregate in the plaza and once together addressed them impressing upon them the obligation they had to give thanks to God, Our Lord, and to His Majesty for such mercy as they had received. And he advised them to live a good life from this point forward, they should live as Christians, serving His Majesty with great loyalty and fealty, and said other things as were fitting. To this they all responded with great humility that they would do as he said.

This done, the *señor* doctor advised that they should hear Mass, in a small wooden house that had been made for that purpose on the site that had been selected for the pueblo's church. The mass was said by pastor and preacher Fray Diego Guillén, of the order of Saint Francis, with the assistance of the *señor* doctor. The sermon conformed to what the *señor* doctor had previously instructed and extorted the *negros* to lead good, Christian, wholesome lives. The church was dedicated to the blessed Saint Sebastian, who was selected to be the patron and intercessor for the pueblo. . . .

Later, with everyone gathered at the door of the church, the *señor* doctor proposed that the *negro* captains elect and propose one from among them, whom they all recognize as a *mayoral* [leader],[6] to be placed so that all would be subject to him as governor and magistrate who in the name of His Majesty would maintain justice and defend them from harm, in the manner of a *cacique*, so that they know what best to do and that in their name he might petition and confer with the Royal Audiencia about that which might be necessary. Having understood this, the captains and *negros* who were present, with common accord, named as their leader Juan Jolofo because he was old, of good reason, and regarded by all as a father. The *señor* doctor accepted the nomination as *mayoral* and ordered that the *negros* obey him and follow his orders, and to follow all the commands that the *gobernador* and *justicia mayor*, who will be placed in this pueblo, will give in the name of His Majesty, for he will be superior to everyone. The *negros* accepted this with great happiness, promising to fulfill that which was ordered.

Later, the *señor* doctor stated that he named as his *gobernador* and *justicia mayor* Captain Juan de Magán, who had worked very hard during the war and in whom could be found all the abilities necessary for the office. . . .

Later, Thursday the eighth of February, in the afternoon, after General Pedro de Ortega sent word that some ships and frigates were coming by the sea carrying more *negros* and *indios* that had surrendered to their site and settlement, the *señor* Doctor Alonso Criado de Castilla left the city for a port they call the Las Terneras, located about a league from the city, where the general had landed the ships the night before. The next morning, the *señor* doctor ordered that they disembark and sent them to the ravine that is called Aguas Buenas where they were sheltered for the night. The next day, the ninth of January, they entered the *villa* and site of Santa Cruz la Real, and at the entrance to the site the *negros* and *indios* were counted and listed by the *señor* doctor, in the presence of the current scrivener, as follows:

List of those who were brought in the second trip from the Bayano by General Pedro de Ortega Valencia to the settlement of Santa Cruz la Real, Saturday the tenth of Feburary, 1582.

- Andrés Terranova
- Juan, *criollo*
- Juan Galan
- Pedro Biafara
- Antonio, boy
- Alonso, *criollo* from the *monte*
- Pedro Poto Terranova
- Antón Casanga
- Miguel, *criollo* from the *monte*
- Francisca Mandinga
- Antón, *criollo zambaigo*
- Antón Biafara
- Baltasar, *criollo* from the *monte*
- Salvador, *zambaigo*, *criollo* from the *monte*
- Martín, *criollo*
- Cristobal, *criollo* boy
- Antonico, *zambaigo* boy
- Antonico, *negro* boy
- María Biafara
- Bitoria Biafara
- Madalena Biafara
- Vitoria Casanga
- Felipa, her daughter, a child
- María Bran
- Ysabel, *criolla* from the *monte*
- Diego, *criollo*, her son, a child
- Ysabel Angola
- Domingo, her son, a child
- Francisca Xalonga
- Madalena, *negra* child
- Lucía Zape
- Juana, *criolla* from the *monte*
- Juana, *criolla* child
- Ysabel Conga
- Elena, *criolla* from Santo Domingo[7]
- Franciso, her son, a child
- Ana Angola

> *Negras con sus hijos*

- Juana Mandinga
- Marquesa, *criolla* from the *monte*
- María, *criolla* from the *monte*
- Jeronima, *criolla* from the *monte*
- Martín, her son, a child
- Dominga, *criolla* from the *monte*
- Mariquita, *negra* child
- Ysabel Bran
- Catalina Biocho
- Ana, her daughter, a child
- María Portuguesa
- Gaspar de Avila, *negro*
- Montano, *negro*

The twelve *indios* and *indias* that follow were held by the *negros* in their company, they had been captured in the war and had been held in the bush, they are *ladino*.[8]

- Francisca, *india*
- Luisa, *india*
- María, *india*
- Ysabel, *india*
- Juana, *india*
- Antonico, *zambaigo*, her child
- Pedro de Ortega, *indio*
- Ana, *india*
- Ysabel, her daughter *india*
- Catalina, *india*
- Juan, Christian
- Catalina *india*, translator

And the *indios* that came in peace from the *montes* of the Bayano to the Spanish captains, who are neither *ladinos* nor baptized, and who came together with those of General Pedro de Ortega. . . .

- Antón cacique
- Juan, his son
- another *indio*
- another *indio*

- another *indio*
- another *indio*
- another *indio*
- another *indio*
- another *indio*
- another *indio*
- another *indio*
- another *indio*
- another *indio*
- another *indio*
- another *indio*
- another *indio*
- another *indio*
- another *indio*
- another *indio*
- another *indio*
- another *india*
- another *india*
- another *india*
- another *india*
- another *india*
- another *india*
- another *india*
- another *india*
- another *india*
- another *india*
- another *india* girl
- another *india* girl
- another *india*
- another *india*
- another girl child
- another *india*
- another *india*
- a boy child
- another *india*
- another *india*
- a boy child

- another girl child
- another girl child *india*
- a boy child *indio*
- another *india*

Afterward, the *señor* doctor ordered that the *indios* and their people be gathered together, as they had come intermixed with the *negros* as was recorded in the lists, and be sheltered in a nearby river and given maize and meat.

The next day, Sunday the eleventh of February, the *señor* doctor gathered the *cacique* and principal *indios* and took them to see the land so that they might select a site for their settlement.⁹ Having seen the savannas and bush nearby, the *indios* were satisfied in selecting a convenient place to build their settlement on a level savanna near where the *negros* had their settlement. In between the settlement of the *negros* and that of the *indios* was a river that afforded them access to the fields, rivers, and bush similar to that enjoyed by the *negros*. And as it was understood that the *negros* had been friendly with them and had helped support them, even though should they wish to leave and find another settlement in the company of other *indios* of this kingdom—such as those of the pueblo of Chepo, or those of Parita, or Cubita—they might freely do so . . . , so long as they stayed in this settlement [the *señor* doctor] ordered that the priest of the *negros* might easily teach them doctrine. Similarly, they were to be governed by the *gobernador* Captain Juan de Magán. And so gathered, the *indios* went to their own site where they built a very large house out of wood and thatch alongside individual homes. The *negros* let go voluntarily those [*indios*] whom they had held captive, granting them their freedom. These joined the other *indios* of the settlement and gathered together at the site they gave the pueblo the name and avocation of Saint Anthony of Padua.

The next day, the twelfth of February, the *señor* doctor set about understanding whether there were any disputes or discord between the people, *negros* and *indios*. Knowing that there had been differences, he endeavored to resolve them and come to an agreement, working to return the foreign women that had been held by some [*negros*], and instructing them in Christianity and good living. To better effectuate this, he ordered that messengers be sent to the city of Panama to the prelates of the holy cathedral church, currently *sede vacante*,¹⁰ so that they would send the dean and *provi-*

sor of the cathedral in order to resolve doubts about the baptism of many of the *negros* and *indios* and in order that those who wish to marry may do so and live according to the Christian faith.

Afterward, the next day, don Rodrigo Hernández, dean of the holy cathedral church, came to the site. Having conferred with the *señor* doctor over the doubts pertaining to the Holy Sacraments, [the dean] gave the order to baptize the many children and adults that needed baptism and to celebrate many marriages. The *señor* doctor was present the entire time, and to more greatly please and oblige the *mayoral* and head of the *negros* [he] asked them to serve as godparents at the baptisms and marriages.

1. AGI, Panama 13, R. 21, N. 133.
2. Here the audiencia reveals its desire to separate maroons from the lands they knew in order to better control them.
3. In the early modern world, formal ceremonies served to reinforce hierarchies of civic and political power. Seed, *Ceremonies of Possession;* Curcio, *Great Festivals of Colonial Mexico City.*
4. "Ubala" may not represent an ethnonym. Wheat considers it a term of Biafada origin. Wheat, *Atlantic Africa and the Spanish Caribbean,* 61–62.
5. The term "Beragua" may refer to the Spanish province of Veragua located to the west of Panama in what is now Costa Rica. The pairing of "Biafara" and "Beragua" may indicate that this individual had spent time in Veragua before escaping captivity.
6. The term *mayoral* is most commonly used for a foreman, a leader of workers. The position being described here is similar to that of a cacique, the ruler of an Indigenous community, which the Spanish often termed *gobernador*—as in the case of Santiago del Príncipe. In this case, the term *gobernador* would be reserved for the Spanish magistrate and not used for the leader of the *negros.*
7. Elena was likely born to a slave in the Caribbean town of Santo Domingo.
8. The Spanish may have assumed that these Indigenous persons were captives of the maroons because of their own prejudices.
9. Spanish stereotypes of *negros* as violent and harmful to *indios* fueled the choice to separate the two communities along racial lines.
10. Lacking a bishop.

58. Deposition of Juan Vaquero, May 3, 1582
Source: AGI, Patronato 234, R. 6, fs. 632v–34.

In March 1582, the audiencia knew that some maroons of the Bayano did not know of the peace. Hidden in remote camps and divided into small bands, these maroons remained isolated. To find them, the audiencia dispatched squads led by former maroon leaders to search the region. On May 3, Juan Vaquero, a prominent captain of the Bayano maroons, reported on his expedition.

•   •   •

He stated that his name is Juan Vaquero, one of the captains of the sur-rendered *negros* from the Bayano. After having submitted to the service of His Majesty with the rest of the *negros* who are now settled at the *villa* of Santa Cruz la Real, he stayed at the Real de San Miguel with General Pedro de Ortega Valencia and the soldiers of His Majesty. Pedro de Ortega sent him with Sebastián de Madrid, a surrendered *negro* from Portobelo, and eleven other surrendered *negros*, with some enslaved *negros* of His Majesty serving as porters, to search the *montes* of the Bayano to see if any *negros* remained to surrender and to bring them news of the peace agreed to by the rest. This witness with Sebastián de Madrid and the others left about a month and a half ago from the Real de San Miguel. From there they went straight to Old Bayano to set up camp. Then they traversed to the north sea and its rivers, ravines, bush, and mountains where previously there had been *negro* settlements. In these places and many others of the Bayano's bush they searched for *negros* but found none other than old camps from the time of Captain Carreño.[1] From the Real de San Miguel to these camps is about twenty-five leagues and another twenty-five to the north sea.

From the north sea they went to the Río Membrillos that is about seventy leagues from the Real de San Miguel along the north sea. From there they travelled along the coast to the Río Caracoles that is about one hundred leagues from the Real de San Miguel, fifty leagues from this city, and forty leagues from Nombre de Dios. From the Río Caracoles they came traversing the clearings and mountains of Pacora to the south sea, leaving by way of the Río Chepo and its pueblo of *indios*, seven leagues from this city. In all these places they travelled, they did not find any settlement or *negro* other than camps from long ago.

Asked whether they had left any part of the *montes* of the Bayano where the *negros* might be found and collected and whether this witness knows how many *negros* have stayed or who they are?

He said that they had left the coast of the north sea from the Rio de Mosqui-tos to the city of Nombre de Dios, a straight path of about one hundred

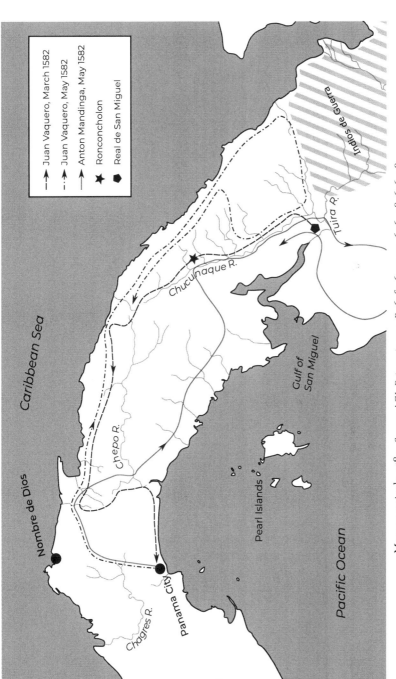

Maroon patrols, 1582. *Source:* AGI, Patronato 234, R. 6, fs. 632v–34, 646–48, 656–58.

leagues, traversing the land from place to place. There are many rivers, ravines, and bush in which some *negros* could settle and hide. There are also about one hundred leagues to the Río de Uraba.[2] This witness did not go there. But when this witness left the Real de San Miguel, other captains and men went to the Río de Uraba. . . . He knows that in the *montes* of the Bayano there is a *negro* named Maçatanba, who has four or five *negros* Zapes and Casangas with him. Maçatanba is a Casanga. He has another three *negras*. There is also Diego Congo who is with Lorenzo Bran, Pedro Bonba, Francisco Bran, Tagale, and Juan Congo, Antón *criollo*, [and] Mariquilla *criolla*. This witness does not know the *negros* who are with Maçatanba.

When asked how he knew that these *negros* were in the Bayano, Juan Vaquero replied that he knew them while living in the bush and that they had not been killed or come in peace. He added that he was very eager to return to the coastline near Nombre de Dios to continue searching. The audiencia agreed and sent the maroons out on another set of expeditions.

---

1. The maroons' recollection of prior camps stretched back over thirty years, demonstrating a continuous collective memory that spanned generations.
2. The Río Atrato in the Gulf of Urabá.

59. Deposition of Antón Mandinga, August 25, 1582
Source: AGI, Patronato 234, R. 6, fs. 646–48.

After Juan Vaquero's initial expedition, the audiencia sent out two more. Once again, Juan Vaquero led one. Antón Mandinga and Pedro Ubala led the other. In August, Antón Mandinga returned with six more maroons and recounted a three-month journey that had taken him almost fifty leagues beyond the Real de San Miguel to the edge of lands controlled by *"indios de guerra."*

• • •

He stated that about three moons ago, this witness left from this city with Captain Pedro Ubala and Juan Vaquero and twenty-five other *negro* soldiers from those that have surrendered to fulfill what this Royal Audiencia ordered of them. Together they went to the Río Caracoles which is in the Bayano along the south sea, forty leagues from this city. At the river they split up. After conferring together with Juan Vaquero, this witness and Pedro Ubala, and sixteen *negros*, went searching along the south sea, all of the bush, rivers, ravines that they encountered. Juan Vaquero went with eight *negros* along the north sea. In this way they divided, and each searched a different place. This witness and Pedro Ubala with the sixteen *negros* went along the south sea searching all the old camps and settlements, rivers, bush, and ravines of the Bayano, a region eighty leagues long and forty leagues wide. Having searched this whole area they did not find any *negros*, or signs of them, until they reached the Río Chongone, which is thirty-five leagues from the Real de Bayano inland along the slopes that flow into the south sea. They found signs that *negros* had cut bananas and been hunting. Following the trail to the Río Ubañe, fifteen leagues beyond the Río Chongone, they spied a camp along the river on top of a hill.

They went to the camp where they found the six *negros* that they brought [back]. They recognized this witness and the others that came with him. This witness and Pedro Ubala told them that they were at peace and had surrendered to the service of God and His Majesty, and they had a pueblo where His Majesty treated them well. The *negros* replied that they wished the same that had been done for their companions. Together they returned with them. A *negro* named Pedro, who saw this witness and the rest, fled, not recognizing them. Not being able to find him, they left him behind. The six *negros* who they brought are those who have been presented. This witness and Pedro Ubala asked these *negros cimarrones* if they knew of any others that were still in the bush. . . . They replied that there was not another *negro* other than Pedro who had fled.

When asked whether there were any places that he did not search, Antón Mandinga replied:

If there is any land that this witness did not search it is from the Río Ubañe, where they found the six *negros*, toward the Río de Uraba. A distance of ninety leagues, it is populated by *indios de guerra* and patrolled by [*indio*] soldiers. This witness has removed all the *negros cimarrones* that were there. If any unknown *negro* remains there, these *indios* will kill him due to the great enmity they have against *negros cimarrones*.

60. Deposition of Juan Vaquero, September 28, 1582
Source: AGI, Patronato 234, R. 6, fs. 656–58.

Juan Vaquero's second expedition lasted a month longer than that of Antón Mandinga.

•   •   •

He said about five months ago, more or less, this witness left this city by order of this royal Audiencia in the company of Captain Antón Mandinga and Pedro Ubala, *negro* from those that have surrendered to the service of His Majesty and are settled in the *villa* of Santa Cruz la Real, to go to the bush in search of Captain Maçatanba and others who remain in the *montes* of the Bayano. They went together, the captains and twenty or so *negro* soldiers. After arriving at the Río Caracoles, thirty leagues from this city, this witness, the other captains, Antón Mandinga and Pedro Ubala, and the other *negro* soldiers conferred to determine which part of the Bayano would be best to search for those that remain at large. They agreed that this witness would go to the mountains of the north sea toward the port of Acla. Antón Tigre and Pedro Ubala would go to the south sea. They split up, and this witness went with ten *negro* soldiers, for of the twelve that he led two returned after falling ill. Antón Tigre and Pedro Ubala went toward the south sea with the remaining *negro* soldiers, about fifteen.

This witness went with his men from the Río Caracoles searching the downslopes and mountains of the north sea, all of the bush, ravines, and rivers that are found on the Río Famina, Río Pueblo Cozcoz, Río Teresa, Río Membrillo, Río Lagarto, Río Indios, Río Santa Cruz, Río de Miel Grande, Río de Miel Chiquito, Río de Rodrigo Maçanga, Río Bonbas, Río Maçatanba— where [this witness] had his pueblo—and Río Playa Grande. From this last one they continued until they reached the Río Tunia, crossing from the mountains of the north sea to the south sea. They then crossed back to the north sea as far as Río Membrillo, Arroyo Chico, also called Hijosuyo. In the headwaters of this river they found signs that they followed for three or four months, after which they encountered Captain Maçatanba near the headwaters of the Río Membrillo.

Before they arrived at the camp, where they had small fields of maize, coming to their huts, Maçatanba and his people startled until they recognized this witness. After recognizing him they willingly came in peace.

This witness told them that he was to bring them in peace and that they would enjoy the freedom that His Majesty has given them. They said they wished the freedom that the other surrendered *negros* enjoy. The *negros* that were with Maçatanba are those that he has brought and presented before this royal Audiencia. . . . They had retreated so far because of the war, and because the soldiers had killed many people. They did not know the favor that His Majesty had offered in pardoning them. . . .

Neither Juan Vaquero nor those who were with Maçatanba knew of any other maroons still at large in the Bayano.

61. Questioning of Maçatanba, September 28, 1582

Source: AGI, Patronato 234, R. 6, fs. 662–64.

The audiencia interviewed Maçatanba and his people to verify that they were the last holdouts from the Bayano war. Appearing to be almost seventy years old, and declaring that he had not been baptized, Maçatanba explained how he had come to settle so far away.

•   •   •

Asked, where Juan Vaquero found this witness and the six *negros* and *negras* that were in his company? He said that [it was] in the headwaters of a river named Satamana, where they had their fields and camp.

Asked, when and why did he go to settle there? He said that out of fear of the war and the soldiers that pursued them, they had killed people. This witness retreated with the people who have come with him. They had been settled there for about one moon. Before they had travelled at night fleeing the soldiers.

Asked, if this witness knew of the peace, surrender, and pardon that His Majesty offered and if [he knew] his companions were settled and tranquil? He said that he did not know of anything in the question because if he had known they would have come. He became aware after encountering Juan Vaquero and knowing this they willingly offered themselves to the service of His Majesty.

Epilogue (1583–1623)

By mid-1583, the two *villas* of Santiago del Príncipe and Santa Cruz la Real were firmly established. Officials noted the regular and occasional services rendered by the residents as part of their peace agreements. In early 1583, maroons undertook several patrols into the Bayano to capture as many as sixty slaves that had fled the city of Panama.[1] Writing in March 1583, *oidor* Criado de Castilla praised their efforts: "When a *negro* flees it is easy for [the former maroons] to capture them such as they have recently done. [The fugitives] barely reach the bush before they are brought back. Because this disturbs the peace of their community, when [the former maroons] find them, they do not treat them well. As a result, we have seen that those who absent themselves choose to return to their masters of their own volition fearing that [the former maroons] come after them."[2] Additionally, the former maroons helped Pedro de Ortega Valencia identify a shorter, faster route between Nombre de Dios and Panama.[3] Unfortunately, few sources speak to the realities of daily life other than frequent comments that the residents of the two settlements lived quietly and peacefully.

The peace agreements had stipulated that the former maroons were to receive food, crops, and livestock to establish their own subsistence base. Yet bad harvests in 1583 delayed the ability of Santa Cruz la Real to produce enough for its residents to support themselves, much less generate any income.[4] Such pressures may have led maroons to leave the towns for the nearby cities or create smaller dispersed settlements in the hopes of better meeting their subsistence needs.

Records suggest that Santa Cruz la Real experienced a steady decline in numbers during its first fifteen years. In 1589, Antonio de Salazar, a newly arrived member of the audiencia, noted that Santa Cruz la Real had about one hundred married men.[5] This observation suggests a slight decline from its founding population of around three hundred fifty.[6] Three years later, the audiencia claimed that Santa Cruz la Real had sixty-six married men, twenty-eight single men, and four single women but did not enumerate children.[7] In the same letter, the audiencia described the population of Santiago del Príncipe as being forty married men. Approximately ten years after their founding, Santa Cruz la Real appears to have shrunk by at least 40 percent, while Santiago del Príncipe remained roughly the same size. Two events in the mid-1590s further contributed to the decline of each city.

In December 1593, the Crown ordered that the Atlantic port be moved from Nombre de Dios to Portobelo.[8] Work began immediately on clearing a site for the new city and identifying the best route between Portobelo and Panama. During this time, residents of Santa Cruz la Real helped scout the new road, discovering a trail that would take the name of their Spanish *gobernador*, Juan de Magán.[9] Enslaved Africans represented the primary labor force for new construction. Although the commissioners overseeing the project asked the Crown to purchase two or three hundred slaves, the treasury had to rent most of the enslaved laborers from local slaveowners. In order to support the construction efforts, the commissioners proposed that both free-Black communities be merged and moved to the outskirts of the new port.[10] They argued that the communities could provide much-needed food and continue to help scout and clear the new roads. Before the plan was enacted, an English fleet led by Francis Drake invaded the region.

On January 6, 1596, coastal sentinels posted by Santiago del Príncipe spied at least forty sails approaching Nombre de Dios.[11] That day, between six hundred and nine hundred Englishmen captured Nombre de Dios. Spanish resistance in the port city was light, its residents having fled in advance of the English. The most serious resistance came from the men of Santiago del Príncipe who destroyed a bridge hoping to impede the English advance.[12] Twenty or thirty former maroons set up an ambush, armed with firearms and bows and arrows. They succeeded in killing an English officer and wounding several others.[13] After the ambush, the residents of Santiago del Príncipe retreated into the bush. The community also sent two messengers to Panama warning of the English landing.[14]

Outside of Nombre de Dios, the Spanish had established a robust defense in the weeks preceding the fleet's arrival.[15] The Spanish correctly determined that Drake would not content himself with taking Nombre de Dios and that he hoped to reach Panama City. Consequently, the local commander, Alonso de Sotomayor, established an ambush along the road to Panama City in a pass named Capirilla.

The residents of Santa Cruz la Real played a part in these plans. Sotomayor ordered men from Santa Cruz to join Spanish militiamen at Venta de Cruces. These forces formed part of a reserve unit that could be mobilized should the English break through the ambush. A unit of free-colored militiamen from Panama City also formed part of Sotomayor's defensive deployment.

The ambush worked. Although vastly outnumbered, the Spanish suffered only seven fatalities, four of whom were African soldiers, possibly former maroons or free men of color.[16] The following day, January 11, the English retreated to Nombre de Dios. They sacked and burned the city. As they departed, the English made a retaliatory attack against Santiago del Príncipe for their earlier ambush and for killing over twenty Englishmen as they resupplied their water. When the English reached the settlement they found it burned. The maroons had burned their homes rather than allow the enemy to occupy them, employing one of the tactics that they had previously used against Spanish assaults.[17]

After spending several weeks at sea, the English returned to Portobelo, capturing the bay and scattering the workers. The fleet remained in the harbor for three weeks but did not attempt any overland assaults. The English departed soon after Drake was buried at sea, having died of dysentery.

In the wake of the English attack, the residents of Santiago del Príncipe immediately worked to rebuild their town and to help the residents of Nombre de Dios. Nevertheless, their numbers began to decline. In May of 1596, *oidor* Salazar noted that the town had between twenty-five and thirty married residents, a reduction of 25 percent from the previous count. In the same letter, Salazar again proposed that Santa Cruz la Real and Santiago del Príncipe be merged.[18] Together their tithes would fully pay the priest dedicated to their spiritual care and eliminate the cost of one Spanish *gobernador*.

No document specified an exact date of implementation, but the plan appears to have been been carried out in early 1597.[19] In January of that year, some residents from Santa Cruz la Real were relocated to Portobelo to aid in its defense. Additionally, for the first time, a single Spaniard, Ruy Díaz

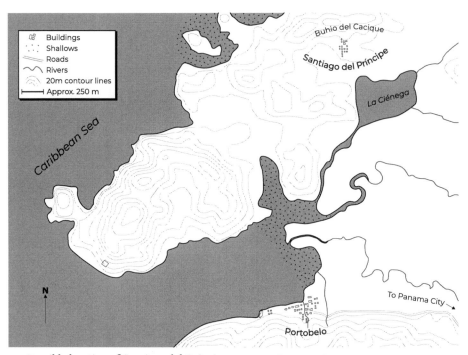

Possible location of Santiago del Príncipe, ca. 1597. *Sources*: AGI, Panama 14, R. 10, N. 57;
Panama 16, R. 1, N. 4; "Descripción corográfica de algunos lugares de las indias . . . ,"
Biblioteca Nacional de España, Madrid, Mss. 364, fs. 217.

de Mendoza, held the position of *gobernador* for both communities.[20] These
moves suggest that initially each community retained its corporate integ-
rity even as Spanish authorities consolidated their physical location and
Spanish oversight. After 1597, Santa Cruz la Real disappears from Spanish
documentation.[21]

These changes paralleled the abandonment of Nombre de Dios and the
relocation of its residents to the new city of Portobelo. In early 1596, faced
with the imminent arrival of the fleet from Spain, authorities authorized
the disembarkation of the fleet at Nombre de Dios and ordered the hasty
construction of huts to house the newly arrived merchandise and people.
After the fleet arrived, the provisional city saw major fires in August and
September 1596. These tragic events only accelerated authorities' desires to
finalize the relocation. By mid-1597, the formal move of the city's residents
had begun.[22] Concurrently, Santiago del Príncipe moved from its former
site near Nombre de Dios to a new site outside the still unfinished Porto-

View from Portobelo toward Bohío del Cacique (*center distance*).
Photograph by the author.

belo.[23] The move represented a homecoming of sorts. Only eighteen years
before, the maroons of Portobelo had left that bay to reside near Nombre de
Dios.

Their knowledge of the region allowed them to identify a site for their
new town. In 1594, don Luis Maçanbique and don Pedro his *maestre de
campo* testified that a half league from the future port there was a site called
Bohío del Cacique. The location would be an ideal place to establish an agricultural community for the support of the port.[24] In 1607, a description of
Portobelo said that a half-league from Portobelo lived the "*mogollon* soldiers
who had been *negros cimarrones* from the Bayano."[25] The account further
noted that residents of the new Santiago del Príncipe lived on the shores of
a lake called "the swamp" (*la ciénaga*) and travelled in canoes down a small
river to reach the city.[26] Given the short distance, the town's residents went
back and forth "day and night," bringing agricultural produce and domestic fowl to the port. From their new location, residents of the town maintained a coastal watch from the Bohío del Cacique.[27]

By the early seventeenth century, official reports began to complain of
marronage once again. In 1599, five enslaved Africans working in Portobelo escaped. These men fled down the coast toward Acla and the heart of
the old maroon territory. In January 1602, ten more slaves fled Portobelo
assisted by some of those who had escaped three years before. In response,
President Alonso de Sotomayor sent out twenty men from Santiago del
Príncipe under the command of their Spanish *gobernador*, Captain Diego
Chumacero. They only succeeded in capturing two runaways.

On July 5, 1602, fifteen more enslaved Africans escaped.[28] This mass
flight prompted further action. Captain Chumacero led thirty men from
Santiago del Príncipe and twenty Spanish soldiers. They were joined by a

separate twenty-man expedition from the presidio of the Bayano. The expedition found a settlement near the bay of Acla supported by fields of rice and maize. After raiding the village and scattering its residents, they scoured the area, eventually capturing fourteen of its thirty-seven residents.

In 1607, officials complained that at least one hundred maroons had reestablished themselves in the Bayano. Some of these maroons had attacked a group of shipwrecked Spaniards. The maroons killed seven of thirteen shipwreck survivors, including a priest.[29] The retaliatory expedition included twenty-five soldiers from the Bayano presidio and five men from Santiago del Príncipe.[30] After almost a month of searching they encountered a settlement and many small camps. Although they burned the settlement, the party had to retreat to the coast to be resupplied.

Twenty-five soldiers from Portobelo and five more men from Santiago del Príncipe reinforced the expedition along with the supplies. This larger party attacked a maroon settlement presumed to house thirty-five men and seven women. They killed seventeen maroons and captured six.

As the expedition returned, it stumbled on four Portuguese sailors from a slave ship that had run aground. They related that after the crew and enslaved Africans had gone ashore, they had been set upon by *indios de guerra*. A patrol of the region encountered some Indigenous settlements and four Africans hiding in the bush. Although they did not have a translator, the recovered Africans made clear that Indigenous people had attacked, killing the Portuguese quartermaster and taking away many of the other Africans.

During 1608 and 1609, further patrols sought to locate the shipwrecked Africans and prevent them from establishing new communities. Eventually the patrols captured two maroons and five of the shipwrecked Africans.[31] From these they learned of the location of a maroon settlement between Acla and the Pacific. In late 1609, two expeditions flanked the community; one entering the region from the Caribbean side and the other travelling overland from Gulf of San Miguel. The expeditions killed fourteen and captured eleven maroons.[32] Writing in early 1610, officials reported that there was no need to send out further patrols.[33]

In 1606–7, one hundred fifty-two people lived in Santiago del Príncipe. The community had thirty-nine married men, thirty-three unmarried men of various ages, fifty-eight women, and twenty-two slaves.[34] Amazingly, don Luis Maçanbique continued to lead the community at the reported age of 110. The presence of slaves indicates that at least some members of the community had acquired enough capital to purchase their own enslaved laborers. Moreover, it suggests that despite their own prolonged fight for freedom, the former maroons accepted slavery as a legitimate institution and incorporated it into their community.[35] Although certainly a sizable community, the new Santiago del Príncipe, ostensibly home to residents of both former maroon towns, housed fewer people than had been resident in Santa Cruz la Real in 1592.

The decline likely reflected various factors. At their inception, neither community had balanced sex ratios: men outnumbered women almost two to one.[36] Men unable to find spouses within the communities may have gravitated to the nearby Spanish cities in the hopes of finding a partner. Similarly, neither community had many children at their foundation. This demographic gap would have both delayed and impeded natural increase of their residents. Death and disease undoubtably claimed some members of these communities and exacerbated the existing demographic impediments to natural increase. The destruction of Santiago del Príncipe during Drake's 1596 attack, the forced relocation and merger of Santa Cruz la Real, and the forced relocation to Portobelo each afforded moments when former maroons may have chosen to leave their towns to establish themselves elsewhere.

The city of Panama likely represented the primary destination for residents choosing to leave. By 1607, the city numbered almost six thousand residents, three-quarters of whom were persons of African descent.[37] While the majority of these residents were enslaved, the city boasted over six hundred free *mulatos* and *negros*. By the early seventeenth century, both of these racial groups had balanced sex ratios. The city also had at least sixteen *zambaigos*, eleven men and five women. In all likelihood some or all of these individuals were former maroons born from African-Indigenous unions in the Bayano.[38] Moreover, given the large size of the city, former maroons or their descendants may have been able to establish new social networks otherwise unavailable in the free-Black towns. An adventurous few may even have turned to the sea to work the ships trading in the Pacific.

Some evidence suggests that when the authorities ordered the relocation of Santa Cruz la Real, many residents chose to remain in the area dispersed on small rural estates. In 1608, President Valverde de Mercado reported that at least three hundred *negros* and *mulatos* lived in the countryside outside Panama City. Complaining that they led scandalous lives, he proposed that they be gathered and resettled about a half league from the former site of Santa Cruz la Real. The new settlement would be called Santa Cruz la Nueva.[39] Although the plan received royal approval, no evidence suggests that it came to fruition. Nevertheless, it reveals that ten years after its forced abandonment, hundreds of persons of African descent lived in the environs of the former Santa Cruz la Real. Given the meager size of the new Santiago del Príncipe, it is quite possible that many of the original inhabitants of Santa Cruz la Real resisted their relocation and simply chose to remain on the hills and plains that bordered their former home.

In 1608, the king requested opinions as to whether the residents of Santiago del Príncipe should be moved into Portobelo.[40] The request sought to eliminate the expense of the town's Spanish *gobernador* and priest. Responding in 1609, President Valverde de Mercado rejected the plan.[41] He noted that they would be unable to continue their agricultural production in the city. The only other arable lands were over a league away, and if they had to work those lands they would still live outside the city. The royal order had been prompted by reports that the community had shrunk to only forty people. The query appears to have confused the number of men capable of engaging in military service for the total size of the community.[42] With the community's total size of one hundred thirty free persons, including seventy-two men, forty men of fighting age would seem appropriate.

During the second decade of the seventeenth century, few official documents shed light on the community. In 1614, twelve men from Santiago del Príncipe accompanied twenty-five solders on an anti-maroon expedition to the Bayano.[43] An ambush by *indios de guerra* killed most of the party. Only two or three soldiers from Santiago del Príncipe survived. Two years later, the president of the audiencia reported that increased fighting against *indios de guerra* had led to the deaths of over seventy Spanish soldiers and "many *negros*" from Santiago del Príncipe.[44] These losses would have been devastating to the community. The ten soldiers killed in 1614 represented a quarter of the community's working-age adult males. The additional losses alluded to in 1616 may imply that the community lost a significant percentage of its able-bodied men to conflicts with Native groups in only a few short years.

In 1620, the audiencia reported that Santiago del Príncipe existed in name only, with its full-time residents numbering less than fifteen.[45] Most of the community lived in Portobelo, as did its Spanish *gobernador* and priest. The *fiscal* again proposed eliminating these positions since they represented an unnecessary expense.[46] This plan was not acted on, as at least one more Spaniard served as *gobernador* through 1623. Nevertheless, after 1623 no known documents refer to Santiago del Príncipe. In all likelihood, by the mid-1620s its residents had gravitated to Portobelo and become part of its already sizable free and enslaved Black community.

After over four decades, Santiago del Príncipe faded into obscurity. Yet the story of its founders and its residents reveals a largely unknown history. For almost six decades, thousands of enslaved Africans fled Spanish settlements to find autonomy and refuge in the wilds of the isthmus. Their lives should not be romanticized. Every day represented a struggle for food and shelter. They needed to practice constant vigilance to protect their communities from Spanish attacks.

Further, maroons could not just hide in the woods far from Spanish Panama. The lack of resources, especially manufactured goods, required that they raid Spanish settlements and trade routes. The need to gain new members, especially female members, led them to free other Africans from enslavement. When other Europeans arrived in the region, maroons recognized the value of establishing alliances with enemies of Spain. While these alliances furthered maroon goals, they also precipitated strong Spanish responses. Facing a war of "fire and blood," maroons persevered, disbanding into small groups to avoid capture and maintain their freedom.

After decades of struggle, runaway slaves in colonial Panama forced Spanish authorities to negotiate a peaceful solution that granted the maroons freedom and self-governance. The maroons of Portobelo became the first Africans in the Americas to successfully resist a European power. Joined by the maroons of the Bayano, these men and women established the first formal free-Black communities in Spanish America. Even though these settlements would disappear within fifty years, their struggle helped establish a pattern that other maroons could exploit. The future free-Black towns of Yanga, Amapa, San Lorenzo de las Minas, and San Basilio owe their existence in part to the efforts of Panama's maroons. Moreover, the impact of their struggle crossed imperial lines. In 1739, the Leeward Maroons and Windward Maroons of Jamaica secured a negotiated peace with the British and self-governing communities in part because colonial authorities consciously mirrored the model used by the Spanish 150 years prior.[47] Thus, although largely unknown, the impact of Panama's maroons and their successful struggle against slavery was echoed in the lives of enslaved Africans in the Americas for centuries.

Notes

1. AGI, Panama 13, R. 22, N. 147, bloque 3, fs. 5–6.
2. AGI, Panama 13, R. 22, N. 144.
3. AGI, Panama 13, R. 22, N. 146.
4. AGI, Panama 13, R. 22, N. 150.
5. AGI, Panama 14, R. 5, N. 27.
6. There were 116 women in 1582. If they were all married, the initial settlement would have had 116 married men.
7. AGI, Panama 14, R. 8, N. 40.
8. Mena García, "El traslado de la ciudad," 86. As early as the 1560s, Spanish observers had noted that the Bay of Portobelo offered a more protected and defensible harbor than Nombre de Dios.
9. AGI, Panama 14, R. 11, N. 60. At this time the English and Spanish used different calendars. The Spanish had switched to the Gregorian calendar, while the English retained the Julian calendar. English accounts using the Julian calendar give the date of arrival as December 27, 1595.
10. AGI, Panama 14, R. 10, N. 56.
11. Hidalgo Pérez, "Historia atlántica," 317.
12. AGI, Panama 14, R. 12, N. 68, bloque 2.
13. "The voyage truely discoursed, made by Sir Francis Drake," in Hakluyt, *Principal Navigations*, 10:237. The English author of this account confused the former maroon settlement for "an Indian town."
14. Hidalgo Pérez, "Historia atlántica," 318.
15. Spanish spies had known of the fleet prior to its departure. After an Englishman was captured on a raid in the Canary Islands, Spanish authorities sent warnings to all American ports. These preparations allowed the Spanish to foil his attacks on San Juan (Puerto Rico). He also raided Río de la Hacha and Santa Marta, but the residents of both settlements fled prior to his arrival. Andrews, *Drake's Voyages*, 168; Kelsey, *Sir Francis Drake*, 382–88.
16. AGI, Panama 14, R. 12, N. 68, bloque 2.
17. Some Spanish sources credited the town's Spanish *gobernador*, Juan de Tejada, for destroying the town rather than see it captured. Regardless of who made the decision, the residents of Santiago del Principe knew the tactic well. Hidalgo Pérez, "Historia atlántica," 326.
18. AGI, Panama 14, R. 12, N. 74.
19. Writing in 1609, Francisco Valverde de Mercado, president of the audiencia, noted that the former maroons had experienced two relocations, one from Santa Cruz la Real to Nombre de Dios and then the move to Portobelo. AGI, Panama 16, R. 1, N.4.
20. "N. 171 Petición de advertencia de Juan de Ibarra, contador de las cuentas" in Jopling, *Indios y negros en Panamá*, 413–14.
21. In 1623, Diego Chumacero de la Vega noted that he had served as *gobernador* of both towns in the early seventeenth century, further reinforcing the probabil-

ity that they continued as separate corporate entities even as they merged physically. AGI, Panama 63B, N. 5.

22. AGI, Panama 32, N. 23.

23. In June 1597, the audiencia wrote to the king concerning the "good governance" of the *"pueblo de los negros,"* suggesting that by this time Santiago del Príncipe and Santa Cruz la Real comprised a single settlement. AGI, Panama 14, R. 13, N. 86.

24. AGI, Panama 14, R. 10, N.57, bloque 1.

25. "Descripción corográfica de algunos lugares de las indias," in *Descripción de Indias*, Biblioteca Nacional de España, Madrid, Mss. 3064, fs. 217, http:// bdh-rd.bne.es/viewer.vm?id=0000023116&page=1. The term *mogollon* conveyed the meaning of "someone who is financially supported by someone else" and alluded to the fact that their community had been royally subsidized for many years. Hidalgo Pérez notes that the reference to the maroons of the Bayano further supports the claim that Santiago del Príncipe had incorporated the residents of Santa Cruz la Real. Hidalgo Pérez, "Historia atlántica," 355.

26. "Descripción corográfica de algunos lugares de las indias," in *Descripcion de Indias*, Biblioteca Nacional de España, Mss. 3064, fs. 217v–18; "Descripción de la ciudad de San Phelippe de Puertobelo," in *Descripcion de Indias*, Biblioteca Nacional de España, Mss. 3064, fs. 129v, http://bdh-rd.bne.es/viewer.vm?id =0000023116&page=1.

27. AGI, Panama 16, R. 1, N. 4.

28. AGI, Panama 15, R. 3, N. 31.

29. AGI, Panama 15, R. 8, N. 19.

30. AGI, Panama 15, R. 9, N. 94.

31. AGI, Panama 16, R. 1, N. 4.

32. AGI, Panama 16, R. 2, N. 16.

33. AGI, Panama 16, R. 2, N. 18.

34. "Descripción de la ciudad de San Phelippe de Puertobelo," in *Descripcion de Indias*, Biblioteca Nacional de España, Mss. 3064, fs. 153, http://bdh-rd.bne.es /viewer.vm?id=0000023116&page=1.

35. The sparse reference to slaves in the community does not offer evidence for the cultural manifestation of slavery. Did the slavery practiced by the former maroons follow African patterns of enslavement and servitude or had they acculturated to European forms?

36. Tardieu, *Cimarrones de Panamá*, 194, 214.

37. "Descripción de Panama," in *Descripcion de Indias*, Biblioteca Nacional de España, Mss. 3064, fs. 63–64, http://bdh-rd.bne.es/viewer.vm?id=0000023 116&page=1.

38. Given the tiny Indigenous population of Panama City, twenty-seven total, it is unlikely that all of the *zambaigos* of Panama City were born from African-Indigenous unions in the city. On the Isla del Rey, one of the Pearl Islands,

there was at least one African-Indigenous couple that bore four *zambaigo* children. "Descripción de Panama," fs. 63v, 81v–82.

39. AGI, Panama 15, R. 9, N. 94.
40. AGI, Panama 229, L. 1, fs. 195.
41. AGI, Panama 16, R. 1, N. 4.
42. AGI, Panama 46, N. 1. A marginal notation in this document reported that the community had forty men capable of bearing arms.
43. AGI, Panama 16, R. 6, N. 69.
44. AGI, Panama 16, R. 8, N. 103.
45. AGI, Panama 17, R. 4, N. 52.
46. AGI, Panama 34A, N. 40a.
47. Campbell, *Maroons of Jamaica*, 100–101.

References

Aguado, Pedro de. 1919. *Historia de Venezuela*. 2 vols. Madrid: Real Academia de la Historia.

Alegre, Francisco Javier. 1956. *Historia de la provincia de la compañía de Jesus de Nueva España*. New ed. 4 vols. Rome: Institutum Historicum S.J.

Altman, Ida. 2007. "The Revolt of Enriquillo and the Historiography of Early Spanish America." *Americas* 63, no. 4: 587–614.

Anderson, Charles L. G. 1914. *Old Panama and Castilla del Oro*. Boston: Page.

Anderson, Robert Nelson. 1996. "The Quilombo of Palmares: A New Overview of a Maroon State in Seventeenth-Century Brazil." *Journal of Latin American Studies* 28, no. 3: 545–66.

Andrews, Kenneth R. 1968. *Drake's Voyages: A Re-assessment of Their Place in Elizabethan Maritime Expansion*. New York: Scribner.

Arrom, José Juan. 1951. "Criollo: Definición y matices de un concepto." *Hispania* 34, no. 2: 172–76.

Barcia, Manuel. 2014. *West African Warfare in Bahia and Cuba: Soldier Slaves in the Atlantic World, 1807–1844*. Past and Present Book Series. New York: Oxford University Press.

Behrendt, Stephen D., Anthony J. H. Latham, and David Northrup, eds. 2010. *The Diary of Antera Duke, an Eighteenth-Century African Slave Trader*. New York: Oxford University Press.

Bilby, Kenneth, and Diana Baird N'Diaye. 1992. "Creativity and Resistance: Maroon Culture in the Americas." In *Festival of American Folklife*, edited by Peter Seitel, 54–80. Washington, D.C.: Smithsonian Institution.

Campbell, Mavis Christine. 1988. *The Maroons of Jamaica, 1655–1796: A History of Resistance, Collaboration & Betrayal*. Granby, Mass.: Bergin & Garvey.

Candido, Mariana. 2013. *An African Slaving Port and the Atlantic World: Benguela and Its Hinterland*. Cambridge: Cambridge University Press.

Carney, Judith Ann, and Richard Nicholas Rosomoff. 2009. *In the Shadow of Slavery: Africa's Botanical Legacy in the Atlantic World*. Berkeley: University of California Press.

Casimir de Brizuela, Gladis. 2004. *El territorio cueva y su transformación en el siglo XVI*. Panama City: Instituto de Estudios Nacionales, Universidad de Panamá, Universidad Veracruzana.

Cassiani Herrera, Alfonso. 2003. "San Basilio de Palenque: historia de la resistencia, 1599–1713." In *150 años de la abolición de la esclavización en Colombia: Desde la marginalidad a la reconstrucción de la nación*, 70–91. Bogotá: Ministerio de Cultura; CERLALC; Fundación Beatriz Osorio Sierra; Aguilar; Convenio Andres Bello; Museo Nacional de Colombia.

Castillero Calvo, Alfredo. 1995. *Conquista, evangelización y resistencia: Triunfo o fracaso de la política indigenista?* Panama: Editorial Mariano Arosemena; Instituto Nacional de Cultura.

———. 2004a. "Conflictos sociales, guerra y Pax Hispana." In *Historia general de Panamá*, edited by Alfredo Castillero Calvo. Panama: Comité Nacional del Centenario de la República.

———, ed. 2004b. *Historia general de Panamá*. 3 vols. Panama: Comité Nacional del Centenario de la República.

Ceballos, Jorge Díaz. 2018. "New World Civitas, Contested Jurisdictions, and Inter-Cultural Conversation in the Construction of the Spanish Monarchy." *Colonial Latin American Review* 27, no. 1: 30–51.

Chambers, Douglas B. 2001. "Ethnicity in the Diaspora: The Slave-Trade and the Creation of African 'Nations' in the Americas." *Slavery and Abolition* 22, no. 3: 25–39.

Colección de documentos inéditos relativos al descubrimiento, conquista y colonizacion de las posesiones espanolas en america y occeania (CDI-DCC). 1864. Madrid: Imprenta de Manuel de Quirós.

Curcio, Linda Ann. 2004. *The Great Festivals of Colonial Mexico City: Performing Power and Identity*. Albuquerque: University of New Mexico Press.

Deive, Carlos Esteban. 1980. *La esclavitud del negro en Santo Domingo*. 2 vols. Santo Domingo: Museo del Hombre Dominicano.

———. 1985. *Los cimarrones del maniel de Neiba: Historia y etnografía*. Santo Domingo: Banco Central de la República Dominicana.

———. 1989. *Los guerrilleros negros*. Santo Domingo: Fundación Cultural Dominicana.

Diez Castillo, Luis A. 1981. *Los cimarrones y los negros antillanos en Panamá*. Panama City: Impresora R. Mercado Rudas.

Diouf, Sylviane A. 2014. *Slavery's Exiles: The Story of the American Maroons*. New York: New York University Press.

Du Bois, W. E. B. 2007. *The World and Africa; Color and Democracy*. Oxford W. E. B. Du Bois. New York: Oxford University Press.

Eagle, Marc. 2019. "The Early Slave Trade to Spanish America Caribbean Pathways, 1530–1580." In *The Spanish Caribbean and the Atlantic World in the Long Sixteenth Century*, edited by Ida Altman and David Wheat, 139–60. Lincoln: University of Nebraska Press.

Encinas, Diego de. 1945. *Cedulario indiano: Reproducción facsímile de la edición única de 1596.* 4 vols. Madrid: Ediciones Cultura Hispánica.

Fernández de Navarrete, Martín, ed. 1829. *Colección de los viages y descubrimientos que hicieron por mar los españoles desde fines del siglo XV.* 5 vols. Madrid: Imprenta Real.

Ferreira, Roquinaldo. 2012. *Cross-Cultural Exchange in the Atlantic World: Angola and Brazil during the Era of the Slave Trade.* Cambridge: Cambridge University Press.

Florentino, Manolo, and Márcia Amantino. 2011. "Runaways and *Quilombolas* in the Americas." In *The Cambridge World History of Slavery,* edited by David Eltis and Stanley L. Engerman, 708–40. New York: Cambridge University Press.

Fortune, Armando. 1967. "Los primeros negros en el Istmo de Panama." *Revista Lotería,* no. 144: 56–84.

———. 1975a. "Bayano, precursor de la libertad de los esclavos." *Revista Lotería,* no. 234: 1–15.

———. 1975b. "El esclavo negro en el desenvolvimiento económico del Istmo de Panamá durante el descubrimiento y la conquista (1501–1532)." *Revista Lotería,* no. 228: 1–16.

———. 2018. "Los negros cimarrones en tierra firme y su lucha por la libertad (1971)." In *Antología del pensamiento crítico panameño contemporáneo,* edited by Marco A. Gandásequi, Dídimo Castillo Fernández, and Azael Carrera Hernández, 309–77. Buenos Aires: CLASCO.

García Casares, Joaquín. 2008. *Historia del Darién: Cuevas, cunas, españoles, afros, presencia y actualidad de los chocoes.* Panama: Editorial Universitaria.

Green, Toby. 2011. *The Rise of the Trans-Atlantic Slave Trade in Western Africa, 1300–1589.* Cambridge: Cambridge University Press.

Guardia, Roberto de la. 1977. *Los negros del Istmo de Panamá.* Panama City: Ediciones INAC.

Guillot, Carlos F. 1961. *Negros rebeldes y negros cimarrones: Perfil afroamericano en la historia del Nuevo Mundo durante el siglo XVI.* Buenos Aires: Librería y Editorial "El Ateneo."

Hakluyt, Richard. 1904. *The Principal Navigations, Voyages, Traffiques and Discoveries of the English Nation.* 12 vols. Glasgow: James MacLehose and Sons.

Hall, Gwendolyn Midlo. 2005. *Slavery and African Ethnicities in the Americas: Restoring the Links.* Chapel Hill: University of North Carolina Press.

Hamm, Brian. 2019. "Between Acceptance and Exclusion: Spanish Responses to Portuguese Immigrants in the Sixteenth-Century Spanish Caribbean." In *The Spanish Caribbean and the Atlantic World in the Long Sixteenth Century,* edited by Ida Altman and David Wheat, 113–38. Lincoln: University of Nebraska Press.

Helms, Mary W. 1979. *Ancient Panama: Chiefs in Search of Power.* Austin: University of Texas Press.

Hidalgo Pérez, Marta. 2018. "Una historia atlántica en el Panamá del siglo XVI: Los 'Negros de Portobelo' y la villa de Santiago del Principe." PhD diss., Universitat de Barcelona.

Hoopes, John 2001. "Late Chibca." In *Encyclopedia of Prehistory*, edited by Peter N. Peregrine and Martin Ember, 239–56. New York: Kluwer Academic–Plenum Publishers.

Jopling, Carol F., ed. 1994. *Indios y negros en Panamá en los siglos XVI y XVII: Selecciones de los documentos del Archivo General de Indias* Antigua: Centro de Investigaciones Regionales de Mesoamérica.

Kelsey, Harry. 1998. *Sir Francis Drake: The Queen's Pirate*. New Haven: Yale University Press.

King, James Ferguson. 1943. "Descriptive Data on Negro Slaves in Spanish Importation Records and Bills of Sale." *Journal of Negro History* 28, no. 2: 204–19.

Landers, Jane. 2006. "*Cimarrón* and Citizen: African Ethnicity, Corporate Identity, and the Evolution of Free Black Towns in the Spanish Circum-Caribbean." In *Slaves, Subjects, and Subversives: Blacks in Colonial Latin America*, edited by Jane G. Landers and Barry Robinson, 111–45. Albuquerque: University of New Mexico Press.

Lane, Kris E. 1998. *Pillaging the Empire: Piracy in the Americas, 1500–1750*. Armonk, N.Y.: M. E. Sharpe.

Las Casas, Bartolomé de. 1876. *Historia de las Indias*. 5 vols. Madrid: Imprenta de Miguel Ginesta.

Law, Robin. 1997. "Ethnicity and the Slave Trade: 'Lucumí' and 'Nagô' as Ethnonyms in West Africa." *History in Africa* 24: 205–19.

López de Velasco, Juan. 1894. *Geografía y descripción universal de las Indias*. Madrid: Real Academia de la Historia.

Lovejoy, Henry B, and Olatunji Ojo. 2015. "'Lucumí,' 'Terranova,' and the Origins of the Yoruba Nation." *Journal of African History* 56, no. 3: 353–72.

Lovejoy, Paul E. 2000. "Identifying Enslaved Africans in the African Diaspora." In *Identity in the Shadow of Slavery*, edited by Paul E. Lovejoy, 1–29. New York: Continuum.

Mena García, Carmen. 1983. "El traslado de la ciudad de Nombre de Dios a Portobelo a fines del siglo XVI." *Anuario de estudios americanos* 40: 71–102.

Mena García, María del Carmen. 1984. *La sociedad de Panamá en el siglo XVI*. Sevilla: Excma. Diputación Provincial de Sevilla.

———. 2011. *El oro del Darién: Entradas y cabalgadas en la conquista de Tierra Firme (1509–1526)*. Sevilla: Centro de Estudios Andaluces (Consejería de Presidencia); Consejo Superior de Investigaciones Científicas.

Nemser, Daniel. 2017. *Infrastructures of Race: Concentration and Biopolitics in Colonial Mexico*. Austin: University of Texas Press.

Nichols, Philip. 1910. "Sir Francis Drake Revived." In *Voyages and Travels: Ancient and Modern*, edited by Charles W. Eliot, 125–203. New York: P. F. Collier and Son.

Orr, Julie M. 2018. *Scotland, Darien and the Atlantic World, 1698–1700*. Edinburgh: Edinburgh University Press.

Oviedo y Valdés, Gonzalo Fernández de. 1851. *Historia general y natural de las Indias islas y tierra firme del mar Océano*. 4 vols. Madrid: Real Academia de la Historia.

———. 2006. *Writing from the Edge of the World: The Memoirs of Darién, 1514–1527*. Translated by G. F. Dille. Tuscaloosa: University of Alabama Press.

Pike, Ruth. 2007. "Black Rebels: The Cimarrons of Sixteenth-Century Panama." *Americas* 64, no. 2: 243–66.

Recopilación de leyes de los Reynos de las Indias. 1973. 4 vols. Madrid: Ediciones Cultura Hispánica.

Restall, Matthew. 2000. "Black Conquistadors: Armed Africans in Early Spanish America." *Americas* 57, no. 2: 171–205.

———. 2003. *Seven Myths of the Spanish Conquest*. New York: Oxford University Press.

Romoli, Kathleen. 1987. *Los de la lengua de Cueva: Los grupos indígenas del istmo oriental en la época de la conquista Española*. Bogota: Instituto Colombiano de Antropología.

Sauer, Carl Ortwin. 1966. *The Early Spanish Main*. Berkeley: University of California Press.

Schwaller, Robert C. 2011. "'*Mulata, Hija de Negro y India*': Afro-Indigenous *Mulatos* in Early Colonial Mexico." *Journal of Social History* 44, no. 3: 885–910.

———. 2018. "Contested Conquests: African Maroons and the Incomplete Conquest of Hispaniola, 1519–1620." *Americas* 75, no. 4: 609–38.

Seed, Patricia. 1995. *Ceremonies of Possession in Europe's Conquest of the New World, 1492–1640*. New York: Cambridge University Press.

Spicksley, Judith. 2015. "Contested Enslavement: The Portuguese in Angola and the Problem of Debt, c. 1600–1800." *Itinerario* 39, no. 2: 247–75.

Stone, Erin Woodruff. 2013. "America's First Slave Revolt: Indians and African Slaves in Española, 1500–1534." *Ethnohistory* 60, no. 2: 195–217.

Sweet, James H. 2009. "Mistaken Identities? Olaudah Equiano, Domingos Álvares, and the Methodological Challenges of Studying the African Diaspora." *American Historical Review* 114, no. 2: 279–306.

Tardieu, Jean-Pierre. 2009. *Cimarrones de Panamá: La forja de una identidad afroamericana en el siglo XVI*. Madrid: Iberoamericana Editorial.

Thompson, Alvin O. 2006. *Flight to Freedom: African Runaways and Maroons in the Americas*. Kingston, Jamaica: University of the West Indies Press.

Thornton, John K. 1998. *Africa and Africans in the Making of the Atlantic World, 1400–1800*. 2nd ed. New York: Cambridge University Press.

Utrera, Cipriano de. 2014. *Historia militar de Santo Domingo (documentos y noticias)*. 3 vols. Santo Domingo: Editora Búho.

Vega, Garcilaso de la. 1617. *Historia General del Peru*. Cordoba: Viuda de Andres Barrera.

Vila Vilar, E. 1987. "Cimarronaje en Panamá y Cartagena. El costo de una guerrilla en el siglo XVII." *Cahiers du monde hispanique et luso-brésilien* 49: 77–92.

Wheat, David. 2016. *Atlantic Africa and the Spanish Caribbean, 1570–1640*. Chapel Hill: University of North Carolina Press.

Wright, Irene Aloha. 1932. *Documents concerning English Voyages to the Spanish Main, 1569–1580*. London: Hakluyt Society.

Index

Page numbers in *italics* indicate illustrative matter.

abductions: English, of enslaved *negros*, 103, 163; laws regarding, of enslaved Africans, 93–96, 124; maroon, of enslaved Africans, 41–42, 45–46, 52, 83–86, 89, 91–94, 203

Acla: depopulation of, 43; dissolution of, 12; English corsairs in and around, 135, 138–40, 142–43, 146, 149, 152, 159–60, 216; founding of, 8; French in and around, 172; garrison established, 213; maroons in, 44; maroon settlements near, 226, 258; municipal government, 14; resettlement of, 216. *See also* Gulf of Acla

African Americans, 2, 76n24

African customs, 58–59, 75n20, 109, 181, 185n1, 234

African ethnonyms: importance of, to maroon social organization, 217; origins and significance of individual, 152n3, 165n2, 177nn3–5, 184n8, 185n2, 185n4, 187nn2–3, 190n1, 210nn1–3, 211n7, 211n9, 224nn2–3, 224n6, 224nn8–9, 225n10, 245n4; as second names and expressions of identity or origin, 20–21. *See also individual ethnonyms*; ethnic categories

African martial practices, 25, 30n74, 74n7, 109, 181

African-Indigenous unions, 59–60, 218–23, 234, 237–39, 259. *See also zambaigo(s)*

Africans, stereotypes of: as barbarous, 57, 59, 176, 212; as bestial, 24, 25, 60, 128; construction of, 20; as fearsome, 52, 63, 76n26, 107, 113, 245n9; as primitive, 68–69, 162; and their physical prowess, 53–54, 56, 59, 64, 67; as untrustworthy, duplicitous, or unreasonable, 66, 200–202, 214

Aguado, Pedro de, 50–51, 74–77, 111n5, 111n13

Aguirre, Lope de, 47, 51, 52, 74n3

Aguirre, Wrath of God (film), 74n3

Amapa, 27, 261

Andagoya, Pascual de, 12, 22

Angola (ethnonym): defined, 210n2; as surname of maroons on census lists, 205–7, 209, 222–23, 236–37, 241. *See also* African ethnonyms; ethnic categories

Angola, Juan, 122n2, 214, 233

Archivo General de Indias (AGI), xiv–xv, xvii

Arles, Juan de, 64

arrows and arrowheads: of Indigenous peoples, 214; of maroons, 41, 52, 54–56, 63, 83, 109, 132–33, 137, 141, 171, 179, 181, 184, 187, 201, 254; types of, 105. *See also* weapons

Arroyo Chico, 250

Arson: of food stores and crops, 143, 147, 161; of English fort, 139–40; of maroon settlements, 19, 25, 27, 39, 46, 48, 137, 147, 149, 151, 157, 159, 164, 255, 258; of Spanish settlements and property, 17, 41, 68, 83–85, 112, 119, 255; as strategy of war, 162n1; of vessels, 147, 155

artillery, 117, 146, 154, 156; calivers, 130; cannon, 122n3, 141, 142n3, 143, 171; versos 139, 143. *See also* weapons

Arze, García de, 52, 64

Audiencia of Lima, 15, 152

Audiencia of Panama: authorization by, of marronage laws, 90, 93; authorization by, of military action against maroons, 86, 122–29; conflict between officials in Peru and, 15, 146, 148, 152; contrasting strategies of, against maroons, 121; establishment of ordinances for free-black communities by, 193–99, 240; military strategy of, against English, 160–62, 164, 176; representatives commissioned by, 85, 123–24, 142, 186, 194, 198, 200, 240; requests by, for royal funds in pursuit of war, 144; role of, in peace agreements with maroons, 1, 19, 123–25, 174, 178, 180, 184–86, 188–89, 193, 226, 229–30, 245, 248

audiencia, defined, xvii, 14

Avila, Gonzalo de, 46

Ayora, Juan de, 7, 8, 13

Azevedo, Pedro de, 37

Badajoz, Gonzalo de, 8, 9

Balboa, Vasco Nuñez de: companionship of, with Olano, 15; expeditions led by, 6, 8, 10, 13; strategies of negotiation and conquest of, 5

bananas: cultivation of, 63, 92, 143, 164; destroyed groves of, 164; as indicators of maroon presence, 249; for sustenance; 64, 72, 152, 156, 172

Bañol (ethnonym), 185n2, 217–18, 220–21, 235. *See also* African ethnonyms; ethnic categories

Bañol, Antón, 185, 200–202

barbs, 56. *See also* weapons

Barís (ethnonym). *See* Motilones (ethnonym)

Barrionuevo, Francisco, 23

Bautista de Señor, Juan, 39

Bayano: disambiguation of, xiii-xiv

Bayano (maroon leader), 18, 38, 45–50, 58–60, 66–74

Bayano (region): census lists of maroons from or at large in, 216–24; census list of maroons resettled from, 234–39, 241–44; English access to, 106–7, 135, 153–54, 175; expeditions to reach maroons at large in, after peace negotiations, 244–51; fortresses and settlements in, 148–49; geography of, 215, 249; maroon persons and populations from, 26, 98n4, 154, 173n9, 192, 198, 209; naming of, 18; negotiations between Spanish and maroons of, 174–84, 188, 203, 229–30; reestablishment of maroons in, 253–58; resettlement of maroons from, 230–33; Spanish military action against settlements in, 86, 157–65, 204, 211–14, 225, 258. *See also* Catalina (maroon

Made in the USA
Middletown, DE
14 February 2022

61106311R00182